Praise for *Reinventing Management*

"Change isn't just for the rank-and-file anymore; it's coming for you. Instant access to information and global resources have changed the world we live and work in. Julian Birkinshaw shows that 19th century industrial management won't work in a 21st century fluid workplace. Read this, or prepare to be 'game-changed' by someone who has."
Jack Hughes, CEO, TopCoder

"Julian Birkinshaw provides a comprehensive, articulate, and important overview of the role of management in contemporary organizations' successes and failures. In so doing, he guides managers to think differently about how they do their job and researchers to ask somewhat different and more important and interesting questions. Birkinshaw is unique in his ability to cover this material with wisdom and rigor."
Jeffrey Pfeffer, Professor, Stanford Graduate School of Business and author of *What Were They Thinking? Unconventional Wisdom About Management*

"Technological and social changes are having an enormous impact on the world of business, and on the way companies are managed. In this book, Julian Birkinshaw provides a roadmap for making sense of how the world of management is changing, and he provides useful advice for companies who want to harness the potential that Web 2.0 has to offer."
P.V. Kannan, CEO, 24/7 Customer

"We have used Professor Birkinshaw's ideas at DiGi, and they have helped us to frame our internal discussions about what our current management model is, and how we plan to evolve it in the years ahead."
Johan Dennelind, CEO DiGi Telecommunications, Malaysia

"Management is an important key quality which is frequently misunderstood. It is in fact a profession. Julian Birkinshaw provides a fresh

new look at what management is really about and provides a useful framework to help executives make smarter choices in their work. The book is an estimable read for anyone who cares about improving professionalism and quality of management in the business world."
Sir John Ritblat, Honorary President, The British Land Company

"The need for an inside-out approach to management is brought out powerfully by Julian Birkinshaw in his latest work. Julian's book provides us with an 'alternate' view on reinventing management in today's changing environment. A refreshing read for managers and leaders."
Vineet Nayar, CEO, HCL Technologies

"We are the first human beings to live in an exponential age, and the first to be faced with a radically accelerating pace of change. Problem is, our organizations aren't up to the challenges this new reality imposes. The top-down, overly bureaucratic management model found in most companies was invented in the early decades of the 20th century, when chance was much better behaved. In this important new book, Julian Birkinshaw helps us look beyond our legacy management practices, and imagine bold new ways of leading, managing and organizing. Filled with mind-expanding examples, Reinventing Management is a must read for managers who want to build an organization that's truly fit for the future."
Gary Hamel, best-selling author of *The Future of Management*

"...a stimulating new book..."
BNET.co.uk, May 2010

"He discusses important issues and provides invaluable insights and suggestions that can help to develop a distinctive management model."
Professional Manager, September 2010

"This is an excellent, absorbing and thought provoking book. A must read."
Edge, September 2010

Reinventing Management

Revised and Updated Edition

Smarter Choices for Getting Work Done

Julian Birkinshaw

JOSSEY-BASS
A Wiley Imprint
www.josseybass.com

This revised and updated edition published 2012
© 2012 John Wiley & Sons, Ltd
Originally published in 2010

Under the Jossey-Bass imprint, Jossey-Bass, 989 Market Street, San Francisco CA 94103-1741, USA
www.jossey-bass.com

Registered office
John Wiley & Sons Ltd, The Atrium, Southern Gate, Chichester, West Sussex, PO19 8SQ, United Kingdom

For details of our global editorial offices, for customer services and for information about how to apply for permission to reuse the copyright material in this book please see our website at www.wiley.com.

The right of the author to be identified as the author of this work has been asserted in accordance with the Copyright, Designs and Patents Act 1988.

A catalogue record for this book is available from the British Library.

ISBN 978-1-118-37590-7 (hardback)
ISBN 978-1-118-38966-9 (ebook)
ISBN 978-1-118-38967-6 (ebook)
ISBN 978-1-118-38970-6 (ebook)

Set in 12/15pt Goudy by Toppan Best-set Premedia Limited
Printed in Great Britain by TJ International Ltd, Padstow, Cornwall, UK

This book is dedicated to Laura, Ross, Duncan, and Lisa

Contents

Preface

This book tells you what management is, why it is important, and how you can generate competitive advantage for your company by taking it seriously.

You might expect there to be a lot of books on this subject, given the enormous numbers of people who are managers, and the poor quality of management that exists in many organizations. But the reality is that few management writers write specifically about the nature of *Management*. A few lonely voices—most notably Peter Drucker and Henry Mintzberg—have continued to remind us of its importance over the years, but most writers have preferred to focus on more alluring themes, such as leadership, change, and strategy.

There are a couple of prejudices about the practice of management that help to explain why it has struggled for attention. The first prejudice suggests that management is simple, timeless and unchanging. People have been managing others since the time of the Pyramids, it is argued, and the basic tasks of coordinating and controlling haven't changed since then. So is there really anything new to learn? Yes, in fact, there is. While the *functions* of management have changed very little over the years (in terms of what needs to be done), the *methods* of management (in terms of how it gets done) have changed dramatically. And the technological and social changes afoot in the business world today will result in even greater changes in the years ahead.

The second prejudice suggests that what organizations really need is leaders, not managers. Leadership is probably the biggest single category of business books today, and every business school offers courses to help you improve your leadership skills. Management now sits firmly in the shadow of leadership, often viewed as a necessary but rather tedious activity.

But it's not obvious that this recent focus on leadership has really helped to improve the agility or competitiveness of our business organizations. Indeed, if there is a problem today in the world of business, it is that companies don't implement their grand plans as effectively as they should. There is a gap between our goals and our ability to achieve them. And I believe it is the job of management, the discipline of getting work done through others, to fill that gap.

Management and leadership, in other words, are both equally important. They are two horses pulling the same cart. We need to pay much greater attention to management to put it back on an equal footing with leadership.

Interestingly, since this book first came out in 2010, there has been a genuine upturn in interest in the field of management. For example, other titles that came out the same time as this one included *Manager Redefined* by Thomas Davenport and Stephen Harding, *The Leaders Guide to Radical Management* by Stephen Denning, *Management Reset* by Ed Lawler and Christopher Worley, *Good Boss, Bad Boss* by Bob Sutton, and *Being the Boss* by Linda Hill and Kent Lineback. It is too early to claim victory in the fight to put management back on an equal footing with leadership, but at least there is some momentum afoot. Another important development has been the emergence of the Management Innovation Exchange (www.managementexchange.com), the first serious attempt to create an online community where management ideas can be discussed and developed in real time, and without mediation.

My own research on management began five years ago, when I first started collaborating with Gary Hamel, a Visiting Professor at the London Business School and the founder of *Strategos*, a Chicago-based consulting firm. We shared an interest in helping companies to become more resilient and more entrepreneurial, and we quickly came to the view that the biggest single blocker to change was the antiquated approach to management used by most large companies. The concept of the Management Innovation Lab (MLab) was born, with support from London Business School, UBS, the David and Elaine Potter Charitable Foundation, the CIPD and AIM Research.

We decided that the mission of MLab was to "Accelerate the evolution of management." A lot of people scratched their heads when we explained this to them. How can you innovate *management*? What is management anyway? Surely you mean leadership, not management? All the old prejudices came out, but we stuck to our guns. We began working with a few progressive companies to help them dream up and try out innovative management methods. And we built relationships with management innovators in dozens of companies around the world—people who had put their own experimental approaches to management in place, and wanted some reassurance that they were on the right track. The Management Innovation Exchange (MIX), mentioned above, was one of the natural outgrowths of these pioneering efforts to work with companies in a new way. Created by Gary Hamel, the MIX is proving to be a really valuable resource to people looking for inspiration and practical ideas for developing new ways of working.

Four years ago, I published *Giant Steps in Management* with my colleague Michael Mol. It was an attempt to make sense of the history of management innovation—how 50 key innovations including Total Quality Management, Brand Management, and Activity Based Costing, had influenced the development of management as a field. We were interested in understanding how these individual innovations had come about, and also how they had collectively brought about a transformation (over a 150-year period) in the nature of management work.

In this book, I turn my attention to the future. Rather than look at individual management innovations, my focus is on what I have come to call the company's *Management Model*—the conscious choices made by its top executives to define how work gets done. I believe it is not sufficient simply to look for ways of improving individual components of management, such as enhancing the compensation system, or making the planning system more efficient. Rather, the challenge is to think about how these discrete choices fit together, and to figure out how your Management Model, as a whole, supports and enriches your company's strategy.

This book provides you with the frameworks and tools you need to reinvent management in your company. It will describe the full range of methods companies use to coordinate activities, make decisions, set objectives, and motivate people. And it will help you to make smarter choices—in the context of your own particular circumstances—for getting work done.

Acknowledgements

This book is the culmination of more than five years' work, and it has involved interviews with many hundreds of executives and conversations with many dozens of colleagues. While it will not be possible to acknowledge everyone who helped me put the book together, I would like at least to acknowledge my main sources of inspiration and insight.

It was Gary Hamel who got me started on the journey that led to this book, when we first started talking about the need for management innovation back in 2004. I helped Gary to create the Management Innovation Lab (MLab), and over the years it has become an important vehicle for trying out and focusing our ideas. Many of the ideas in this book came out of conversations with Gary, for which I am truly grateful. Thanks also to the other individuals involved in MLab: Jules Goddard, Jeremy Clarke, Alan Matcham, Lisa Valikangas and Stuart Crainer. MLab was sponsored by UBS, the David and Elaine Potter Charitable Foundation, the CIPD and the Advanced Institute of Management Research.

I am indebted to all my co-authors who have helped me to get my ideas into shape and ready for publication in academic and managerial journals. Some of the papers we have written together are explicitly referred to in this book; others have influenced this book more indirectly. So thanks to: Tina Ambos, Cyril Bouquet, Andrew Campbell, Cris Gibson, Jules Goddard, Huw Jenkins, Morten Hansen, Suzanne Heywood, Susan Hill and Michael Mol.

I interviewed perhaps two hundred executives in preparation for writing this book. I have not kept good records of all these interviews, but I would like to acknowledge the following individuals who all offered useful examples or insights: Francesca Barnes, Tod Bedilion, Ed Bevan, Tim Brooks, Randy Chase, Jack Hughes, Lianne Eden, Hari Hariharan, Modestas Gelbudas, Jeff Hollender, Larry Huston, Huw Jenkins, P.V. Kannan, Terri Kelley, Graham Kill, Lars Kolind, Srinivas Koushik, John Mackey, Dena McCallum, Jim McKeown, Michael Molinaro, Sunil Jayantha Narawathne, Vineet Nayar, Hillary Neumayr, Jeremy Palmer, John Perkins, David Potter, Robyn Pratt, Hema Ravichandrar, Bruce Rayner, Peter Robbins, Eric Schmidt, Art Schneiderman, Ross Smith, Toni Stadelmann, Henry Stewart, Claudius Sutter, Reto Wey, Mike Wing and David Yuan.

London Business School has been my professional home for the last decade, and it provided me with the perfect environment for developing the book. Its twin focus on academic rigor and managerial relevance helped me to make my ideas as practical as possible while not losing touch with the scholarly debates on which I am building. So thanks to Deans Laura Tyson, Robin Buchanan and Andrew Likierman, and also to my colleagues who have helped to shape the book, including Lynda Gratton, Michael Jacobides, Costas Markides, Phanish Puranam, Don Sull and Freek Vermeulen. Sumantra Ghoshal, of course, was also an enormously important influence in my first few years at London Business School, and his departure was a great loss to all of us. My former employers, the Stockholm School of Economics, the University of Toronto and the Richard Ivey School of Business, were all influential in shaping pieces of what ultimately came together in this book.

The actual writing process for this book was pretty quick, taking roughly three months from mid-July to early October in 2009. This speedy production process would not have been possible without the enormous effort put in by Karen Sharpe, who converted my first draft text into something coherent and readable. She also helped enormously with several of the company case studies. The other reason that the writing process was so rapid was because of the large number of pre-existing case studies that had been put together by the MLab team. I would particularly like to thank Stuart Crainer, Des Dearlove and Simon Caulkin for their help in this respect. Nigel Owens, Laura Birkinshaw, Allister Maclellan and Rosie Robertson all helped along the way during the writing process, by reviewing draft chapters and helping me with fact checking.

Finally, from Wiley/Jossey-Bass I would like to thank Rosemary Nixon and Kathe Sweeney for showing such enthusiasm for the original proposal in summer 2008, and for encouraging me throughout the writing process.

About the Author

Julian Birkinshaw is Professor and Chair of Strategic and Entrepreneurship at the London Business School. He has PhD and MBA degrees in Business from the Richard Ivey School of Business, University of Western Ontario, and a BSc (Hons) from the University of Durham, UK. He was awarded an Honorary Doctorate by the Stockholm School of Economics, 2009.

Professor Birkinshaw's main area of expertise is in the strategy and management of large multinational corporations, and on such specific issues as corporate entrepreneurship, innovation, subsidiary–headquarters relationship, knowledge management, network organizations and global customer management.

He is the author of 10 other books, including *Giant Steps in Management* (2007), *Inventuring: Why Big Companies Must Think Small* (2003), *Leadership the Sven-Goran Eriksson Way* (2002) and *Entrepreneurship in the Global Firm* (2001), and over 70 articles in such journals as *Harvard Business Review*, *Sloan Management Review*, *Strategic Management Journal* and *Academy of Management Journal*. He is active as a consultant and executive educator to many large companies, including Rio Tinto, SAP, GSK, ABB, Ericsson, Kone, Petrofac, WPP, Bombardier, Sara Lee, HSBC, Akzo Nobel, Roche, Thyssen Krupp, UBS, PWC, Coloplast, BBC, Unilever and Novo Nordisk.

In 1998 the leading British management magazine *Management Today* profiled Professor Birkinshaw as one of six of the "Next generation of management gurus." He is regularly quoted in international media outlets, including CNN, BBC, *The Economist*, the *Wall Street Journal* and *The Times*. He speaks regularly at business conferences in the UK, Europe, North America and Australia.

Professor Birkinshaw is co-founder with bestselling author Gary Hamel of the Management Innovation Lab (MLab), a unique partnership between academia and business that is seeking to accelerate the evolution of management.

1

WHY MANAGEMENT FAILED

Here is a simple thought experiment. About forty years from now you receive a text message from your grand-daughter. She has been given an assignment at school: *what were the causes of the Great Recession of 2007-13?* "You were working during that era," she says, "Can you tell me the answer?"

Of course, we have all developed our own views about how the current economic crisis came about, and we are inevitably drawn to the proximate causes, such as excessive borrowing, low interest rates, and a lack of financial regulation. But as these events recede into history, our understanding of what happened will evolve. Many of the proximate causes will gradually be downplayed. And other less-obvious and less-proximate causes will become more apparent.

What are these less-obvious and underlying causes? Well, only time will tell. But I believe part of the answer is that we have focused too much on the "policy" side of the story up to now—on the decisions made by central bankers, government officials and regulators. Of course their decisions are important, but these players can only do so much. They set the rules, they operate a few vital levers of control, and they have the right to penalize those who break the rules.

But in a capitalist economic system, I believe *firms are the real agents of change.* They are the producers of the goods and services that drive economic growth. They employ the majority of people. They have the capacity to act decisively, to put money behind big opportunities, to invest in people and new technologies. They also have the capacity to get it wrong on a large scale—by putting resources into poorly-thought out projects, by allowing negligent and irresponsible behavior, and by creating demotivating and uninspiring places to work.

So here is a prediction. Forty years from now, a discussion of the causes of the "Great Recession of 2007-13" will not just talk about low interest rates, excess leverage and lax regulation. It will also include a recognition of the flawed model of management that most large firms were using in the 1990s and 2000s; a model that led to short-term decision making, poor risk-management, and the creation of ill-thought-out incentive systems. The flaws in this model, it will be argued, exacerbated the problems created by policymakers, and contributed significantly to the length and the depth of the recession.

I don't know if this seems like a surprising argument, but it isn't hard to make the case that bad management is part of the problem we are facing today. Consider the following examples from the last twelve months.

- Spring 2011: The National Commission report on BP's oil spill in the gulf put the blame squarely on the shoulders of management. "The Macondo disaster was not, as some have suggested, the result of a coincidental alignment of disparate technical failures. While many technical failures contributed to the blowout, the Chief Counsel's team traces each of them back to an overarching failure of management."[1]

- Summer 2011: Rupert Murdoch's News Corp was dragged through the mud following the phone-hacking scandal at the *News of the World* paper. One group of shareholders sued News Corp for "failing to exercise proper oversight and take sufficient action," leading to a "piling on of questionable deals, a waste of corporate resources, a starring role in a blockbuster scandal, and a gigantic public relations disaster."[2]

- Fall 2011: The beleaguered Swiss bank, UBS, recorded a $2.3b loss from rogue trader, Kweku Adoboli, despite a tightening up of its risk management systems in the post credit-crisis years. According to one observer, "that sort of fraud is only possible at a financial institution with very lax risk oversight. There has to be a huge gap in terms of internal controls."[3]

- Winter 2011: The long-awaited report from the UK's Financial Services Authority (FSA) into the collapse of Royal Bank of Scotland was published on December 12. It concluded there were "underlying deficiencies in RBS management governance and culture which made it prone to make poor decisions."[4]

Of course, it is trite to say that "management is to blame". Any problem in a firm is, by definition, the responsibility of the people at the top. But we can go much deeper here in articulating the precise ways in which management failed. We will do this by comparing two recent, high-profile failures: Lehman Brothers and General Motors.

Lehman Brothers

Since 1993, Lehman had been led by Dick Fuld, a legendary figure on Wall Street, and a "textbook example of the command and control CEO."[5] Fuld inspired great loyalty in his management team, but his style was aggressive and intimidating. In the words of a former employee, "His style contained the seeds of disaster. It meant that nobody would or could challenge the boss if his judgment erred or if things started to go wrong."

And things did go wrong. The company made a record $4.2 billion profit in 2007, but it had done so by chasing low-margin, high-risk business without the necessary levels of capital. When the sub-prime crisis hit, Lehman found itself exposed and vulnerable. Fuld explored the possibility of a merger with several deep-pocketed competitors, but he refused to accept the low valuation they were offering him. And on September 15, 2008, the company filed for bankruptcy.

What were the underlying causes of Lehman's failure? While Dick Fuld's take-no-prisoners management style certainly didn't help their cause, we need to dig into the company's underlying Management Model to understand what happened. Contributory factors included:

Its risk-management was poor. Like most of its competitors, Lehman failed to understand the risk associated with an entire class of mortgage-backed securities. But more importantly, no one felt accountable for the risks they were taking on these products. By falling back on formal rules rather than careful use of personal judgment to take into account the changing situation, Lehman made many bad decisions.

It had perverse incentive systems. Lehman's employees knew what behaviors would maximize their bonuses. They also knew these very same behaviors would not be in the long-term interests of their shareholders—that's what made the incentive systems perverse. For example, targets were typically based on revenue income, not profit, and individual effort was often rewarded ahead of teamwork.

There was no long-term unifying vision. Lehman wanted to be "number one in the industry by 2012," but that wasn't a vision—it was simply a desired position on the leader board. Lehman did not provide its employees with any intrinsic motivation to work hard to achieve that goal, nor any reason to work there instead of going over to the competitors. And that vision was far from unifying—there were ongoing power struggles between the New York and London centers.

Of course Lehman Brothers was not alone in pursuing a failed Management Model. With a few partial exceptions such as Goldman Sachs and JP Morgan, these practices were endemic to the investment banking industry. It was the combination of Lehman's model, its fragile position as an independent broker-dealer, and its massive exposure to the sub-prime meltdown that led to its ultimate failure.

The key point here is that a more effective Management Model could have made all the difference. Instead, it was almost as if management didn't matter. An encapsulated definition of what a Management Model is, something we fully explore in the next chapter, is the set of choices we make about how work gets done in an organization. One of the well-kept secrets of the investment banks is that their own management systems are far less sophisticated than those of the companies to which they act as advisors. For example: people are frequently promoted on technical, not managerial, competence; aggressive and intimidating behavior is tolerated; effective teamwork and sharing of ideas is rare.

Nor are these new problems. In 2002 The *Economist* reviewed the state of the banking industry and called the investment banks "among the worst managed institutions on the planet."[6] And back in 1993, following an earlier financial crisis, the CEO of Citicorp, John Reed, wrote himself a memo, documenting all the managerial failings in his company: "I was frustrated by the bureaucracy...I believe that 75% of our management process is unneeded...we need the courage to change our ways."[7] The harsh truth is that most investment banks have been poorly managed for decades despite—or because of—the vast profits they have made. The financial crisis of 2008 has finally exposed these problems for all to see.

General Motors

General Motors (GM) is another company with a long and proud history. In the post-war period, GM was the acme of the modern industrial firm, the leading player in the most important industry in the world. But from a market share of 51 percent in 1962, the company began a long slide down to a share of 22 percent in 2008. New competitors from Japan, of course, were the initial cause of GM's troubles, but despite the fixes tried by successive generations of executives, the decline continued. The financial crisis of 2008 was the final straw: credit dried up, customers stopped buying cars, and GM ran out of cash, filing for bankruptcy in May 2009. After a restructuring, GM returned to the stock market in November 2010.

As is so often the case, the seeds of GM's failure can be linked directly to its earlier successes. GM rose to its position of leadership thanks to Alfred P. Sloan's famous management innovation strategy—the multidivisional, professionally managed firm. By creating semi-autonomous divisions with profit responsibility, and by building a professional cadre of executives concerned with long-term planning at the corporate center, Sloan's GM was able to deliver economies of scale and scope that were unmatched. Indeed, it is no exaggeration to say that GM was the model of a well-managed company in the inter-war period. Two of the best-selling business books of that era—Sloan's *My Years with General Motors* and Peter F. Drucker's *Concept of the Corporation*—were both essentially case studies of GM's Management Model, and the ideas they put forward were widely copied.[8]

So where did GM go wrong? The company was the model of bureaucracy with formal rules and procedures, a clear hierarchy, and standardized inputs and outputs. This worked well for years, perhaps too well—GM became dominant, and gradually took control not just of its supply chain but of its customers as well. We can be sure that economist John Kenneth Galbraith had GM in mind when he made the following statement in his influential treatise, "The New Industrial State," in 1967:

> "The initiative in deciding what is to be produced comes not from the sovereign consumer who, through the market, issues the instructions that bend the productive mechanism to his ultimate will. Rather it comes from the great producing organization which reaches forward to control the markets that it is presumed to serve.[9]"

This model worked fine in an industry dominated by the Big Three. But the 1973 oil-price shock, the arrival of Japanese competitors, and the rediscovery of consumer sovereignty changed all that. At that point, all GM's strengths as a formal, procedure-driven hierarchy turned into liabilities—it was too slow in developing new models, its designs were too conservative, and its cost base was too high. A famous memo written by former Vice Chairman Elmer Johnson in 1988 summarized the problem very clearly:

> "...our most serious problem pertains to organization and culture... Thus our hope for broad change lies in radically altering the culture of the top 500 people, in part by changing the membership of this group and in part by changing the policies, processes, and frameworks that reinforce the current mind-set...The meetings of our many committees and policy groups have become little more than time-consuming formalities... Our culture discourages open, frank debate among GM executives in the pursuit of problem resolution... Most of the top 500 executives in GM have typically changed jobs every two years or so, without regard to long-term project responsibility. In some ways they have come to resemble elected or appointed top officials in the federal bureaucracy. They come and go and have little impact on operations"[10].

A similar, though more succinct, diagnosis was offered by former U.S. presidential candidate Ross Perot when he sold his company, EDS, to GM in the 1980s: "At GM the stress is not on getting results—on winning—but on bureaucracy, on conforming to the GM System."[11] GM found itself killed off, in other words, by the very things that allowed it to succeed in the postwar years—formalized processes, careful planning, dispassionate decision-making, and an entrenched hierarchy.

This story is now well known. Here's the point: GM's bankruptcy was caused in large part by a failure of management just as Lehman's was. But the *mistakes made by* GM were *completely different from the mistakes made by Lehman*. To wit:

- Lehman motivated its employees through extrinsic and material rewards, and used incentives to encourage individualism and risk-taking. GM paid its employees less well, it hired people who loved the car industry, and it promoted risk-averse loyal employees.

- Lehman used mostly informal systems for coordinating and decision-making. GM emphasized formal procedures and rules.

- Lehman had no clear sense of purpose or higher-order mission. GM had a very clear and long-held vision—to be the world leader in transportation products.

Like Lehman, GM's demise can be explained by any number of factors. Some of these are purely external, such as Japanese competitors and rising oil prices in the case of GM, and poor regulation and policymaking in the case of Lehman.

My view—and the thesis of this book—is that we have to look inside, to the underlying *Management Models* that both companies adopted, subconsciously or not. We will examine shortly what a Management Model is, but for the moment we can think of it as the set of choices we make about how work gets done in an organization. A well-chosen Management Model, then, can be a source of competitive advantage; a poorly chosen Management Model can lead to ruin. And Lehman and GM illustrate nicely—but in contrasting ways—the downside risk of sticking with a Management Model that is past its sell-by date. As do Enron and Tyco, for example, which also went through high-profile bankruptcies.

Disenchantment with Management

Management as we know it today is struggling to do the job it was intended to do. But we can also see evidence of a creeping disenchantment with management as a discipline. Here are some examples:

Management as a profession is not well respected. In a 2008 Gallup poll on honesty and ethics among workers in 21 different professions, a mere 12 percent of respondents felt business executives had high/very high integrity—an all-time low. With a 37 percent low/very low rating, the executives came in *behind* lawyers, union leaders, real estate agents, building contractors, and bankers.[12] In a 2009 survey by *Management Today*, 31 percent of respondents stated that they had low or no trust in their management team.[13]

Employees are unhappy with their managers. The most compelling evidence for this comes from economist Richard Layard's studies of happiness.[14] With whom are people most happy interacting? Friends and family are at the top; the boss comes last. In fact, people would prefer to be alone, Layard showed, than spend time interacting with their boss. This is a damning indictment of the management profession.

There are no positive role models. We all know why Dilbert is the best-selling business book series of all time, and why "The Office" sitcom was a big hit on both sides of the Atlantic—it's because they ring true. The Pointy-Haired Boss in Dilbert is a self-centered halfwit; Michael Scott (or David Brent, if you watched the UK version) is entirely lacking in self-awareness, and is frequently outfoxed by his subordinates. If these are the figures that come into people's minds when the word "manager" is used, then we have a serious problem on our hands. Interestingly, the phrase "leader" has much more attractive connotations, and some positive role models—but we will come back to the leader versus manager distinction shortly.

Managers don't usually go to work in the morning thinking, "I'm going to be an asshole today, I'm going to make my employees' lives miserable." But some behave that way anyway, because they are creatures of their environment—a working environment that has taken shape over roughly the last 150 years. The harsh reality is that today's large business organizations are—with notable exceptions—uninspiring places to spend our working lives. Fear and distrust are endemic. Aggressive and unpleasant behavior is condoned. Creativity and passion are suppressed. The good news is that the opportunity for improvement here is vast and, if we *do* improve the practice of management, the payoffs—for pioneering companies, for all their employees, and for society as a whole—are substantial.

Let's be clear upfront that there are no simple solutions to this problem. Many thinkers and business pioneers have tackled the same set of issues, and made limited progress. But we should at least recognize that this is a problem worth working on. Management has failed at the big-picture level, as the employees and shareholders of Lehman and GM will attest. Management has also failed at the personal level, as every one of us has observed.

We need to rethink management. We need to help executives figure out the best way to manage, and we need to help employees take some responsibility—to get the managers they deserve. These are the challenges we come to grips with in this book.

The Corruption of Management

Where did management go wrong? We cannot put it down to a few rogue executives or bad decisions, and we cannot single out specific companies or industries. The problem is systemic, and it goes way back in time. Big-company executives may be the ones in the hot seats, but many other parties are complicit in the problems of management, including policymakers, regulators, academics, and consultants.

Before discussing where things went wrong, we need a clear definition of management. Leading academics from Mary Parker Follett, Henri Fayol, and Chester Barnard through to Peter Drucker, Henry Mintzberg, and Gary Hamel have all offered a view on this, but I am going to keep things simple and use the Wikipedia definition:

"Management is the act of getting people together to accomplish desired goals and objectives."

Please think about these words for a few moments. There is a lot of stuff missing from this definition—no mention of planning, organization, staffing, controlling, or any of the dozen other activities that are usually associated with management. There is also no mention of companies or corporations, and absolutely nothing about hierarchy or bureaucracy. And that is precisely the point—management is a social endeavor, which simply involves getting people to come together to achieve goals that they could not achieve on their own. A soccer coach is a manager, as is an orchestra conductor and a Cub Scout leader. At some point we need to qualify this definition to make it relevant to a business context, but for now let's use the word in its generic form.

I believe that management—as a social activity, and as a philosophy—has gradually become corrupted over the last 100 years. When I say corrupted, I don't mean in the sense of doing immoral or dishonest things (though clearly there have been quite a few cases of corrupt managers in recent years). Rather, I mean that the *word has become infected or tainted*. Its colloquial usage has metamorphosed into something narrower, and more pejorative, than Wikipedia or Webster's Dictionary might suggest. In talking to people about the term, and in reading the literature, I have noticed that managers are typically seen as low-level bureaucrats who are "internally focused, absorbed in operational details, controlling and coordinating the work of their subordinates, and dealing with office politics."[15]

Whether accurate or not, this is a sentiment everyone can recognize. But it is a very restrictive view of the nature of management. And such sentiments also feed back into the workplace, further shaping the practice of management in a negative way. This is why I argue that the word has been corrupted.

Why has this corruption taken place? There are two major reasons:

Large industrial firms became dominant—and their style of management became dominant as well. A careful reading of business history indicates that large companies, of the type most of us work in today, first came into existence about 150 years ago. Back in 1850 nine out of ten white male citizens in the US worked for themselves as farmers, merchants, or craftsmen. The biggest company in the UK at the time had only 300 employees.[16] But the industrial revolution sparked a wholesale change in the nature of work and organization, with mills, railroads, steel manufacturers, and electricity companies all emerging in the latter part of the nineteenth century. Helped along by management pioneers like Frederick Taylor, Frank and Lilian Gilbreth, and Henri Fayol, these companies put in place formal structures and processes and hierarchical systems of control that we would still recognize today, and which were all geared toward efficient, low-cost production of standardized products.

Of course this industrial Management Model was a spectacular success, and became one of the key drivers of economic progress in the twentieth century.[17] But it had an insidious effect on the concept of management, because the term came to be associated exclusively with the hierarchical, bureaucratic form of work practiced in large industrial firms. For many people, even today, the word management conjures up images of hierarchy, control, and formal procedures, for reasons that have nothing to do with the underlying meaning of the term. "Management" and "large industrial firm" became intertwined in the 1920s, and they are still tightly linked today.

Such a narrow model of management gets us into trouble for a couple of reasons. First, it blinds us to the range of alternative Management Models that exist. Sports teams, social communities, aid organizations, even families, operate with very different principles than large industrial companies, and these alternative principles are potentially very useful today. It is interesting to note that management thinker Mary Parker Follett's prescient ideas about empowerment and trust emerged from her work as a community organizer in Boston in the 1920s.[18] While the other writers of that era were studying large industrial companies, she was studying management in voluntary organizations. Unsurprisingly she came up with some novel and belatedly influential ideas and accurately pointed out that management happens in a wide variety of social settings. There is a need for many more management writers like her to make sense of some of these alternative contexts.

The other reason that a narrow view of management gets us into trouble is that it leads us to assume, incorrectly, that large industrial companies are inherently superior to other forms of organization. Of course there are certain industrial processes that are best suited to economies of scale and scope, but we would be misunderstanding history if we assumed that mass production was the only feasible model of industrial organization. In a fascinating article called "Historical Alternatives to Mass Production,"[19] academics Charles Sabel and Jonathan Zeitlin made the case that other viable forms of organizing existed during the industrial revolution, including confederations of independent firms working collaboratively within a municipality, and loosely-linked alliances of medium and small firms linked through family ties and cross-shareholdings. Often concentrated in "industrial districts" such as Baden-Wurtemberg in Germany and Emilia-Romagna in Italy, these models were quite workable in the late 1800s and many are still in existence today. Sabel and Zeitlin weren't trying to suggest that mass production took us down the wrong path. Rather, they were arguing for pluralism—for the need to recognize that Management Models *other than the hierarchical, bureaucratic organization* have their own important merits. Again, this is a lesson from history that has enormous resonance today.

The aggrandizement of leadership came at the expense of management. The second body blow to "management" was the apparently inexorable rise of "leadership" as a field of study. While the classic texts on business management are now more than a century old, books on business leadership are a more recent phenomenon, emerging in the post-war years and really taking off in the 1970s. Today there are more business books published on leadership than any other sub-discipline. A few writers stuck with management—Peter Drucker and Henry Mintzberg being the most notable cases—but in most books management has been entirely subordinated to leadership.

It's very clear what happened. To make room for leadership—which back in the 1970s was a poorly understood phenomenon—business writers felt compelled to diminish the role of management. Managers, in this new worldview, were passive, inert, and narrow-minded, while leaders were visionary agents of change. And the consequences of this leadership "revolution" were predictable: people flocked to this new, sexy way of working, while management took a step backward. Here is one example of what I mean. A few years ago three UK-based academics, Michael Brocklehurst, Chris Grey and Andy Sturdy, asked their part-time MBA students to describe their work. Not one of them used the word "manager". When pressed further, the students said, in essence, that they did not want to be labeled with such a pejorative term: "I equate management with bossy, insecure, weak people trying to intimidate," said one. "A manager is someone who interferes with someone else's work," said another.[20]

Let's look more closely at the leadership versus management debate. Table 1-1 summarizes the arguments of two of the most

Table 1.1: Leadership versus Management[21]

	Role of a Manager	Role of a Leader
Warren Bennis	Focuses on efficiency Accepts the status quo Does things right	Focuses on effectiveness Challenges the status quo Does the right things
John Kotter	Coping with complexity Planning and budgeting Controlling and problem-solving	Coping with change Setting direction Motivating people

influential leadership thinkers, John Kotter and Warren Bennis. Kotter sees managers as being the ones who plan, budget, organize, and control, while leaders set direction, manage change, and motivate people. Bennis views managers as those who promote efficiency, follow the rules, and accept the status quo, while leaders focus on challenging the rules and promoting effectiveness. Needless to say, I believe this dichotomy is inaccurate and, frankly, insulting. Why, for example, does "motivating people" lie beyond the job description of a manager? And "doing things right" versus "doing the right things" is a nice play-on-words but a rather unhelpful distinction. Surely we should all be doing both?

Now, Kotter and Bennis are smart, thoughtful people who are more right than they are wrong. And they have a logically flawless response to my critique: namely, that "leadership" and "management" are *roles* that the same individual can play at different times. I can put on my leader hat in the morning when speaking to my team about next year's plans, and then in the afternoon I can put on my manager hat and work through the quarterly budget. This makes sense. But I still think the aggrandizement of leadership at the expense of management is unhelpful, because management—as a profession and as a concept—is vitally important to the business world. We should be looking for ways to build it up, rather than tear it down.

Here is my view on the management versus leadership debate. Leadership is a process of social influence: it is concerned with the traits, styles, and behaviors of individuals that causes others to follow them. Management is the act of getting people together to accomplish desired goals. To make the distinction even starker, one might almost argue that leadership is *what you say and how you say it*, whereas management is *what you do and how you do it*. I don't want to fall into the trap of making one of these seem important at the expense of the other. I am simply arguing that management and leadership are complementary to one another.

Or to put it really simply, we all need to be leaders *and* managers. We need to be able to influence others through our ideas, words, and actions. We also need to be able to get work done through others on a day-to-day basis.

How do political leaders get elected? Think back to recent elections in your own country. Often, we elect people on their perceived qualities of leadership—vision, charisma, in touch with the people. But once politicians are in office, they need first and foremost to be effective managers—they need to deliver on election promises, resolve competing agendas, and prioritize the issues that land on their desk. Leadership is still part of the job, to be sure, but the ability to "get things done" is ultimately how we judge our political leaders.

To summarize: the concept of management has been gradually corrupted over the years, partly because of the success of large industrial companies and their particular model of management, partly because of the popularity of leadership, which has grown at management's expense. To make progress, we need first to reverse out of the cul-de-sac that management has been driven into. We need to rediscover the original meaning of the word, and we need to remind ourselves that leadership and management are simply two horses pulling the same cart.

Management in a Changing World

I have painted a somewhat gloomy picture so far, and the picture gets gloomier still, at least for the moment. The failure of management might not be such a concern if the business world were as predictable and stable as it had been in the post-war years. But a great deal has changed since then. The major shifts in the business environment are well documented, so we won't go through them in any detail, but they are worth summarizing:

- We have undergone a period of economic and political transformation, the result of which is a more tightly integrated world economy, with new markets opening up in previously closed regions, and new competitors emerging, often with very different operating norms to those we are used to.

- We have also lived through the Information and Communication Technology revolution, leading to the emergence of the "World Wide Computer"[22] that provides access to information on an unprecedented scale.

- We have experienced many social changes as well: people are living and working longer, but with far more loyalty to their own professional identity than to the organization they work for. And they are seeking engagement in their work, not just a paycheck.

These trends have led to a fundamental change in the economic logic of the firm. In the traditional model, capital was the scarce resource, and the strategic imperative of the firm was to transform inputs into outputs as efficiently as possible. Today, the scarce resource is knowledge, and firms succeed not just on the basis of efficiency, but also creativity and innovation.

These trends have also led to changes in the nature of management. The onset of global competition has made it necessary to adapt the traditional Anglo-American model we are most familiar with to the cultural norms of the countries in which we are working. The rise of "knowledge workers," individuals who own their own means of production, has changed the relationship between boss and employee. And the invention of the Internet has made it possible to access information and work together in a dispersed manner that was never possible before.

Of course, depending on your worldview, these trends are either threats or opportunities. They are threats insofar as they make it even harder than before to retreat back into our traditional models of management. And they are opportunities because new ways of working are opening up before our eyes.

Management was in need of reinvention anyway. But with these technological, economic, and social changes afoot, the urgency of the task has become that much greater. We pick up on these themes and play out their implications for management in the chapters ahead.

Reinventing Management

So what is the future of management? In the face of all these challenges, can management be reinvented to make it more effective as an agent of economic progress and more responsive to the needs of employees?

One school of thought says management cannot be reinvented. The argument here can be summarized as follows: management is fundamentally about how individuals work together, and the basic laws of social interaction have not changed for centuries—if ever. While the business context will evolve, the underlying principles of management—how we set objectives, coordinate effort, monitor performance—are never going to change. For example, Stanford Professor Harold Leavitt's most recent book *Top Down* argued the case for hierarchy:

> "Hierarchies have structured human activity for centuries. They've learned to cloak themselves in the commoners' clothes in order to do business in egalitarian cultures, but don't let that fool you.... Hierarchy remains the foundational shape of every large human organization."[23]

Several other leading thinkers, including Henry Mintzberg and Peter Drucker, have put forward similar points of view. In Mintzberg's recent award-winning book, *Managing*, he argues that the nature of managerial work has hardly changed for decades: "Managers deal with different issues as time moves forward, but not with different managing. The job does not change."[24] Indeed, it is interesting to note that most of the major innovations in management—the industrialization of R&D, mass production, decentralization, brand management, discounted cash flow—occurred before 1930. Most of the recent innovations—Six Sigma, the balanced scorecard, re-engineering, for example—have been little more than incremental improvements on existing ideas, rather than entirely new ideas in their own right. If we extend this train of thinking, we could conclude that the evolution of management has more or less run its course, that, to use Francis Fukayama's famous expression, we've reached "the end of history" with regard to management progress.

But we haven't. Of course there is some validity in arguing that the basic laws of human behavior are not going to change. But the practice of management is enormously context-dependent, and as the nature of business organizations evolves, so too will management. Yes, there will always be the need for some sort of hierarchical structure in a large organization, but the nature of that hierarchy—as we discuss in Chapter 4—can potentially change dramatically.

The other reason I disagree with the argument that "management cannot be reinvented" is that *there must be a better way of running large companies*. The first part of this chapter documented some of the problems with management as it functions today, and I believe we cannot just accept that our current model is as good as it gets.

Another school of thought says we are on the cusp of inventing an entirely new model of management. The argument here runs as follows: management as we know it today was developed for the industrial era, in which capital was the scarce resource. Today, it is knowledge. Firms gain advantage not by working efficiently but by harnessing initiative and creativity. And, most vitally, the information technology revolution is making it possible for entirely new ways of working to emerge. MIT Professor Tom Malone has made this case clearly:

> "We are in the early stages of another revolution... that promises to lead to a further transformation in our thinking about control. For the first time in history, technologies allow us to gain the

economic benefits of large organizations, without giving up the human benefits of small ones. This revolution has begun."[25]

Many other writers have made similar claims. For example, technology writer Howard Rheingold observed that "the most far-reaching changes [from new technology] will come, as they often do, from the kinds of relationships, enterprises, communities, and markets that the infrastructure makes possible."[26] *Wired* editor Jeff Howe argues that the internet-driven phenomenon of crowdsourcing "will change the nature of work and creativity."[27] Again, the argument is persuasive, and one that we can all relate to as we try to come to grips with the potential ramifications of Internet technology.

The trouble is, I have a nagging concern that we have been here before. All the arguments around decentralization and empowerment have been debated for a very long time. *Fortune* magazine ran a series of articles on "The New Management" in 1955 in which these themes were discussed. And every generation of management writers since then, including such luminaries as Peter Drucker, Gary Hamel, Rosabeth Moss Kanter, and Sumantra Ghoshal, has also argued for its own version of revolutionary change in the years ahead.

Harvard Professors Robert Eccles and Nitin Nohria wrote a very thoughtful critique of this perspective in *Beyond the Hype*. Writing in 1992, they observed five principles of the "new organization" that were being preached to managers—smaller is better than larger, less diversification is better than more diversification, competition must be replaced by collaboration, formal authority must be diminished, and time cycles must become shorter. Needless to say, these five principles are still being preached 20 years on. And Eccles and Nohria's rhetorical question—are we [really] moving from one historical epoch to another, during which radical and fundamental changes are taking place in organization and work[28]—is still as germane as it was back then.

Is there a third way here? Can we identify a useful way forward that avoids the extreme positions of these other two schools of thought? I believe there is.

We don't need to throw up our hands and say management has gone as far as it can, because that would accept the failures of management as something we must just live with. And we don't need to create a whole new model of management—we have plenty of ideas from the world of theory and insights from the world of practice to guide us.

We need to develop a more comprehensive understanding of what management is really about to make better choices. By going back to a basic definition of management—the act of getting people together to accomplish desired goals—we can frame our discussion of the activities and principles of management much more explicitly. And armed with this new understanding, we can help managers make better choices within the universe of known possibilities, rather than suggest they invent something that has never been thought of before.

Here is an example. Why should we assume that all important decisions get made by the people at the top of the organizational hierarchy? Traditionally this was certainly the case, but is it possible that important decisions might be made in less-hierarchical or non-hierarchical ways? Yes it is. In fact, entire books have been written on the "wisdom of crowds" and "crowdsourcing" techniques for aggregating the views of large numbers of people to make better decisions.[29] So it would be wrong to assume that all decisions made in the future will be made exclusively by those at the top of the hierarchy, and it would be equally wrong to assume that crowdsourcing will entirely replace traditional decision making structures.

The prosaic truth is that *it depends*—the right model depends on a host of contingencies, including the nature of the decision being made, the company's size and background, the interests and capabilities of the employees, and so on. In the next chapter we explore just what a Management Model is. We develop a framework outlining the four key activities of management, and the traditional and alternative principles by which each activity can be managed. *The right Management Model for your company is the one based on the most appropriate choices you make within that framework.*

The Key Messages in this Book

In the field of business strategy it is often argued that there are two different and complementary pathways to success—devising a distinctive strategic position and implementing a particular strategy effectively. Southwest Airlines, Dell Computer, and IKEA have prospered because they developed and protected a distinctive strategic position. Toyota, McDonalds, and Tesco have prospered by executing their plain-vanilla strategy better than anyone else in their industry.[30]

The same logic applies in the field of management: you can make distinctive choices about the Management Model you are going to use, and you can have high-quality managers who simply do their jobs well. Ultimately there is no trade-off needed between these two approaches. High-performing companies typically do both well. But I make the distinction to emphasize that this book is focusing on the former—it is about how you choose the best Management Model for a given situation. Of course the quality of the individuals you employ, and the extent to which they do their jobs well, are important, but such issues are the subject of another book. The focus here is on the overall architecture of management—the choices we make about how we work. We make these choices through four linked steps (Figure 1-1).

Figure 1.1:   The four key steps in making smarter choices

Understanding: You need to be explicit about the management principles you are using to run your company. These principles are invisible, and often understood only at a subconscious level, but they drive the day-to-day processes and practices through which management work gets done. Chapter 2 describes a framework for clarifying what these principles are and it provides a tool to help you diagnose your company's implicit choices.

Evaluating: You need to assess whether your company's management principles are suited to the business environment in which you are working. There are risks associated with whatever principles you employ, so you need to understand the pros and cons of each one so that you can choose wisely. Chapters 3-6 take you through the four major activities of management (coordinating activities, making decisions, setting objectives, motivating people), discussing in detail the pros and cons of each. Chapter 7 then puts forward an integrative framework for looking at these choices in a comprehensive way.

Envisioning and experimenting: You need to be prepared to try out new practices as a way of reinforcing your choices. Your Management Model can only become a source of advantage if you find ways of working that separate you out from the crowd. So it is important to take a creative approach to management, by envisioning new ways of working and experimenting with them. Chapters 8 and 9 therefore focus on *how* you innovate your Management Model, with Chapter 8 addressing the challenges of enacting change from a mid-level position in a large company and Chapter 9 looking at the same issues from the position of the Chief Executive Officer. Chapter 9 closes with a step-by-step guide to the process of management innovation.

Lehman Brothers and GM Revisited

Before moving on to look carefully at what precisely a Management Model is, let's revisit for a moment the cases of Lehman Brothers and General Motors. I suggested that Lehman suffered from a couple of fatal flaws: it lacked any sort of higher-order purpose to guide or motivate its employees, and it focused on extrinsic rewards (i.e. money) at the expense of all else, thereby driving out teamwork, institution-building, and loyalty. GM suffered from excessive bureaucracy and overly formalized management processes, and a mistaken belief that it could control its business environment. Underlying these characteristics, in each case, was an implicit point of view about the company's Management Model, about the guiding principles on which particular practices were built.

And it's not as though there were no other options available to these two companies. Goldman Sachs' partnership model was built on very different underlying principles (and with much greater success) than the free-agent model that Lehman adopted. In the automobile industry, Toyota was founded on a set of beliefs about how to get the best out of employees that was dramatically different from that of the Big Three, but GM was unable to fully internalize those principles. Indeed, GM was never able to shed Alfred Sloan's legacy. Peter Drucker observed, when commenting on GM's long decline, "To the GM executives, policies were 'principles' and were valid forever."[31]

It's worth noting that these companies got it wrong in two distinct (though linked) ways. Mistake number one was that the executives subconsciously assumed (incorrectly) that there was only one valid Management Model in their industry, i.e. the one they had always used. Mistake number two was to fail to adapt their existing Management Model to the changes underway in the business environment, with the result that their earlier strengths turned gradually into liabilities.

It's very easy to go astray. For example, a decade ago, the mantra in many large companies was "bring the market inside"— use market-like mechanisms to overcome the stifling problems of bureaucracy and hierarchy. This advice was aimed at companies like GM. It worked well in Shell and others, as they created Venture Capital-like seed funding systems such as GameChanger.

But it was disastrous in Lehman and the other investment banks, which were destroyed by opening themselves up to market forces. And it was disastrous in Enron. The message, in other words, is that the right Management Model for a big oil company is not necessarily the right Management Model for an investment bank. But more importantly—how crucial it is to get it just right.

Chapter 1: Key Points

Management is the act of getting people together to accomplish desired goals and objectives. Unfortunately this meaning has become corrupted over the years, with the result that many people now see management as a narrow and overly-mechanistic activity. This corruption occurred for two main reasons. First, the growth of the modern industrial corporation led people to equate the style of management practiced in a large factory with the practice of management in general. Second, the rise in popularity of thinking about leadership was at management's expense, so that the job description of management ended up becoming narrower and less attractive over the years.

The 2007–2008 financial crisis was a failure of management as much as it was a failure of policy, governance, or regulation. The underlying cause of Lehman Brothers demise was a poorly chosen Management Model that encouraged bankers to pursue their own interests at the expense of their employees and shareholders. The collapse of General Motors, on the other hand, was the result of an entirely different set of management mistakes that prioritized conforming to the GM system ahead of adapting to changing market demands. In contrasting ways, both companies' problems point to the need for greater attention to be paid to management in large companies.

This book seeks to bring management back into focus. It argues that companies should invest as much time thinking about improving their management practices as they think about developing new products and services. This need is driven both by the flaws in our current models of management and by the new opportunities that Web 2.0 technologies offer us.

There are two views of management out there at the moment. One view suggests that management as a discipline is essentially the same as it has ever been, the other view suggests that we need to radically rethink our basic principles of management. This book suggests a third way—it suggests that managers become more conscious of the choices they have subconsciously made about how they get work done, and it shows how they can make smarter choices in the future that build on the opportunities for improvement, while also being aware of the downside risks.

2

WHAT'S YOUR MANAGEMENT MODEL?

Picture the following scenario. Your firm competes in a highly competitive industry sector with tight margins. Your customers view your product as a commodity—they might pay marginally more for a leading brand (yours is not one of them), and there are no obvious points of differentiation. There is little scope for technological innovation—new ideas are quickly copied. Employee turnover is high.

How do you compete? How might you gain competitive advantage?

Two very different firms—Happy Ltd with 40 employees and HCL Technologies with tens of thousands—took a novel approach to this dilemma. They decided to differentiate themselves on the basis of their Management Models.

Building Competitive Advantage through Management Model Innovation

Happy Ltd (Happy) is a $3 million IT training company in London founded by Henry Stewart.[1] With a failed start-up under his belt and an affinity for people, Stewart set out in the mid-1990s to build a great company designed around a distinctive set of management principles. The underlying philosophy is simply that people work best when they feel good about themselves. Managers are chosen for their ability to manage, and employees can change managers if the current one is not right for them. The manager's job is to inspire and support their team, not look over their employees' shoulders. New recruits are never asked for qualifications but are chosen for attitude, potential, and how well they respond to feedback on their training style. Mistakes are celebrated, and all major projects are pre-approved (i.e. staff are able to implement the solution they come up with, without referring back to their manager).

Explained Stewart: "The most radical thing we believe is that managers should be chosen according to how good they are at managing people. Too often, managers are chosen for technical competence and how long they've been in the job. As a result, one of the biggest reasons people leave a company is to get away from their manager."

How has Stewart's novel approach fared in the UK IT training market? Client satisfaction is currently at an industry-leading 98.7%, and is the single most important performance indicator at Happy because it leads to follow-up business. "Our basic philosophy of marketing is to deliver a great service and wait for the phone to ring," commented Stewart. Happy sells its training courses for £200 per day, more than double the £90 per day the leading competitor charges. And while the industry contracted by 30% during the period 2001–2007, Happy's revenues doubled. Employee turnover is half the industry average, and 2000 people are on a waiting list for vacancies at the company. Not surprisingly, Happy has been listed in the top 20 workplaces in the UK for the last five years. It has also been rated the best company in the country for customer service (by *Management Today*), the best for well-being (*Financial Times*), and the best small business for positive impact on society (Business in the Community).[2]

HCL Technologies (HCL) is one of the leading Indian IT services companies with 85 000 employees and $6 billion in revenues in 2010[3] (there is also a sister company, HCL Infosystems). Vineet Nayar became president in 2005 after 20 years in the company (and later CEO), and on taking the helm he faced exactly the dilemma outlined above. The market for IT services was growing, but customer demands were becoming increasingly complex, and there was no real differentiation between suppliers.

At that time, HCL was a second-tier Indian brand in a sector dominated by giants including IBM, EDS, and Accenture.

Faced with this situation, Nayar had a Eureka comment: he saw that IT services had become a commodity market. Everyone claimed to be customer focused, but he believed that the one person who can actually create a solution is the employee. What brings most value in the industry, he recognized, is what employees do when they interact with customers. "So the higher quality of employee you have in terms of capability, enablement, engagement, the better value gets created in that interface," he noted.

The first step in getting HCL to face up to this opportunity was to take a leaf from a fairy story. Explained Nayar: "Most of us spend our time bullshitting, telling everyone what a great company we are. So we launched a huge concept we called 'Mirror, Mirror on the Wall' and we dragged up the dirt on the company. We brought it out in front of all the employees, and I met every one of them. It unleashed an energy that was unparalleled by anything I have seen in my life. Honesty really does pay."

With the genie out of the bottle, Nayar then began a process of changing the entire social fabric of HCL—everything with the aim of "spoiling" the employees and giving them the confidence and skills to do their best. Innovations included:

- **Reverse accountability.** The company launched company-wide 360-degree appraisals for all managers and placed the results on the web for all to see. Some 1500 managers have been appraised in this way, and Nayar determined it an enormous success. The surveys are not linked to pay or promotion, but the public nature of the exercise is enough for managers to take it very seriously.

- **Parallel hierarchy.** Recognizing that "we are obsessed by the idea that hierarchy gives us certainty," Nayar wanted to destroy the concept that there is one person who takes the decision. And so HCL launched "Destroy the Office of the CEO." They created a parallel hierarchy organization of 32 communities of interest where people can collaborate and create opportunities outside their hierarchy, making it impossible for one person to have control. After three years, 20% of HCL's revenues from ideas and initiatives was created out of the communities of interest.

- **Hygiene.** It's easy to say employees come first, but how do you prove it? HCL's answer is the creation of service level agreements between administrative departments and the employee. For any employee complaint—from a broken chair to a contested bonus—an employee opens a service ticket on a portal and sends it to the department in question. Crucially, it is only the employee who can close the ticket, and since service desks are measured on their response rates and times, there is a strong incentive for rapid closure.

Through these and other initiatives, HCL is sending a powerful signal that it is the front-line employees who create the value, and the organization is there to support them, rather than the other way round.

The results of these initiatives? Compared to its peers, HCL is growing faster and has lower levels of employee turnover. In 2009 the company won the Financial Times *Boldness in Business* readers' award and Hewitt's *Best Employer in India* award. Its compound annual growth rate from 2008 to 2011 was an industry-leading 24%. Explained Nayar: "For the last three years we have not gone into any new markets; all we have done is focus on employees. And we are growing faster than anybody else. We are either bloody lucky, or we must be doing something right."[4]

Happy and HCL illustrate *the power of an innovative Management Model*. Both companies are doing well, because their leaders have chosen to think creatively about how they manage—both in terms of the underlying philosophy of management and the specific practices they use to reinforce their philosophy. They have made conscious and unusual choices in how they approach the four areas that comprise the core activities of management:

- **New ways of coordinating activities.** HCL Technologies has put in place new ways of matching employees up with projects rather than allocating all projects from above. Happy is small enough that coordination happens through personal relationships; Stewart actively resists bureaucracy.

- **New ways of making decisions.** Stewart "pre-approves" all requests for funding, and Nayar encourages employees to take responsibility for coming up with creative solutions for clients. In both cases, they are pushing decision-making down to the people *doing* the work.

- **New ways of defining objectives.** Happy and HCL Technologies both say explicitly that "the customer comes second." Employee satisfaction is what they care most deeply about—everything else follows from that (we discuss this point at length in Chapter 5).

- **New ways of motivating employees.** Both companies are looking for ways of bringing out employees' underlying desire to do a good job—by creating a more supportive and more enjoyable working environment.

The similarities between the two approaches are important here. But so are the differences. Remember, Happy is a 40-person firm still run by its founder. Stewart had the opportunity to shape his company to suit his philosophy. And he took that opportunity. It is never easy to develop a new model of management, but at least Stewart had the luxury of choosing every one of the people who works for him—people who share his view of the world.

Vineet Nayar had a more difficult job: at the time he took over as CEO, he had to persuade an entrenched management team—and 55 000 employees—that there was a need to change, and that his unusual ideas would help the company move forward.

We explore the challenges of *implementing* new management ideas in detail in Chapters 8 and 9, but for the moment it is simply worth acknowledging that developing a new Management Model in an established company is difficult—but not impossible. HCL is proof of that.

So here's the key point: in a competitive market, where your new products and services are rapidly copied by your competitors, what possible sources of competitive advantage do you have? There is some evidence that a distinctive *business model* (defined below) can generate long-term benefits. I believe a distinctive *Management Model* can also do that. In the cases of Happy and HCL, Management Model innovation has generated higher levels of employee engagement, which in turn has led to improvements in customer satisfaction and financial performance. But the argument is broader than that: Management Model innovation can also enable dramatic improvements on many different strategic imperatives. For example, over the course of the book we discuss:

- How the Swiss private bank UBS Wealth Management *eliminated its traditional budgeting system* in 2001 to drive organic growth.

- How Danish hearing-aid company Oticon created a *project-based spaghetti organization* in the 1990s to achieve higher levels of strategic agility.

- How Dutch digital TV company Irdeto created a *dual-core headquarters* in 2006 to establish a global mindset across the organization.

- How the UK oil major BP put in place a *peer review system* in the 1990s to encourage cross-unit collaboration.

In these cases, executives were looking to deliver on important strategic objectives (organic growth, agility, innovation, global presence, collaboration) and they turned to Management Model innovation (eliminating budgeting, spaghetti organization, dual-core headquarters, peer review) as the mechanism by which they would effect change. Sometimes these innovations had enduring value, sometimes their impact was temporary. But in all cases, the central notion was that changes to the company's Management Model could generate strategic benefits.

So what exactly is a Management Model, and how can it be used to create competitive advantage? We look at these questions next.

Defining What a Management Model Is

One enduring change in the management lexicon brought about by the dotcom revolution was the term *business model*—how a firm makes money. The concept had been in existence for decades, but the competition between "old" and "new" economy firms, with very different business models, helped to demonstrate its importance as a way of thinking about the basic choices firms make when it comes to their sources of revenue, their cost structure, and their make-or-buy options.

In the post-dotcom era, firms have continued to experiment with new business models, with some success. But genuinely new business models are hard to come by, and they aren't as easily defended as they once were. Firms are therefore on the lookout for new forms of competitive advantage—they are looking for sources of distinctiveness that are enduring, hard to copy, and valuable in the marketplace.

One emerging and intriguing possibility, as suggested by Happy and HCL's experiences, is the idea that a firm's *Management Model* can become a source of advantage. In fact, asking, "What is your Management Model?" is as important as asking "What is your business model?" Peter Drucker argued that an organization's business model—the "theory of the business" in his words—has three parts: assumptions about the environment of the organization, the specific mission of the organization, and the core competencies needed to accomplish the organization's mission.[5] Together these assumptions define what an organiz-ation gets paid for, what results it considers meaningful, and what it must excel at to maintain its competitive position. But knowing the answers to these questions is only half the story: these are answers to the *what* and the *why* of business. The other half of the story—your Management Model—answers the equally important question *how*.

And just what is a Management Model? Here is a formal definition:

> A Management Model is the choices made by the executives of a firm regarding how they define objectives, motivate effort, coor-dinate activities, and allocate resources—in other words, the defi-nition of *how* work of management gets done.

This definition has two important features. First, it is about *making choices*. In the airline industry there are several coexisting business models (the full-service, fly-everywhere flag carrier; the no-frills, point-to-point scheduled airline; the peak-season charter airline; the business-only airline), and every firm knows it has to make an explicit choice about which business model it will adopt. Similarly, some industries already feature competing Management Models. For example, Linux, Google, and Microsoft all operate with very different Management Models (Linux is run through an open-source software community; Google has a highly informal, university-like model; Microsoft has a more traditional, hierarchical structure), yet they compete head-to-head in the desktop operating system market. Toyota operated for decades with a different Management Model from those of GM and Ford, despite having a very similar business model.[6] And of course Happy and HCL are both examples of companies pushing to develop distinct Management Models in their respec-tive industries.

The second feature of the definition is that the *discipline of management has four specific dimensions*. Managers have to decide

Table 2.1:   Four perspectives on the activities of management[7]

Management Writer	Activities of Management
Henri Fayol	Prevoyance (forecasting and planning), Organizing, Commanding, Controlling
Luther Gulick and Lyndall Urwick	Planning, Organizing, Staffing, Directing, Coordinating, Reporting, Budgeting
Peter Drucker	Setting Objectives, Organizing, Motivating and Communicating, Measurement, Development
Henry Mintzberg	Framing and Scheduling, Communicating and Controlling, Leading and Linking, Doing and Dealing

where their organization—or their department or unit—is going (*define objectives*), and they have to get people to agree to go in that direction (*motivate effort*). The means by which they do this is to manage across (*coordinate activities*) and to manage down (*making decisions*).

Is this a comprehensive list of the activities of management? No it is not. In fact, over the years many other management writers have come up with their own, often much longer, lists. Table 2.1 lists some of the well-known lists, including those of Henri Fayol, Peter Drucker, and Henry Mintzberg.

In comparing their lists of activities to mine, you can see that there is enormous overlap, and clearly I have chosen to "lump" certain things together while others have chosen to "split" them up. But a more important difference is that I have tried to use terms that do not assume all management occurs in a large hierarchical firm. As made clear in Chapter 1, one of the problems with the term management is that its usage has become overly narrow. So words like staffing, controlling, and directing send entirely the wrong signals because they assume a particular model. Do managers *need* to control and direct their employees? Or can we imagine an alternative model in which employees take control of their own activities and set their own direction? As much as possible, I believe we should define the dimensions of management in a context-neutral way, so that they are as relevant to a symphony orchestra as they are to an auto plant.

Hence the four key activities, or dimensions, of management in my definition. They are all "value-adding" activities that collectively enable the organization to achieve its aims. They are conceptually separate. And they also form the structure for the next four chapters of the book.

Two omissions are worth commenting on briefly. First, I have not included "controlling" (or "monitoring") as a separate activity, because in my mind it cuts across all four activities. It also has big-brother overtones that may or not be appropriate in a modern organization. Second, I have not included "developing people" as a separate activity. Clearly as a business school professor I believe developing people is enormously important, but in this particular worldview it fits within the "motivating effort" box, rather than getting a box of its own.

Organizing Framework: Four Dimensions, Eight Principles

To make this definition useful as both an organizing structure for the book and as a practical guide for managers, we need to add one additional layer of complexity—the framework that pulls together practices, processes, and principles.

The work that happens on a daily basis in organizations can be thought of as the *practices* of management. Common practices include 360-degree feedback systems, quality circles, and scenario planning. These practices are sometimes generic ways of working that all companies use, and they are sometimes unique to a single company.[8]

Practices are then linked together into a set of *management processes*. Typical examples are the resource-allocation process, the performance-management process, the new-product development process, and so on. These processes are the mechanisms by which organizations fulfill their overall objectives. They *indirectly* add value by ensuring that the business processes (supply, manufacturing, order fulfillment, for example, which turn inputs into outputs) are working efficiently and effectively.

Finally, management processes are built on a set of underlying *management principles*. A principle is simply an assumption or belief about the way something works or should work. One deeply held management principle, for example, is extrinsic motivation —the notion that employees need material and direct rewards to keep them performing well. Management principles are often subconsciously held and rarely challenged. But they are also vitally important because they shape the management processes and practices that are used on a daily basis. And as you should have gathered by now, one of the key themes of this book is to help firms raise their awareness of the management principles they are using.

It is useful to apply the iceberg metaphor here. Practices are the visible, day-to-day things that people do at work. Processes lie just below the surface of the water, not visible to the casual observer but well understood by the architects of the organization. Principles lie a long way below the surface—no one can see them, and many people don't even know they exist.

Here's a brief example: the *bonus system*, used and abused by investment banks, is a management practice that is part of a broader *performance management process* designed to get the best out of people. The practice is based on an academic theory called *expectancy theory*, which attempts to explain what motivates individuals to work harder. Obviously most managers have no understanding of expectancy theory, and neither would we expect them to. But it exists and, alongside many other obscure theories, it has influenced the design of our specific processes and practices.

In each of the next four chapters, we take the four dimensions of management in turn, and we consider two divergent principles for each. The first might be considered the *traditional principle* that firms have implicitly used for generations. The second is the *alternative principle* that is either just beginning to be adopted, or has been talked about for a long time but has not been widely used. Figure 2.1 provides a quick summary of these

Figure 2.1:   The four dimensions of management

		1	2	3	4

MEANS
- Managing across: activities — Bureaucracy ←——→ Emergence
- Managing down: decisions — Hierarchy ←→ Collective wisdom

ENDS
- Managing objectives — Alignment ←——→ Obliquity
- Managing individual motivation — Extrinsic ←——→ Intrinsic

Table 2.2:   Definitions of management principles used in Figure 2.1

Bureaucracy is a means of coordinating economic activity that relies on formal rules and procedures to ensure conformity of behavior and to generate consistent outputs.

Emergence is the spontaneous coordination of activities achieved through the self-interested behaviors of independent actors.

Hierarchy is a way of structuring work that provides managers with legitimate authority over their subordinates, and vests this power in them because it values their experience and wisdom.

Collective wisdom suggests that under certain conditions the aggregated expertise of a large number of people can produce more accurate forecasts and better decisions than those of a small number of experts.

The principle of *alignment* in a business context states that all employees are working directly toward the same common goals.

The *oblique* principle states that goals are often best achieved when pursued indirectly.

Extrinsic motivation comes from outside the person—for example, money, coercion, and the threat of punishment.

Intrinsic motivation comes from the rewards inherent to a task or activity itself—for example, playing the piano, walking in the countryside, or solving a puzzle.

dimensions and principles. Admittedly, some of these words, particularly *obliquity*, may seem unduly complex to you. For now, it's important that the overall structure makes sense—the details become clear in the chapters that lie ahead. Figure 2.1 portrays this framework graphically, and Table 2.2 provides a quick overview of what these terms mean.

Now, this framework immediately provokes a couple of questions. First, does it suggest that there will be an inexorable shift, over time, to the right-hand side—to these alternative management principles, the ones with the alluring names? Second, if competitive advantage is about choosing a distinct Management Model, is there some advice available about which principles to adopt? Does it sometimes make sense to choose the ones on the left, rather than the right? And are there certain clusters of principles that you need to link together?

We tackle these questions shortly. But before doing so, we need a short digression into the way management thinking and practice has evolved over the years.

Same As It Ever Was?

There is a long history of innovation in management thinking. In an earlier book, *Giant Steps in Management*, I described the 50 most important "management innovations" of the last 150 years, and many other writers, such as Mauro Guilen, Daniel Wren, and Eric Abrahamson, have contributed interesting perspectives. But as observed in Chapter 1, the evolution of management is not straightforward—we do not see a logical, linear development of new management practices. Instead, we see ideas falling in and out of fashion (see Box 2.1: Management Innovation at Ozco). For example, at the time of writing, the alluring concept of *employee engagement* is a hot idea in companies and consultancies around the world. Employee engagement is concerned essentially with making work more fulfilling and less machine-like. It is an important issue, no question, but how new is it? Well, in short, it is not remotely new. Every generation for the last 150 years has used its own words to pursue the same objective of making work more fulfilling and less machine-like: in the early 1990s the word was empowerment; in the 1970s, Quality of Working Life; in the 1960s, Socio Technical Systems thinking; in the 1930s,

Box 2.1:   Management Innovation at Ozco

Ozco is a large company in the extraction and processing sector.[9] In the early 1980s, executives in Ozco picked up on the ideas of an academic consultant called Elliot Jaques. Jaques had an impressive academic background. He was best known for his studies showing that people at more senior levels in an organizational hierarchy had longer time horizons and dealt with more complex problems. Packaged as *Stratified Systems Thinking (SST)*, the work had been well received but not without some controversy because it was a reaffirmation of the importance of hierarchy.

Ozco liked Jaques' ideas, and embarked on a systematic program to incorporate them into the structure and management of the company. This involved surveying everyone, analyzing their answers, putting in a new structure with new job descriptions, and rethinking the training and development activities. The company stuck with this program for several years. It was used consistently, and many people felt SST provided a clear and logical way of structuring the company.

But after five years or so, SST fell out of favor. Ozco merged with another company and the techniques were not picked up in the newly merged entity. Today, 10 years on, sediments remain—some senior managers still use SST terminology, and reflect back on the clarity of the structure it provided—but Ozco has moved on, and is now working with other management ideas.

Why did SST run out of steam? Here are the views of people who lived through the whole process:

- Diminishing returns to effort: After five years, the major benefits of SST had already been achieved, and it wasn't worth any additional investment.
- Other priorities: SST continued to have merit, but other things, including the merger, got in the way and distracted us.

- Skepticism of fads: Some people took up SST as a personal crusade, almost zealot-like in their enthusiasm. This had the opposite effect on others, whose interest quickly faded.
- Tired rhetoric. SST was valuable for a period, but its pro-hierarchy message became outdated. When it no longer fitted the *zeitgeist*, it was dropped.

Many readers will recognize these concerns, and will have lived through similar cycles of organizational change. From the skeptic's point of view, this is another example of a failed management innovation, because it did not last. But the outcome was more positive than that. The program of change certainly helped Ozco in a number of important ways and—in the language of this book—it helped the company to sharpen and refine its Management Model. But the fact that the language of SST subsequently fell out of use does not make the program a failure. Management frequently evolves in a "two steps forward, one step back" manner.

the Human Relations movement; and in the 1890s, the Welfare Work movement.

So are we making genuine progress in the field of management or are we spinning our wheels? It seems likely that there is truth in both extremes, but most observers are justifiably frustrated at how slowly the practice of management is actually changing.[10] So it's important to ask: *Why do we see so few genuine improvements in the practice of management?* Here are my four partial answers that collectively help to explain what is going on:

- **Ingrained thinking is hard to break.** The language of management is a century old, and is based on a combination of industrial-era manufacturing practices and military analogies. Thus, we talk about the *chain of command, line versus staff,* and *superiors and subordinates.* These terms affect how we view our work, which in turn affects how we behave. So like the fish that have no concept of water, most employees have no concept of a non-hierarchical, non-structured work environment.

- **New work practices are fragile.** Many companies have experimented with alternative ways of working, and their experience is that a new model can be made to work as long as enormous energy is put into maintaining it. For example, Rolls-Royce, the UK aircraft engine manufacturer, was a pioneer in self-directed work teams. Studies showed that 49 work practices had to be in place for these self-directed teams to function effectively, and if more than a few were missing, the teams reverted to type—they fell back on the old command-and-control structure. In other words, it's not just the old language that holds people back—it's the fact that new management models involve changes in behavior that don't come naturally.

- **Companies are more interested in results than improved practices.** In the book *Beyond the Hype,* Bob Eccles and Nitin Nohria argued that it doesn't really matter whether companies are actually delivering on the promise of new Management Models—what matters is that the rhetoric of change is spurring people to take action. For example, Ozco's experiments with SST, which we discuss in Box 2.1, led to useful changes in the way that roles and responsibilities were assigned, and it gave a focus to those changes. It doesn't matter, according to this view, whether they were demonstrable, lasting improvements in the company's management practices.

- **In difficult times, companies are afraid to try something new.** At the time of writing, most companies were still coming to terms with a contracting economy, uncertainty in demand, and a future of higher taxes. We are all familiar with the saying "don't let a good crisis go to waste"—the idea that a downturn is the time to push through changes that would not be acceptable when times are good. But human nature actually pushes us in the opposite direction—we circle the wagons, and we fall back on proven ways of keeping things under control. There are certainly exceptions, as we will see in this book, but most executives have little enthusiasm for experimenting with new ways of working when the economy is in bad shape.

- **External regulations pull us back.** Finally, even if a company's executives have the courage to try something new, they don't always have the degrees of freedom to allow them to act. As the fall-out from the financial crisis of 2008 continues, the only certainty facing publicly-listed companies is a future with more regulation and greater external scrutiny. And it goes without saying that these additional checks and balances are making companies more conservative, more process-oriented, and more tightly controlled from the centre.

There is, in other words, a great deal of inertia in the system of management that has emerged over time. Some of this inertia comes from ingrained behaviors and outdated terminology. Some of it comes from a lack of strong evidence that alternative models are superior. A computer technologist can prove—using objective data—that a new microprocessor is twice as fast as the old processor. But the champion of Stratified Systems Thinking at Ozco (see Box 2.1) cannot show in a definitive way that the new Management Model is better than the old one, though there are indicators, including greater employee longevity, improved efficiency, and enhanced productivity. There is much more room for interpretation and subjective evaluation in the world of management than in the world of technology.

The purpose of this discussion is simply to underline the important point that the visible practices of management do not change quickly or easily. They never have done, and we shouldn't expect them to do so in the future. Even the "Total Quality Management" revolution that was inspired by W. Edwards Deming and executed by Toyota was actually a 10-year process of change. What looks in retrospect like revolution, in the field of management at any rate, always feels like evolution at the time.

Is there *a window of opportunity* here to help companies develop new Management Models? Is there anything about the current business environment that would help to overcome all this inertia? Is there anything that might make our proposals about developing new Management Models a little easier? Yes there is. We saw earlier that there are some broad changes under way in the business environment. Let's take a closer look at four of these—specific technology and social changes that might provide a window of opportunity for the development of innovative new Management Models:

- **Web 2.0.** The first generation of the Internet was about one-way communication: users could read company websites and make online purchases. The second generation of the Internet, also known as Web 2.0, saw users become contributors: we wrote reviews on Amazon, we started blogging, we voted for our favorite stories, and we became members of online social communities. As many writers have observed, the interactive Web or "world wide computer" allows people to interact in entirely new ways. For example, we tend to evaluate blogs and comments on the basis of their actual content, rather than according to the status or hierarchical position of those who posted them. We contribute to joint projects (e.g. Wikipedia) through an innate desire to get involved, rather than to gain material rewards. And if we don't like the official version of a story, we will quickly share our contrary point of view with the world.[11] It doesn't take much imagination to realize that these behaviors, which are antithetical to the norms in most large firms, have the potential to spur significant changes in how we conduct ourselves at work.

- **Generation Y.** The generation born after 1980, whose members are now entering the workforce in significant numbers, bring with them a different set of expectations about work and a different set of skills from those of their Generation X and Baby Boom forebears. Technology writer

Don Tapscott has summarized the differentiating character-istics of this group: they want freedom in everything they do; they love to customize and personalize; they are the col-laboration and relationship generation; they have a need for speed.[12] Of course, it is debatable whether these are life-stage, rather than generational, differences, but even the most skeptical observers recognize that Generation Y is far more technology-savvy and able to multi-task than we boomers are. Again, the potential implications for the workplace of the future are big.

Here is one piece of relevant data: in a study done by UK-based flexible benefits provider, You at Work, the Generation Y employees who were *more* committed to the companies they were working for were also the ones who were spending *more* time online using Facebook and other social networking sites during their working hours.[13] As You at Work CEO Bruce Rayner observed, "For these individuals, there was no bound-ary between work and play, or between employees and non-employees." It's an important insight and, judging by the number of companies that still ban Facebook at work, it's one that many have not yet recognized.

- **Online gaming.** The scale of the computer-based game industry is staggering. By one estimate, there are more than 150 million casual game players today, using one or more of their PCs, mobile phones, or games consoles.[14] But probably the more important trend is the rise of massively multiplayer online role-playing games (MMORPGs) like *World of Warcraft*. These require gamers to join virtual teams of two to 40 people, divide up roles and responsibilities, and agree on and implement a strategy to complete a particular quest. The analogies to the world of work are obvious and very real, and as we will see in Chapter 6, some companies are already experimenting with "productivity games" as a way of getting traditional work done in a more effective manner. *World of Warcraft*, by the way, has some 9 million subscribers, typically paying $15 per month, and it is just one of many MMORPGs out there. So it is big business.

■ **Social awareness.** Finally, there is a more diffuse, but no less real, trend toward greater environmental and social awareness. This is manifested in the growth of many non-governmental organizations (NGOs) like Greenpeace, the anti-capitalist groups protesting at the annual G8 meetings, the acceptance by big business of the reality of global warming, and the growth of so-called social enterprise organizations that are driven by a social mission rather than profitability. One defining characteristic of Generation Y employees is their interest in corporate integrity and openness when deciding what to buy and where to work, and this comes in large part from their having grown up in a world where concerns about the environment and globalization are ever-present. The implications of this trend for management are less obvious, but may be highly significant. In Chapter 5, we explore how managers set objectives for their companies—for example, Seventh Generation's overarching goal is to make the world a better place—and the roles of various stakeholders in shaping those objectives.

We have to steer a fine line here. Are we living in a time of great change? Yes we are. Did previous generations also live in times of great change? Yes they did. So we need to be aware of the changes afoot, but at the same time not get bowled over by them.

Follow the Trend or Stick to the Knitting?

While there is a window of opportunity for companies to make dramatic changes to their Management Models, driven by the technological and social changes under way, there is also the reality that management generally does not evolve very fast. The smart thing, then, is for a company to pick the right Management Model rather than seek novelty for its own sake.

Let me lay my cards on the table. I am an optimist and I like change. I believe executives should be asking "can we do this a better way?" rather than thinking "this is why we've always done it this way," or "this is the new trend, let's follow it." I believe the technological and social changes under way will have a significant and positive impact on the way we manage organizations in the future.

But we face a real risk of companies pursuing new ideas for their own sake. Every new concept that finds its way into the management literature is initially presented as a paradigm-shifting, world-changing discovery. Then gradually its deficiencies become better understood, and the limitations around its effective use get drawn. For example, the phenomenal success of Wikipedia inspired many organizations to try their own form of community-built product. Some were successful, such as istockphoto.com, the royalty-free photo site; some were a partial success, such as IBM's Innovation Jam (discussed at greater length in Chapter 4); some were outright failures, such as A Million Penguins, an attempt to write a wikinovel.[15] Of course, we cannot know in advance what exactly will work and what won't (that's what experimentation is for); but we need commentators and theoreticians to be more thoughtful—and more honest—about how widely a particular concept should be applied.

The stance in this book is therefore one of *qualified* optimism. So when we explore the emerging management principles on the right-hand side of the framework and the specific practices associated with them, we carefully look at the risks and limitations in applying them. The fact is, these *new practices are not for everyone*, and the clearer we can be about the types of companies they suit, and the type they do not suit, the better.

In summary, I foresee a gradual shift toward the right-hand side of Figure 2.1 for many companies. Indeed, I did a brief survey, and the respondents confirmed this view: their estimates of where they expected to be five years from now were consistently to the right of where they were today (Figure 2.2). Equally, though, there were companies in my survey who did not foresee any

Figure 2.2: How people see their management model changing

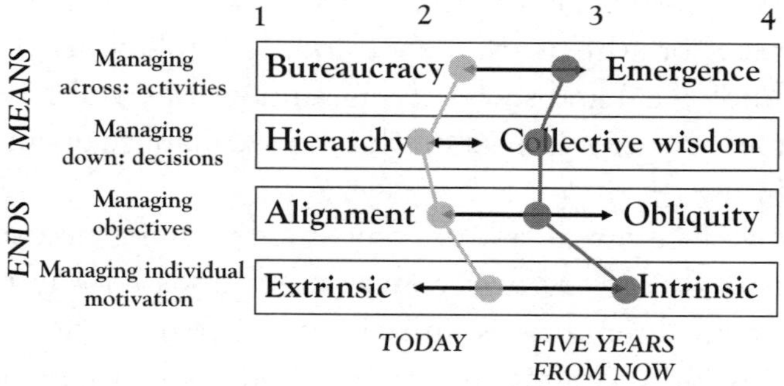

change, and there will be others who don't make the shift they are predicting.

Here is one interesting example to underline this point. Management thinker Gary Hamel wrote a highly influential article in 1999, "Bringing Silicon Valley inside."[16] He argued that most large firms have management structures inspired more by Soviet-style central planning than by free-market principles, and that we should develop Silicon Valley-style internal markets for allocating people and capital to ideas. Many companies picked up on this idea, some with considerable success. For example, in the article Hamel mentioned GameChanger, Royal Dutch Shell's extraordinarily successful process for seed-funding innovative technology projects in the energy industry that have the potential to "change the game" (we discuss GameChanger in detail in Chapter 3). But Enron followed a variant of this model, by giving its employees enormous freedom to pursue opportunities and jobs within the company's "internal market," and the consequences were disastrous.

And think, for a moment, where the Silicon Valley Management Model sits on Figure 2.2. A pure market system is built on material rewards and short-term goals (both on the left side) coupled with emergent coordination and decentralized decision-making (both on the right side). Suddenly, the picture is rather more complex: the Silicon-Valley Management Model involves a blend of left- and right-side principles, and it worked nicely for Shell (as far as they took it), but it destroyed Enron (who took it too far). We pick up and explore these themes in more detail later in the book. For now, the point is simply to understand that there is no inexorable trend to the right side of this framework. Nor is there one-Management-Model-fits all. The winners will be the companies who make wise choices and refine them as necessary.

Your Turn

Before we move on to examine the core dimensions of management and their corresponding principles, it's useful to evaluate your current Management Model. Table 2.3 can help you do that.

In assessing your model, consider your organization or business unit as a whole. Does the left-hand statement or the right-hand statement better characterize the way your company manages? In cases where your organization attempts to achieve *both* the left and right sides, indicate (by ticking box 2 or 3) the side that is currently more pervasive. Take the average scores for each pair of answers, and plot them on Figure 2.3. The Average Profile on Figure 2.3 refers to the mean scores that were obtained from more than 70 companies in a survey conducted in 2007.

Figure 2.3: Plot your current Management Model

		1	2	3	4	
Put average score for questions 1 → and 2 here	Bureaucracy		●			Emergence
Put average score for questions 3 → and 4 here	Hierarchy		●			Collective wisdom
Put average score for questions 5 → and 6 here	Alignment		●			Obliquity
Put average score for questions 7 → and 8 here	Extrinsic		●			Intrinsic

● =average response across more than 70 companies

Table 2.3:   Evaluate your current Management Model

Statement on Left	1 Strongly Agree with Statement on Left	2 Marginally Agree with Statement on Left	3 Marginally Agree with Statement on Right	4 Strongly Agree with Statement on Right	Statement on Right
1. Outputs are created through management processes, i.e. the formal coordination of inputs and structuring of effort					Outputs are created through mutual adjustment, i.e. the informal and spontaneous coordination of effort by individuals acting in their own best interests
2. Our default assumption is that information about internal processes (e.g. budget numbers, service levels achieved) is confidential and viewed on a need-to-know basis					Our default assumption is that information about internal processes is available and open to the scrutiny of all employees
3. Responsibility for making decisions (and accepting their consequences) is allocated to specific individuals					Responsibility for making decisions (and accepting their consequences) is viewed as a collective responsibility of entire teams/groups

4. Managers prefer to rely primarily on their own experience and deep knowledge of a situation					Managers prefer to tap into and make use of the disparate knowledge of their subordinates and those outside the company
5. There is a preference for narrow and always-explicit objectives					There is a preference for broad and sometimes-implicit objectives
6. There is a concern for short-term achievement against objectives (i.e. quarters/years)					There is a concern for long-term achievement against objectives (i.e. decades/generation)
7. We hire good people by making the salary, benefits, and bonuses attractive					We hire good people by focusing on the sense of achievement they will feel and their contribution to society
8. When people work long hours, it is because they are seeking to get ahead and/or to get a larger bonus					When people work long hours, it is because they enjoy the work

Chapter 2: Key points

One enduring source of competitive advantage for companies is the development of a novel business model—the choices executives make about their sources of revenue, their cost structure, and their make-or-buy options. An equally promising approach is to develop a novel Management Model—a set of explicit choices about how you get the work of management done. Some companies, including HCL Technologies and Happy Ltd, have achieved spectacular results by making conscious and deliberate changes to the way work is done.

The discipline of management consists of four primary sets of activities, or dimensions: Setting Goals, Motivating Employees, Coordinating Activities, and Making Decisions. For each one of these dimensions, it is possible to identify a traditional principle by which it operates (for example, making decisions through hierarchical control), and an alternative principle that is increasingly popular (e.g. making decisions through the collective wisdom of a large number of people). By identifying traditional and alternative poles for each dimension, we can develop a framework that allows you to diagnose your company's Management Model. This allows you to expose the subconscious choices you have made in the past about *how* you manage. Once you understand your management *principles*, it becomes possible to make changes to the management *processes* and *practices* that are based on those principles.

The practice of management does not change very quickly. Ingrained habits are hard to break, and new work practices are fragile. However, we have a window of opportunity, driven by the emergence of Web 2.0 technologies and the increasing numbers of Generation Y employees in the workforce, for making more substantial changes to the practice of management than was possible in recent decades.

This chapter provides the framework on which the rest of the book is built, with the next four chapters considering each dimension in turn, and then Chapter 7 pulling these four dimensions together to suggest four generic Models of Management.

3

COORDINATING ACTIVITIES: FROM BUREAUCRACY TO EMERGENCE

Drachten is not the sort of town that attracts a lot of tourists. Located in the north part of the Netherlands, it is windswept and rainy, and until recently was best known for its canals, its history of peat farming, and its Philips electronics factory. But since 2000, it has embarked on a fascinating experiment in traffic engineering that has attracted a steady stream of visitors from around the world. And these visitors are not just urban planners—they also include journalists, sociologists, and management consultants, all interested in the wider implications of Drachten's experiments.

The pioneer of what has come to be called the *Shared Space* concept was Hans Monderman, a Dutch road traffic engineer with a contrarian mindset. He had the simple notion that to make roads safer, you have to make them more dangerous. He believed that road systems had become so congested with signs and markings that people had stopped thinking—they had stopped figuring out for themselves what the best way of interacting with other road users would be. According to Monderman, "The trouble with [most] traffic engineers is that when there's a problem with a road, they always try to add something. To my mind, it's much better to remove things."[1]

Monderman persuaded the local town council to try out his unusual ideas. The centerpiece of the scheme, built in 2000, was the reconstruction of the key traffic intersection, Laweiplein, in the middle of Drachten. A traditional road junction with traffic lights and separate lanes for cars, cyclists, and pedestrians was ripped up to form a visually appealing square with a roundabout in the middle. The road signs, the cycle lane, and even the pedestrian sidewalk were all taken out and replaced with a grassy island, a minimal number of white lines on the road, and an array of fountains round the edge. The objective: "to promote communication and contact between all users as both a means to achieve highway objectives of safety and traffic flow, and to achieve the objective of spatial quality."[2]

What was the outcome of these changes? An official report, written in January 2007, gave it top marks: traffic appeared to flow at a relatively constant rate, which improved the dynamic between all users; pedestrians and cyclists now crossed the intersection without significant delay; and traffic safety seemed to have improved. And for Hans Monderman, who died in 2008, this was an important vindication of his original ideas. "Pedestrians and cyclists used to avoid this place, but now, as you see, the cars look out for the cyclists, the cyclists look out for the pedestrians, and everyone looks out for each other. You can't expect traffic signs and street markings to encourage that sort of behavior. You have to build it into the design of the road." Shared Space thinking is now being picked up in many countries around the world, including Denmark, the UK, and the USA.

So what are the implications of Monderman's experiments in Shared Space for the world of management? Hopefully they are obvious. Think of the traffic signs and road markings as your organization's procedures for capital budgeting, strategic planning, and performance appraisal. These were all put in place by well-intentioned managers trying to make your organization run more smoothly. But by requiring people to follow such procedures, you are implicitly saying that it is OK for them to stop thinking for themselves. Shared Space is about turning this logic on its head: if you provide very few rules and very little structure, most people will figure out for themselves the best thing to do, and the best way of coordinating their activities with those of others. It's a very simple point, but one that appears to be lost on most town planners—and on most organization designers.

Shared Space, in other words, is a powerful metaphor for understanding an alternative model for how coordination happens in some large organizations. The standard model—the one GM and other pioneering industrial companies perfected over the last 60 years—is known as bureaucracy, a term properly explained below, and it puts responsibility for coordination in the hands of CEOs and their central teams. The alternative model is called *emergence*, or self-organizing, where the rules are much looser and the responsibility for coordinating work lies with the individuals doing it.

Now, we all know that bureaucracy has its problems. Indeed, the word has become tainted over the years, a sort of shorthand for everything that is bad about large companies. But my view is more nuanced: the original concept of bureaucracy had very positive connotations, and as a mechanism of coordination it still has enormous benefits, as well as costs. And while the notions of emergence and self-organizing are attractive, they are not panaceas. Hans Monderman never argued that Shared Space thinking would work everywhere—he still believed that highways needed clear markings and speed limits, and he felt that a communal approach to road usage would work particularly well with the socially minded Dutch people. Equally, the application of emergent thinking to organization design has its limitations, as we see later.

In this chapter, we explore the choices managers face in how they coordinate activities. We look at what bureaucracy really means, what emergence looks like, and the conditions for choosing one or the other. And while some level of balance is always needed, the challenge and opportunity for most companies is to move toward the emergent end of the spectrum. The basic philosophy here is *less is more*—most organizations have too much bureaucracy, and can usefully have fewer formal processes for getting work done. Knowing what to change, and how, is the key.

Bureaucracy is not a Four-letter Word

It is ironic that the concept of bureaucracy has become so tainted, because in its original usage it was seen as the antidote to bad management. German sociologist Max Weber argued that organizations are built in one of three ways: on the traditional beliefs and norms of what has gone before (*traditional domination*); on the charisma of their leader (*charismatic domination*); or on a system of rules and procedures (*legal domination*). For Weber, the third model was a more rational and efficient form of organization than the other two. If the traditional model was related to the monarchy as a system of government, and the charismatic model was similar to a dictatorship, then the legal model—with bureaucracy at its center—was akin to democracy: an impersonal and law-based approach to organizing that transcended the idiosyncrasies of a particular situation or person.

Bureaucracy can be seen simply as a means of coordinating economic activity that relies on formal rules and procedures to ensure conformity of behavior and to generate consistent outputs. Bureaucracy is often confused with the principle of hierarchy, but in the schema of this book it is very different. Bureaucracy is a *horizontal* process through which work gets coordinated. Hierarchy is a *vertical* process through which decisions get made and information gets channeled.[3] While the two are obviously related, the key point is that managers see the choices they make on these two dimensions as being distinct and separable.

The pervasive use of bureaucracy in large organizations today is testament to its value. As Weber argued, if an organization's goals are efficiency, consistent quality and reduction of waste, bureaucracy is probably the ideal way of structuring work.[4] But, as with any management principle, bureaucracy has its limitations, namely it relies on formal rules and procedures, and this depersonalizes work and can lead to weak customer responsiveness, ineffective processes, and disengagement on the part of employees—the very problems afflicting GM that we talked about in Chapter 1.

Management researchers Paul Adler and Brian Borys summarized the two views of bureaucracy as follows:

> According to the negative view, the bureaucratic form of organization stifles creativity, fosters dissatisfaction, and demotivates employees. According to the positive view, it provides needed guidance and clarifies responsibilities, thereby easing role stress and helping individuals be and feel more effective.[5]

An example from a non-business context highlights the potentially deleterious effects of bureaucracy. In 2008 there was a high-profile and tragic case in the UK of an infant, Peter Connelly, being abused and ultimately killed by his mother and stepfather. The UK social services had been aware of the situation and had visited the child on some 60 occasions, but they had not acted in time. On further investigation, it became apparent that the local social services organization had built a highly bureaucratized system, with strong information technology support, clearly demarcated roles, and explicit rules for responding to and following up on cases. Presumably this had created cost savings and efficiencies. However, it also meant that social workers were spending 60 to 80% of their time on paperwork, rather than being out in the field talking to the families of at-risk children. And the 60 separate appointments with the child and his mother had been assigned to many different social workers, so the full story had not emerged until too late. One investigation into this case concluded that the computer technology "replaced a system where social workers wrote case notes in narrative form, which [...] made it easier for different officials to quickly pick up the details of complex cases."[6] Or in our terminology, the bureaucratic model—through computer monitoring and nationally imposed targets—squeezed out the personal ownership that many would see as the essence of effective social work.

While this is an extreme case, it illustrates the impersonal, efficiency-oriented nature of bureaucracy as it is often applied. The position we take in this chapter, in other words, is to view bureaucracy as an established management principle that worked well under a rather traditional set of circumstances, but is increasingly poorly suited to the knowledge-intensive business environment we see today.

Under such circumstances, where the imperative is for innovation, adaptability, or personal engagement in an issue, the alternative principle of *emergence* offers greater potential.

But before discussing emergence, there is one further wrinkle to consider. In a thoughtful critique, Paul Adler and Brian Borys argued that not all bureaucracies are created equal. They had spent a lot of time in Toyota's automobile factories, which are the most productive and highest-quality assembly plants on the planet, but also among the most bureaucratic in terms of formal rules and procedures. The two management researchers argued that some bureaucracies are *coercive* (they force people to conform to a set of procedures) while others are *enabling* (they provide the tools and methodologies for continuous improvement). It is not so much the formal procedures that define how things work; rather, it is the way those procedures are interpreted and used by the company's managers.

Emergence

The concept of emergence, as used here, refers to spontaneous coordination through the self-interested behaviors of independent actors.[7] When we see cars, cyclists, and pedestrians finding their own way, unscathed, through Laweiplein; when we see a community of freelance programmers coming together to build a new open-source software product; and when we see an army of termites building a 20-foot high tower, we are witnessing the principle of emergence at work.

There has been enormous academic interest in emergence, and its sister concept, self-organizing, over the last 15 years.[8] Building on insights into non-linear dynamics in the world of physics, researchers in the social and natural science fields have asked how "order" emerges when there is no one doing the "ordering." The answer, in essence, is that individual units are programmed to follow a small number of simple rules. When tens or hundreds of these units interact with one another, some sort of structure or pattern emerges. This is what happens in nature, when swans flock and when bees build a hive. It explains many social phenomena including traffic jams and crowd dynamics. And of course the entire concept of a market economy, based on the self-interested behavior of independent agents, also builds on this basic principle.

Margaret Wheatley, a leading proponent of self-organizing, has written extensively on these issues, and she claims it was the beauty and intricacy of termite towers on the Australian savanna—the tallest structures on earth relative to the size of their builders—that inspired her. She observed:

> On their own, termites are capable of digging only dirt piles. Individual ones are like single neurons, but as a coordinated group they perform like a mind. They emit chemicals for communication. They wander at will, bump up against one another, and then they respond. I think this is an excellent maxim for organizational life.[9]

Wheatley believes, in other words, that emergence isn't just a way of understanding how social order takes shape—it is also an imperative, a prescription, for how we as individuals and as managers *should* be thinking about work. Many others have taken a similar position. In their bestselling book, *Competing on the Edge*, Google executive Shona Brown and Stanford professor Kathy Eisenhardt argued that executives in fast-moving industries should aim to position their organizations at the edge of chaos, where "systems can most effectively change. Systems with more structure ... are too rigid to move; systems with less structure are too disorganized."[10] In their view, emergent behavior—wandering, bumping, responding—is necessary for experimenting with new opportunities, but it needs to be coupled with processes for harnessing and focusing effort.

In its idealized form, emergence is all about spontaneous order. But for the purposes of this book, I agree with Brown and Eisenhardt that, as a *management* principle, emergence means putting in place the guiding structures that will stimulate individuals to coordinate their activities, in a focused way, of their own volition.

Bureaucracy and Emergence– a Never-ending Dance

Emergence, in other words, is the antithesis of bureaucracy, and many companies find themselves oscillating between these two principles as they seek to find a workable synthesis.

Consider the case of Oticon, the Danish hearing-aid manufacturer that became known a few years back for its *Spaghetti Organization*. Faced with a declining market position and a growing competitive threat from Siemens and Philips, CEO Lars Kolind embarked on a radical turnaround plan in 1988, the essence of which was to create a highly responsive and nimble organization that would offer levels of innovation and service that its large competitors could not match. Kolind got rid of the formal organization structure and replaced it with a bottom-up model in which teams would self-organize around development projects they wanted to pursue. In true Darwinian fashion, projects that attracted customer interest and funding survived, while those that did not were killed off. To make this new model stick, Kolind used radical slogans such as "think the unthinkable" and visual symbols, such as a large transparent chute in the middle of the building down which all shredded documents fell.[11]

Oticon's move to a less bureaucratic model of management was enormously successful, and its performance improved dramatically over the following decade. But that is not the whole story. Beginning in 1996, there were a number of structural changes made and many aspects of the spaghetti organization were dropped. Danish economist Nicolai Juul Foss did a follow-up study in the early 2000s, and he observed elements of traditional structure creeping back in. Oticon's headquarters was divided into three business teams; a competence center was set up to review projects and appoint project leaders; and a development group, consisting of all the senior executives, was put in place to steer the company strategy.[12]

These structural shifts are instructive. Lars Kolind inspired the company to experiment with self-organizing, but as the company's performance improved, and as Kolind handed the day-to-day leadership responsibilities on to others, there was a partial shift back toward a more traditional set of principles. At the time of writing, Oticon was somewhere between the two extremes. It is still "characterized by considerable decentralization and delegation of decision-making rights," but many of the elements of the spaghetti organization have been dropped.[13]

There are two important implications from Oticon's experiences for this chapter. First, notwithstanding the allure of emergence and self-organizing as principles for how work will be structured in the future, bureaucracy will continue to be an important feature of the workplace for many decades to come. Not only do managers get some comfort out of procedures for structuring work—it's a style they're quite familiar with—but there is also a lot of evidence that formal procedures are valuable. Indeed, Oticon continues to perform very well, even with a less radical organizational form.

Second, there is an ongoing dance in many organizations between the principles of bureaucracy and emergence. The first step typically takes the form of an emergence-based initiative, such as the introduction of the spaghetti organization in Oticon, or the elimination of the traditional budgeting system in UBS (see Chapter 7). This is followed by a reimposition of bureaucratic controls once the weaknesses in the new model are exposed. As the drawbacks of bureaucracy become manifest, the dance begins again. Companies go through these sorts of cycles all the time, and while they are sometimes derided as "change for change's sake," they can also help provide some sort of dynamic balance between the extremes of either pole.[14]

Bureaucracy and emergence, as we've seen, sit at the extremes of what is, in reality, a continuous spectrum of coordinating mechanisms (see Figure 3.1). On the far left sits the *traditional bureaucracy* that conforms closely to Weber's ideal model and is widely used today in many government departments and certain large companies, such as GM. To its right we find the *flexible bureaucracy* that continues to offer most of the benefits of procedures and rules that typify the traditional bureaucracy, but with

Figure 3.1:   The coordination spectrum: framework for comparing different approaches to coordination

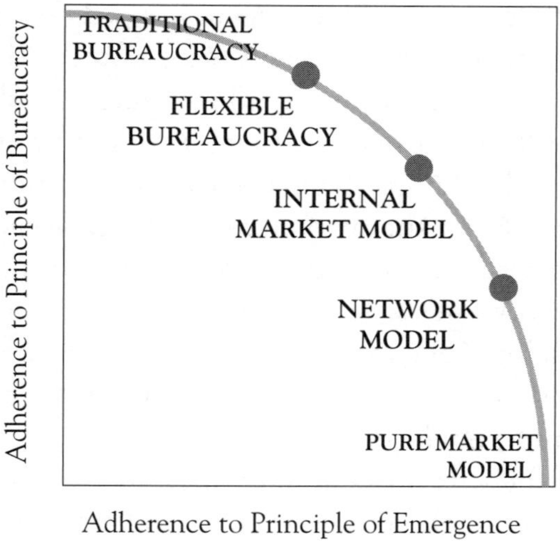

Adherence to Principle of Bureaucracy

TRADITIONAL BUREAUCRACY

FLEXIBLE BUREAUCRACY

INTERNAL MARKET MODEL

NETWORK MODEL

PURE MARKET MODEL

Adherence to Principle of Emergence

fewer of its limitations. In the center we see the *internal market* model, which is best viewed as an emergent process of coordination within the boundaries of an existing company. To the right we see the *network* and *pure market* models that build on the principle of emergence. In the pure market model work is coordinated through purely commercial transactions, whereas in the network model, managers create non-binding ways of encouraging companies and individuals to work closely with them.

This is a well-established framework for understanding the variety of ways that companies and individuals coordinate their efforts.[15] The interesting part of the story is not the far ends of the spectrum (these are well understood), but the range of hybrid models in the middle that reconcile—to some degree—the conflicting principles of bureaucracy and emergence. In the remainder of this chapter we turn the spotlight on these three models—flexible bureaucracy, internal market, and network—and we examine the pros and cons of each.

Flexible Bureaucracy

No large company is entirely immune from bureaucracy. As we see in Chapter 7, the larger a company grows (particularly in terms of employee numbers), the more it tends to develop formal processes for structuring work and for maintaining control. But as we know, such processes have significant costs associated with them, of which the following three are the most important:

- **Formal processes take on a life of their own.** Employees follow them for their own sake, they stop thinking about the reasons they were developed in the first place, and they start to play "games." Nowhere is this more true than with the budgeting process which, according to two leading commentators Jeremy Hope and Robin Fraser, is "time-consuming, adds little value, and prevents managers responding quickly to changes in the business environment."[16]

- **Formal processes make employees internally focused.** Urgent work drives out important work; employees focus their attention on their mostly internally focused processes, and customers get ignored.

- **Employees become disengaged.** As the example of Baby Peter above illustrates, the formalization of work tends to come at the expense of personal ownership. And the less ownership employees feel, the less discretionary effort they are likely to put into their work.

These problems are well known. However, getting rid of formal processes altogether takes drastic measures: Oticon's spaghetti organization was one example of a radical restructuring, and we talk about others in the latter parts of this chapter. So, instead, most companies opt for a more incremental set of approaches that we refer to as *flexible bureaucracy*. Essentially these approaches are designed to retain the benefits of structure and scale that large companies value, while bringing back in some of the flexibility and responsiveness that they typically had when they were much smaller firms.

Now, there are many ways of making a large company more flexible. Some of these actions involve spinning units off, and building market-like systems, as we discuss in the models below. Within the traditional structure, you can take out reporting layers, give more autonomy to people closer to the action; you can eliminate various committees and procedures; and you can clarify roles and responsibilities. All valuable. But our focus here is not on these much-observed practices, but on the underlying principles and lesser-known ways of acting on them.

So what *are* the principles that encourage individuals to coordinate their efforts spontaneously, rather than following rules or doing what some higher-level person told them to do? Three are key:

Peer review. The principle of peer review has a clear and narrow meaning in the world of academia: it holds that we monitor and evaluate each others' research output as equals, rather than through deference to a higher body or a formal set of rules. In a business setting we can therefore think of peer review as a lateral mechanism for shaping and controlling emergent behavior.

What does this mean in practice? One example is BP, the UK-based oil major, which established a sophisticated set of peer-review processes in the late 1990s. The company had moved toward a highly decentralized management model in the early 1990s, wherein each business unit leader agreed on an annual "performance contract" with corporate headquarters, and was given full autonomy to deliver on that contract. To help them achieve their performance contracts, the company then established "peer groups:" each business unit leader was placed in a peer group of leaders running similar businesses (e.g. all early-stage oil fields) and, critically, half of the leader's annual bonus was based on the performance and views of his or her peers. This bonus structure naturally encouraged high levels of collaboration: business leaders met up on a quarterly basis, looking for ways to collaborate and to improve each others' performance. This collaborative spirit was then mirrored many levels below, through so-called "peer assists" in which experts from one business unit traveled to meet their counterparts in another, to help them tackle a performance or productivity problem.

BP's peer group model was, in essence, a non-bureaucratic mechanism for encouraging cross-unit collaboration and performance improvement. It built on the assumption that managers are likely to respond best to advice and challenge from like-minded peers rather than corporate executives. In the words of then CEO John Browne, "There was a very different interaction between people of equal standing when they reviewed each other's work than there was when a superior reviewed the work of a subordinate. We concluded that the way to get the best answers would be to get peers to challenge and support each other, than to have a hierarchical challenge process." This approach helped the desired behaviors to emerge spontaneously, rather than through formal processes. While BP's use of this model has evolved since 2001,[17] it was a central element of the company's dramatic performance improvement through the 1990s.

For a more mundane example of peer review, consider how expense claims are processed in most companies. There are formal rules about what you can and cannot claim, and there is a team of people whose job is to ensure that forms are filled out correctly and rules adhered to. And the more bureaucratic the system, the more employees end up following the letter, not the spirit of the rules. There was a public outcry in the UK in 2009 over the expense claims of some elected Members of Parliament, after a high-court ruling declared that they should be made public. MPs had been claiming for second homes they had never lived in, and for all manner of personal items that had nothing to do with their work, such as a "floating duck island" for £1600, and a moat-cleaning service for £3000. These claims fit the narrow technical rules for MPs' allowances, but did not square with any broader standards of fairness, and the public was understandably outraged.

The solution to this problem was pretty obvious: provide MPs with rough guidelines for what to spend, ask them to use their judgment as to what is sensible, and then post their actual claims online. The media will do the rest, by naming and shaming those MPs who don't comply with the spirit of the rules. A similar approach can be—and often is—used in a corporate setting. This approach is not without risks, as we see below, but it can be an effective and efficient alternative to bureaucratic expense systems.

Transparency. One of the insidious consequences of bureaucracy is that it leaves people in the dark—they see only their part of the system, and this makes it impossible for them to resolve problems or act on opportunities in a thoughtful way. So as a general principle, transparency is a wholly positive thing: it enables employees in different parts of the company to coordinate more effectively; it is also a signal that the company trusts its employees and wants them to understand the bigger picture. And ultimately this results in increased discretionary effort.

Here is a fascinating example of transparency. Skubios Siuntos Ltd is an Authorised Service Contractor for UPS in Lithuania. With 76 employees, its business is delivering and picking up international shipments across the Baltic state of Lithuania. In 2007, its co-founder, Vladas Lasas, was looking for some non-traditional approaches to employee motivation and retention, and he hit on the idea of inviting employees to set their own salaries. He put the following process in place. First, he and his management team set aside a specific budget for salary growth for the coming year of 19 percent, and he asked his team to make an initial estimate of how much extra money each individual should receive. Next, he wrote personally to every employee, with details of every employee's historical compensation data and the company's financial situation with a request that they would answer 5 questions including their bid for a new salary within 24 hours. Once all answers and bids were in, the head of HR and respective manager met with every employee to discuss his proposed salary for the coming year. Some 39% of employees requested increases in salary that were completely in line with their managers' expectations. 40% of employees requested increases that were slightly above expectations, and 21% of employees requested *significantly* more than their managers had estimated. Following this discussion, agreement was promptly reached in 79% of cases. The remaining 21% then met with the head of HR a second time. One employee's salary was raised fully to his desired level, because he proved he was worth it; one employee quit after saying, "Either you give me the money I want or I quit;" and with two employees, a development plan was put in place to show what objectives they would have to achieve to get the salary they had requested.

Six months later, the company went through the same process again, and as before they monitored the feedback. After this second round, 85.5 percent of employees said they were very satisfied (with their salary), 14.5 percent were satisfied, and none were dissatisfied. Moreover staff turnover over this period decreased from 12.8 percent (annual) to 8.4 percent.

Skubios Siuntos' Ltd experiment was an example of what happens when you treat your employees like responsible adults. Employees were encouraged to say how much money they should be paid, within the context of their personal contribution and the overall performance of the company. This became the start of a sensible conversation about what salary they would actually end up with, and what they would achieve in the coming year. Vladas Lasas' view had always been that employees should know more details about the company's financial position, and the "set-the-salary-yourself" initiative built directly on this policy of transparency.

Of course, the principle of transparency is far broader than just sharing information about company performance and salaries. Other settings where transparency can be used to good effect include:

- **Transparency in setting and delivering performance targets.** Back in the 1980s, the manufacturing company SRC Holdings became well known for the concept of *Open Book Management*. Employees were given training in understanding financial information, responsibility for setting and delivering on targets, and a financial stake in how the company performed—with positive results.[18]
- **Transparency in working with suppliers or customers.** Wal-Mart's UK subsidiary Asda, experimented in 2009 with a string of initiatives directed at addressing customers' demands for greater transparency. These included "Window into Asda" to allow customers to see what was happening in Asda factories through live webcams, and through the replacement of brick walls in-store with glass ones, and "Chosen by You," in which regular shoppers are invited to help develop and test new products.[19]
- **Transparency in communicating with external stakeholders.** In the UK the *Guardian* newspaper publishes an annual "social audit" to review its record on environmental,

social, and ethical issues,[20] which an independent auditor then comments on. And the results are not always positive: the 2006 review showed that Pearson Plc, not the *Guardian*, had the best record on environmentally responsible paper sourcing; and the auditor, Richard Evans, criticized the *Guardian* for its reporting on CO_2 emissions.

Personalization. Finally, a third alternative to formal procedures for getting work done is simply personal ownership—give responsibility to key individuals, and require them to live with the consequences of their actions. For example, one of the basic principles that every airline captain knows is: make risk decisions at the appropriate level. The captain may delegate specific decisions to engineering specialists or dispatchers, but the decision to fly the plane rests with him or her—not on the wishes of the air traffic controllers or the airline's chief executive. Formal procedures, in other words, are buttressed with a strong ethos of personal accountability.

This may seem like an obvious point, but consider again why the banking industry got into trouble in 2007. The large investment banks had plenty of people employed in the field of risk management, but they relied entirely on formal processes, using procedures so carefully defined that even well-intentioned managers could no longer see the forest for the trees. According to one report, "the risk governance failings [of the banks] resulted from an over-reliance on low-level risk decisions in siloed businesses, product lines, and trading desks that ignored how these exposures contributed to a firm's overall risk profile."[21]

What the banks needed, in other words, was a much higher level of personal ownership to complement their formal procedures. And interestingly, some of the companies that performed the best through the credit crisis had exactly this approach. For example, one successful hedge fund executive I interviewed in researching this book said, "We have robust informal systems, we communicate naturally, and we develop our own views on what risks to take. We get a return on our judgement." Similarly, JP Morgan Chase, one of the least-affected major players, had a highly cohesive top team that took ownership of its risk management agenda. CEO Jamie Dimon and his team saw early warning signals, back in 2006, of the credit risk on mortgages and the market risk on CDOs, as a result of which they reduced the bank's level of exposure to the mortgage backed securities that crippled so many of their competitors.

Other industries also take the concept of personalization seriously. In the pharmaceutical industry, for example, firms make high-stake investments in new drugs all the time. These firms have sophisticated formal systems and stringent external regulations, but in addition, they are able to rely on the strong ethical norms and professional standards of the medical fraternity—a form of personalization. As one observer wrote, medical experts "are driven by a public willingness to improve collective knowledge of products, rather than by a private or commercial will to distribute them,"[22] and it is this shared accountability among medical professionals that helps to minimize risk.

The risks of flexible bureaucracy. Of course, none of these approaches is risk-free. By moving away from the traditional, formal, and rather secretive way of structuring work, managers are taking a risk that others will take advantage of their new-found openness. So it's worth thinking through the conditions under which these models are most likely to work.

In a fascinating book called Governing the Commons,[23] Nobel prize-winning sociologist Elinor Ostrom described how local communities collectively manage their shared resources. She studied the use of Swiss grazing pastures, Japanese forests, and irrigation systems in the Philippines, and she showed how communities self-organize to ensure that they don't overwork or abuse these shared resources: they have well-defined group boundaries, there is a monitoring system policed by members of the group, there are low-cost conflict mechanisms in place, and individuals can shape their own rules.

Ostrom's findings apply directly to this discussion. Asking employees to make a bid for their own salaries, taking away the expense claim rules, setting performance targets through peer review are moves that are all susceptible to abuse by free-riders who don't care about the consequences for others. So if you have a group with a clear identity that monitors and shapes its own performance, these alternative mechanisms are likely to be valuable. But if not, the risks of abuse are significant.

Internal Market Model

An internal market is by definition a hybrid: it is a market-like mechanism for coordinating activity within the formal boundaries of a company, usually involving transfer prices and service level agreements. This concept has been around for many years. Unfortunately, there is some evidence that internal markets of this type don't get rid of bureaucracy. Indeed, managers frequently comment that it's easier to negotiate with an independent company than with an internal supplier or customers.

But there has been a resurgence of interest in the concept of internal markets over the last decade. I mentioned earlier Gary Hamel's influential article "Bringing Silicon Valley inside." In this piece, Hamel argued that companies should create markets for ideas, capital, and people inside their boundaries (just like venture capitalists in the Valley), rather than use traditional resource-allocation systems that would not have looked out of place in the old Soviet Union. Another influential book was MIT Professor Tom Malone's *The Future of Work*,[24] in which he argued that advances in IT technology were making it possible for companies to dramatically decentralize their decision-making without giving up control.

There are many different types of internal markets in existence today. Those concerned primarily with aggregating the views of large numbers of employees to arrive at a better decision (often called opinion markets) are dealt with in Chapter 4. Here we restrict ourselves to looking at how companies use internal markets to coordinate their activities, i.e. as an alternative to bureaucracy.

Market for ideas. Rather than putting all ideas through a single, formalized screening mechanism, many companies have established some sort of seed fund, or incubator, alongside the traditional process that offers a non-bureaucratic way of trying out new business ideas in a low-cost, low-risk setting. Oil giant Shell's GameChanger is a well-regarded example of this. This unit was set up to fund the development of radical ideas that might develop into entirely new businesses. Today it operates across all the major divisions of Shell (exploration and production, retail, and chemical) and has an annual seed-funding budget of $40 million and a staff of 25 people. Shell employees submit their ideas to the GameChanger website. All ideas are reviewed by members of the unit, and, over the course of six months to a year, the proposals go through various rounds of vetting, prototyping, and funding. Employees take time away from their day jobs to explore their ideas further, and they are compensated for their efforts. As proposals turn into business plans, employees may receive between $300000 and $500000 in initial funding from GameChanger. Project milestones are formally set up, and clear deliverables and progress reviews are required at each stage. Ventures that achieve "proof of concept" (about 10% of all original submissions) leave GameChanger at that point and are either moved into one of the divisions (this happens with most of the projects) or into Shell Technology Ventures, a corporate spin-off vehicle. Since GameChanger was formed in 1996, some 1600 ideas have been submitted. The flow of proposals is constant—between 150 and 200 per year over the past five years. And the unit has now built up a track record of success: 40% of all development projects in the exploration and production sector started out as GameChanger ventures.[25]

Market for capital. The other side of the market for ideas is the market for capital, and in many companies there is a single review committee that holds the purse strings on any and all significant investments.

One company that found its traditional capital allocation model too restrictive is pharmaceutical giant GlaxoSmithKline (GSK). In the late 1990s it had become clear to GSK's executives that they were getting declining yields from their R&D investments, while smaller biotechnology companies were often achieving a great deal more with fewer resources. As observed Tachi Yamada, the global head of R&D:

> Large pharmaceutical companies are very good at the front end of drug discovery which often involves capital intensive screening of compounds. They are also very good at the later stages of drug development—running large clinical trials. It is in the important middle ground of this process—converting promising compounds into viable products—where the flexibility and responsiveness of smaller biotech firms is essential.[26]

Yamada's solution to this threat was a radical restructuring of GSK's drug development operations into seven Centers of Excellence for Drug Discovery (CEDD) that would have bio-tech-like levels of flexibility and autonomy while still benefiting from the scale of GSK's global presence. While each CEDD was given its own distinct therapeutic area, the idea was that they would compete for central funding with one another depending on how well they were doing. And the approach appears to have some merits. The drug development pipeline is so long that the results of this innovation will not be known for several years, but the early indicators of candidate drugs being placed into development are very promising.

Market for talent. Exciting new ventures attract talented people, and many companies have sought to find ways of making this dynamic work within their boundaries. We discussed Oticon's spaghetti organization earlier, the heart of which was the notion that people were free to join whatever projects they were excited about. Another example is W.L. Gore & Associates, Inc. (Gore), the Delaware-based manufacturer of breathable fabrics that has become legendary for its distinctive Management Model. On arrival, new employees, who have been hired according to broad rules rather than for a specific job, are given a sponsor. They are then given short postings in several teams to acclimate themselves to the company, and then with their sponsor's help they have to find a team they can become part of. As Gary Hamel observed, new employees are "in effect, auditioning for a part: it's the sponsor's job to help a new associate find a good fit between his or her skills and the needs of a particular team."[27]

Many other companies, including HCL Technologies, Infosys, BP, and Nokia, have some form of internal job market, where employees are encouraged to take charge of their own career development by applying for jobs across the organization, rather than waiting to be assigned to their next position.

Consider the common themes across these three types of internal market. In all cases, the old bureaucratic system was deemed to be too slow, involving too many layers of management, and without due consideration given to the views of those actually doing the work. Shell's GameChanger succeeded in speeding up and decentralizing responsibility for evaluating new ideas; GSK's center of excellence model also provided speedier decision making and it incentivized scientists to be more commercially minded in their efforts; Gore's internal job market was designed to put responsibility for career management onto the shoulders of individuals, and to give them greater flexibility in identifying their options for development.

The risks of internal markets. So what are the risks of creating these types of internal market systems? Can these sorts of management experiments backfire? Yes they can, and there is a rather interesting case that illustrates all the ways things can go wrong. Think Enron Corporation. If you recall, back in 1999 Enron was the darling of the stock market and of management writers everywhere. It had fully embraced the idea that market-like mechanisms can be brought to bear inside the boundaries of a large company, and for a while its innovative Management Model appeared to work like a dream. But, as we all know, the tower was built on sand, and Enron has now become a cautionary tale of how internal markets can get you into trouble.[28] To wit:

- **Too much space.** Employees need to be given a clear sense of direction to prioritize their efforts toward business, otherwise chaos ensues. In the mid-1990s, Enron was focused on the gas sector, but by the late 1990s, the company moved into electricity trading, online trading, weather derivatives, and broadband networks. And from a goal of being the "best gas distribution company," the language shifted to "the world's best energy company" and then, by 2001, "the world's best company." Within this growing business domain, employees were given enormous latitude to pursue new opportunities. For example, Louise Kitchin, a gas trader in Europe, took the initiative in early 1999 to start an online trading business (EnronOnline) while continuing to work in her existing role. By summer of that year, she had some 250 people working with her on an ad hoc basis and servers in 22 countries—before then-president Jeff Skilling was even aware of the unit's existence.

- **Too few boundaries.** An internal market system needs clear boundaries. While on paper Enron had relatively sophisticated control systems for evaluating investment proposals, the reality is that the official rules and procedures were regularly ignored. Moreover, the top executives Ken Lay and Jeff Skilling would often give individuals who broke the rules a second chance, rather than fire them. From their perspective, this was a deliberate policy to avoid choking the entrepreneurial culture. But it also sent a very clear and dangerous message: it is OK to break the rules.

- **Too little career support.** Enron built an almost unfettered internal labor market. New hires were given a series of six-month assignments with different business units through an "associate" program, but after they completed these rotations all further career steps were their own responsibility. Some individuals proposed new business ideas; others sought out opportunities in exciting new growth areas. The risk–reward mentality in the company meant that the highest-paid individuals were those starting new businesses. As a consequence, business units in high-growth areas attracted talent, but the more established businesses, even if they were profitable, struggled to keep their good people.

Clearly Enron was an unusual company on many dimensions. Here it serves as an example of how things can go wrong if you allow internal market thinking to propagate unchecked inside your company. But we've also seen how when companies retain a careful balance between freedom and control—as Shell did with GameChanger, GSK with its centers of excellence, and Gore with its internal labor market—they are able to benefit enormously from the potential power of internal markets.

Network Model

Unlike the internal market model, where all relationships are managed within a single company, the network model is a way of coordinating activities between independent companies and individuals. It is intended to create high levels of collaboration and trust between parties.

Eden McCallum, the London-based consulting firm, is an interesting example of a company built on network principles. Founded in 2000 at the tail end of the dotcom boom by Liann Eden and Dena McCallum, the company offers strategy consulting services through a network of freelance consultants. Most of these consultants have experience with the big strategy houses like McKinsey, Bain, and BCG, but they value the flexibility of working as freelancers, and this gives Eden McCallum a much lower cost base than traditional consultancies have. By 2010, the firm had grown by more than 50 percent per year, with revenues of more than £16 million, 26 full-time staff and over 400 freelance consultants, making it the second biggest strategy consulting company in London after McKinsey.

Eden McCallum decided to target clients who were put off by, or could not afford, the fees of McKinsey, Bain or BCG. The value proposition was straightforward—we have consultants with the same high-level skills and rigorous approach at approximately half the cost. And we don't have any proprietary methodologies—instead, we will use whatever methodologies are appropriate to solving your problems. And you get to choose the appropriate consultant for your project.

On winning a bid, Eden McCallum puts two to three consultants from its talent pool in front of a client. The client then evaluates who they think will be the best fit, which gives the client a vested interest in making the relationship work. On the completion of projects there is an extensive feedback process focused on the individual consultants and Eden McCallum's performance.

All this makes good sense for the clients. But what about the network of consultants—how does this flexibility help them? Consultants are not employees, nor are they entirely freelance contractors, but they lie somewhere in between. They have considerable loyalty to Eden McCallum, and they get most of their work from the company, but they define their own terms of engagement. This includes choosing which sectors they will accept projects in, how many days per week and how many months per year they work, the logistics around travel, and many other elements as well. To be sure, this arrangement requires constant balancing to keep everyone happy, and it is not for everyone. But by letting their consultants choose their own terms of employment, Eden McCallum generates enormous commitment—turnover among the consultant pool is very low.

Eden McCallum's business model is essentially one of brokering a match between its client base and a talented pool of consultants. And the value-added of the company is in large part about knowing how to scope projects and the quality of the match. Consequently, about a third of its in-house staff are fully employed ensuring that the consultants are the right people in the right jobs, while a half are totally dedicated to developing and nurturing client relationships. It is the ability to match top-quality consultants with the right projects that is the defining capability of Eden McCallum, but, unlike other consulting companies, it is not hindered by capacity management.

The company also invests a lot of time ensuring that the network of consultants feels well treated. One issue is the fee structure which is now entirely transparent: it is based on a banding system whereby consultants are paid according to their seniority and consulting skills. Another common concern in network organizations is how the available work gets shared out. So Eden McCallum tries to be clear about the likely levels of demand for people with different skills sets. It is about "calibrating expectations"—the company's and the consultants' as well.

The rise of the network model. Freelance networks of this type are on the rise, fueled by two major trends. One is of course the Internet, and the emergence of online communities (some pursuing commercial objectives, others based purely on personal interests). The other trend is the increasing willingness of people to pursue self-employment, and to take charge of their own careers. Far fewer people in the X and Y generations expect to spend their lives working for the same company as did the baby-boomers. Many more are exploring freelance work, setting up their own companies, and so-called "portfolio" careers, working part-time for several employers.

Consider how the BBC, the UK's publicly funded broadcaster, tapped into this trend.[29] In the early 2000s it was confronted with the challenge of the new digital media environment.

How should it deal with this major change in its marketplace—by trying to second-guess a massively complex new world through the efforts of a small R&D group? Or by trying to engage a rich variety of players in those emerging spaces via a series of open source experiments?

Their answer was BBC Backstage—a project that sought to do with new media development what the open source community did with Linux and other software development. The model was deceptively simple—developers were invited to make free use of various elements of the BBC's site (such as live news feeds, weather, TV listings, etc.) to integrate and shape innovative applications. The strap line was "use our stuff to build your stuff"—and as soon as the site was launched in May 2005 it attracted the interest of hundreds of software developers and led to some high potential product ideas.

The network model offers several important benefits over other models of coordination. The first is *flexibility*—the ability to scale work up or down without making dramatic changes to employee numbers. Of course, the swings in work volume are then absorbed by the community of freelancers, but this is understood to be part of the deal when people work for themselves.

Second, the network model provides a level of *discipline* in structuring relationships with workers that traditional employment contracts lack. If a freelancer doesn't work out, he or she doesn't have to be sacked, but is simply not invited to do any more work.

Third, an important benefit is *simpler management processes*. It is inconceivable that Eden McCallum would ask its community of freelancers to participate in the types of meetings and discussions that preoccupy full-time employees. Which is not to say that the company has gotten rid of all processes—it requires its consultants to do a detailed review at the end of each project, for example. But the point is that freelancers have almost zero tolerance for non-value-added meetings or procedures, which puts the burden of proof on the manager to justify what purpose a particular meeting or procedure serves. The result: simpler and more value-added processes.

Risks of the network model. While there are enormous benefits in having a flexible labor force, the network model is far from easy to manage and it brings with it a host of additional risks.

The first risk is that *it is hard to maintain a vibrant network*. Eden McCallum's consultants are free to sell their services to others, so if they don't feel they are getting the interesting work and opportunities they need, they are likely to go elsewhere— with the best ones being the first out the door. As a result, Eden McCallum's managers spend a lot of time investing in their communities, looking for ways to make the work more interesting, and listening to their concerns.

The second risk is that by outsourcing the work, *you are giving up control of many of the core competencies* that are essential to your offering in the marketplace. Eden McCallum does not employ consultants, and it does not have any proprietary methodologies, the traditional mainstays of any consulting firm. But it has to have sufficient expertise to evaluate the competencies it is buying, so there is an internal group that stays on the leading edge of practice and ensures that the consultants who are hired are genuinely top quality.

The third risk is that by creating a community of independent experts, *you are potentially creating competitors*. In theory, Eden McCallum's consultants could sell their services directly to the clients in question. In practice, this won't happen as long as the company continues to do its job well. But there have certainly been cases in other contexts where this has happened. Magna, the Canadian auto parts manufacturer, used to see itself solely as a component manufacturer, a sub-supplier, to the likes of GM and Ford. Nowadays it aspires to becoming a fully-fledged manufacturer of automobiles, as its bid for GM's European assets in 2009 shows.

In an entirely different context, Sun Microsystems created its Java Developer Network in the early 1990s. The company initially thought to control the activities of its partners (the independent software companies who were writing Java code). But it quickly realized this would not be possible. "We had no idea of the magnitude of what we were creating," observed George Paolini, the chief architect of the Java initiative.[30] So instead, Sun created an open-source community, which quickly took off and took on a life of its own. It is an important reminder that business networks, like ecosystems, cannot be controlled by any single player in them.

In sum, the network model is quite a challenging one to manage because it means relying on partners that you don't control, and it requires constant adaptation as those partners needs and capabilities evolve. It also means getting to grips with exactly what your own *raison d'être* is as a company. If you are increasingly subcontracting or outsourcing all the key services you offer, what role are you really playing? Box 3.1 provides some thoughts on this point.

Box 3.1: What is your real value-added in a networked world?

If there is a trend toward the pure market and network-based models of coordination, then where does this process end? Hypothetically, you can outsource or subcontract just about any activity, and if you take this process to its logical conclusion you end up running a virtual company: yourself, your assistant, and a network of partners doing all the real work. Does this mean you don't have any real reason to exist? Actually, no. It turns out that there are still three value-added roles your company can play regardless of whether it actually makes or sells anything. These are:

- **Promoter and guardian of a brand.** Product companies like Nike and Dell are happy to use freelancers and subcontractors to do the work, but they are committed to retaining control over their brand. The brand represents a particular value proposition to customers, and indeed to those working for the company, so one of the key jobs of the company's top executives is to nurture and sustain that value proposition.

- **Network broker.** One way of viewing a company is as a network of relationships, and over time enormous amounts of social capital build up in such relationships. So one of the intrinsic qualities of a company, especially network companies like Eden McCallum, is the value they create by brokering relationships between different parties with very different needs and objectives.

- **Systems integration.** This refers to the capability of bringing together and coordinating the actions of many independent people. It is often said that Boeing's core competence is project management, in that the development and assembly of an airplane, much of which is done by independent contractors, is perhaps the most complex project-management job known to man. At a more mundane scale, Eden McCallum and TopCoder (see Chapter 6) both need to be good at managing complicated systems, to ensure that their freelancers are working on the right things in the right order.

Some Final Points

In this chapter we have looked at the pros and cons of three different approaches to coordination, and we have discussed the management challenges associated with each. As we will see with all the other dimensions of management, there is no right solution; it just depends on what fits with your company's immediate circumstances, and with how you want to be viewed in the marketplace.

The single most important message to take away from this chapter is that less is more. In other words, less attention paid to formal management processes will typically lead to more individual initiative and engagement, and in turn greater levels of flexibility and responsiveness. Most companies can benefit enormously from a critical review of their existing processes. Are there processes that can be simplified or rethought? Are there some that should be got rid of altogether? These are important questions that most companies do not spend enough time on.

The second broad message is that the potential for getting work done through networks of loosely affiliated partners is increasing all the time. And as companies move toward the emergent end of the coordination spectrum, the company's purpose must, of necessity, evolve as well. Many companies are becoming more "virtual" by increasingly getting work done through the types of network relationships discussed here; and there is a burgeoning economy of freelance individuals who are willing and able to sell their services to large companies without becoming employees (this is very common in the information technology sector). But even though all this is happening, the predictions that some observers have made about the demise of large, traditional companies are certainly overplayed. In my view, we will continue to see all these different models of coordination existing side by side for many years to come, depending on the particular circumstances faced by each company.

Chapter 3: Key points

The traditional principle for coordinating work in large companies is *bureaucracy*: the use of formal rules and procedures for transforming inputs into outputs. The alternative principle is *emergence*: spontaneous coordination of activity through the self-interested behaviors of independent actors.

This chapter describes three coordinating mechanisms in detail. The *flexible bureaucracy* offers most of the benefits of a traditional bureaucracy with more freedom for personal expression and greater transparency. The *internal market* model encourages emergent processes of coordination within the boundaries of an existing company. With the *network* model, managers create non-binding ways of encouraging companies and individuals who they don't formally employ to work closely with them.

There is an overall trend towards the emergent end of the coordination spectrum, driven by technological changes that make it easier to share information widely, and by social changes that are encouraging individuals to become freelance workers. But the increasing use of emergence-based approaches to coordination will be tempered by the security and stability many people get from formalized rules and procedures.

Each of these three coordinating mechanisms has its own pros and cons. Your challenge as a manager is (a) to understand the relative merits of each mechanism, (b) to evaluate which is the most appropriate one for your particular circumstances, and (c) if you believe there is scope for improvement, to envision and experiment with new mechanisms for coordination that build on these ideas.

4

MAKING AND COMMUNICATING DECISIONS: FROM HIERARCHY TO COLLECTIVE WISDOM

Life as a dedicated sports fan can be tough. You love watching your team play. You live for their victories. You despair when they lose. And, worst of all, you get really upset when the coach makes the wrong calls—selling a star player, picking the wrong team, choosing the wrong tactics. You could do a far better job yourself!

Former soccer journalist Will Brooks was one such enthusiast, and he decided to take action. In April 2007 he set up a website, www.myfootballclub.co.uk, or MyFC for short (football in the UK = soccer in the USA), with the aim of recruiting enough like-minded souls that they could club together and buy their own team—so they could call the shots.

By August 2007, the website had more than 12 000 members (at £35 per head) and more than half a million pounds in the bank. This allowed Brooks to move to phase two—opening talks with half a dozen UK soccer clubs, all with varying degrees of financial difficulties. By January 2008, Brooks had put together a prospective deal with Ebbsfleet United, a lower-league club situated in the south-east of London. He asked the members if they wanted to do the deal: 96% of the 21 000 members, from 70 countries, said yes. The deal was done, and MyFC became the proud owners of Ebbsfleet United for an investment of £635 000.[1]

The MyFC members were delighted by the prospect of getting directly involved in managing the team. And Ebbsfleet's coach,

Liam Daish, was equally positive about the arrangement: "As the coach, I look forward to the challenge of working with thousands of members to produce a winning team."

MyFC's members quickly confirmed Daish's transfer targets (the players he wanted to buy), with 95% in agreement. But when it came to the thorny issue of whether MyFC members should pick the starting line-up for matches, a small majority opted in favor of giving that decision to Daish. It helped that the club was on a roll, with victory in the FA Trophy final in May 2008, but nonetheless this was a significant change from the original plan. The issue was widely debated on online forums, with one member observing: "On a practical stance my view is that the manager should pick the team … it is fine for fans to vote but the final decision should be his … you might think everyone is equal but some people are more equal than others."[2] The members continued to vote on important issues, such as a sponsorship deal from Nike, and whether to sell the club's best player, but they decided to leave the day-to-day decisions to the coach after all.

But even with the FA Trophy in the club's trophy cabinet, the club's prospects were uncertain. The initial enthusiasm of MyFC's membership waned, with many choosing not to renew. By 2010, the membership had dwindled from 32,000 to around 4,000, and Ebbsfleet United were again looking for new sources of funding.[3]

MyFC is a fascinating example of collective wisdom at work. *Collective wisdom* refers to the idea that a large group of individuals with diverse points of view will often reach a better final decision than a single expert. There are many examples of this principle in operation—from Wikipedia to Linux to InnoCentive—but rarely are the tensions involved in this approach to decision-making played out so clearly.

Two important points are worth underlining here. First, lots of people have opinions, but not everyone's has equal value. While the "crowd" was excited about the prospect of picking Ebbsfleet United's team on a weekly basis, to their credit they realized that they did not actually have the detailed knowledge to make such judgments, so they delegated this decision to the coach, Liam Daish.

Second, the level of crowd involvement waned fairly quickly after the initial bout of enthusiasm. Only 492 votes were cast on the key decision about whether Daish should pick the team. And from a high of 32 000 members, the number had dropped to 9500 by February 2009, and to fewer than 4000 in 2010. This is not an unusual pattern in crowdsourcing activities: people like to exercise their point of view, and they like to get involved in new projects, but after the initial bout of enthusiasm they will often move on to other things. MyFC is doing far better than many similar initiatives, but it is still an open question as to whether it will have the numbers on an ongoing basis to fulfill its objectives.

In this chapter we examine the principle of collective wisdom as a contrast to the traditional notion of *hierarchy*, perhaps the oldest management principle of them all. As before, we take a close look at the way these two principles are applied by managers as they make and communicate decisions, and we consider their pros and cons. Unlike some of the other concepts discussed in the book, collective wisdom is well understood and very much in vogue. That is why we are taking a fairly critical look at it—we don't want to fall into the trap of assuming that crowd-based decision-making is necessarily superior to the traditional hierarchical approach just because it is new and trendy. Indeed, this is why we started this chapter with the MyFC story, and the indeterminate messages it sends. Collective wisdom has great potential as an alternative management principle, but it also has significant limitations.

What is Hierarchy?

Hierarchy gives managers direct accountability for the decisions they make, and it provides them with legitimate authority over their subordinates. This power is vested in managers because the underlying assumption of hierarchy is that those at the top have greater experience and superior wisdom. The word hierarchy, as we touched on in Chapter 3, is often used interchangeably with bureaucracy in everyday usage, but strictly speaking it is actually one element of bureaucracy. We separate it out here because it helps us to come to grips with the tensions involved in *managing up and down* (in contrast to bureaucracy, which is about managing *across*). More specifically, in this chapter we examine two of the key activities of management—making decisions and communicating with employees—through the lens of hierarchy.

It is interesting how seldom the term hierarchy gets properly defined. For many people, it is such a central feature of the business world, and indeed other types of social systems, that it doesn't really need defining. But some precision is useful here. In its most basic form, hierarchy refers to the breakdown of a totality into parts in an ordered or structured way. But in a business setting, hierarchy ends up being a multi-layered concept with three overlapping elements: a hierarchy of *position* (where one individual has authority over another by virtue of his or her position), a hierarchy of *knowledge* (where there is more knowledge at the top), and a hierarchy of *action* (whereby action taken by someone at the top defines the actions taken by those below).[4] Traditionally, all these are fully aligned, with the person at the top also being the most knowledgeable and the driver of action. But of course the reality today is that knowledge is dispersed throughout the company (and beyond its boundaries), and individuals are often encouraged to take initiative beyond their formal job description. All of which makes our traditional concept of hierarchy less valid than perhaps it once was.

Now, let's be clear before we go any further that *some level of hierarchy is absolutely essential for large companies to function*. While the trend in recent decades has been toward a delayering of companies and a pushing of decision-making down to the front lines, there are limits to how far this process can go. We saw in

MyFC above, and in Oticon in the previous chapter, that experiments in radical decentralization of decision-making usually end up reintroducing some form of hierarchy. MyFC's members gave the coach the right to make team selection decisions. Oticon reintroduced a central committee to decide which projects would be pursued and which would be stopped. In fact, wherever you look in the world—from the structure of the Linux programming movement, to the way troops of primates organize themselves in the African savanna—we see some sort of hierarchy.

Indeed, some management theorists have gone further in defending the concept of hierarchy. Stanford Professor Harold Leavitt wrote a thoughtful analysis of the "inevitability" of hierarchy. He argued that hierarchies are "psychological magnets that attract achievement-driven men and women. They give us opportunities to achieve power, status, and wealth. And they are great devices for coping with complexity."[5] Canadian management theorist Elliott Jaques, whom we met in Chapter 2, states simply that "hierarchy is the best structure for getting work done in big organizations" and that "properly structured, hierarchy can release energy and creativity, and rationalize productivity."[6]

Even though they defend hierarchy as a concept, both Jaques and Leavitt admit that it still creates problems, largely because it is implemented poorly. What are the biggest problems of hierarchy?

- Hierarchy assumes that the boss always knows best—it confounds the position of individuals on the organization chart with their knowledge. Sometimes this is the correct assumption, but often it is not, with the result that decisions often get made by those with incomplete knowledge of a situation, while others who have something useful to contribute get ignored.

- Information does not move freely between layers. Executives are cautious about revealing sensitive information to those below them in the hierarchy, and subordinates are cautious about how much to say to their bosses, for fear of sending the wrong message. This poor information flow frequently leads to bad decisions being made, and also creates a general air of distrust.

- Not enough managers add real value to the work of their subordinates. Perhaps because the hierarchy has too many layers, managers often intrude on the work of their subordinates and "steal" their decisions. This of course engenders frustration and disenchantment among subordinates.

There are related problems as well, from slow decision-making to a lack of accountability, but these can better be classified as problems with bureaucracy that we discussed in the previous chapter. The three problems above are narrower, in that they are a direct consequence of the hierarchical relationships that exist in most large organizations.

As a result of the dominance of hierarchical thinking, the processes that have emerged in large organizations—from strategic planning to resource allocation to career planning—all build on a presumption that those at the top of the hierarchy have expertise and wisdom that allows them to make decisions on behalf of the entire organization. But this presumption is not always correct, and there are many interesting examples of firms that have experimented with ways of bringing to bear the collective intelligence of their people.

Collective Wisdom

The alternative principle, *collective wisdom*, suggests that under certain conditions the aggregated expertise of a large number of people can produce more accurate forecasts and better decisions than those of a small number of experts.

The principle of collective intelligence has a well-established body of research associated with it.[7] This research inspired the Rand Institute's well-known Delphi Method for advancing knowledge, and it has influenced such things as the design of stock markets, the prevention of accidents, and the prediction of election results. The concept has become popular in recent years, with a spate of best-selling books such as *Smart Mobs*, *Crowdsourcing*, *Wikinomics* and *The Wisdom of Crowds*.[8] And of course there are many visible manifestations of its power, from mass-collaboration projects like Wikipedia or Linux, as mentioned earlier, through to problem-solving communities like InnoCentive or Procter & Gamble's *Connect + Develop* innovation model, which we discuss further along.

But notwithstanding the enormous potential of collective wisdom as an organizing principle, its implications for *management* have so far been underplayed. Consider, for example, how the collaborative world of Web 2.0 currently coexists with the hierarchical world of large companies. Gary Hamel has argued that these two worlds need to be better integrated: "I believe you can glimpse the future of management in the social revolution that is now gathering pace on the Web ... In many ways, the Web *is* the new technology of management."[9] But even if Hamel is correct, we still have a long way to go before the principle of collective wisdom becomes deeply embedded in the work of management in large companies.

In this chapter we describe some of the experiments managers have put in place to incorporate the principle of collective wisdom into everyday work. Some of these experiments worked well, others did not; and we discuss the reasons why this was the case.

To provide some structure to this chapter, we consider four different management tasks, and we examine the ways managers are blending the principles of hierarchy and collective wisdom to undertake these tasks more effectively. The four tasks are: (a) communicating with subordinates; (b) gaining input from subordinates on decisions; (c) making use of subordinates to solve problems and innovate; and (d) making use of external input to improve decision-making. Figure 4.1 illustrates how these four

Figure 4.1: The decision-making spectrum: framework for comparing different activities

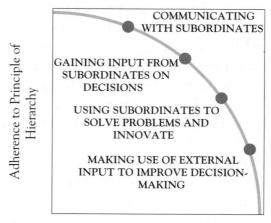

tasks can be mapped against the principles of hierarchy and collective wisdom. As with Figure 3.1 in the previous chapter, the implication of this figure is that the principles are partly conflicting and partly complementary. In other words, large companies need some level of hierarchy, but they would also benefit from greater use of the principle of collective wisdom. The *most effective ways managers typically make and communicate their decisions is through a blend of both principles.*

Communicating with Subordinates

It is frequently stated that one of the critical tasks of a senior manager is communication. "You don't communicate, you *overcommunicate*" was a favorite expression of Percy Barnevik, the former CEO of the engineering firm ABB. But it's a rare company that succeeds in getting its communication strategy right. There are often mistakes made in terms of who gets told, when, and through what media. But my bigger concerns—in the context of this chapter—are that most corporate communications are unidirectional and sterilized. You never get to hear the two sides of the discussion that the board members were preoccupied with when they made a decision, and you never see any account of why something went badly wrong. Contrary or heretical opinions are exorcised from the official record.

Frankly, this doesn't make much sense. One of the pillars of liberal democracy is the right to speak freely, and yet most companies offer no such liberties for their employees. Corporate communications end up looking more like an article from *Pravda* in the 1980s, or a tract of Orwellian Newspeak, than something you would find in a Western newspaper. And the results are entirely predictable. Take a typical "bad news" story such as a plant closure. The company releases its press release. At the same time—or often before—the rumor mill grinds out its unofficial version of events, often corrupting it in the process; and cynical employees gather around the coffee machine, sniping about their senior managers and wondering why they are not better informed.

The Internet has magnified both the severity and the reach of this "rumor mill." First came the anti-company websites, such as microsoftsucks.org and walmartsucks.org, which created a convenient forum for embittered employees and aggrieved customers to share their gripes. The rise of personal blogs subsequently gave even more power to individuals to tell the story their way. And while the first wave of blogs came from outsiders taking pot-shots at a company, they were quickly followed by insiders—company employees putting their own spin on the official story, often with very little regard for corporate etiquette (e.g. scoble.weblogs. com). We also see collective efforts to challenge the official corporate line, such as Friends of the Earth's "The Other Shell Report" in 2002, a carefully researched but highly one-sided analysis of Shell's record on corporate responsibility from the point of view of those "living in the shadow of Shell's operations" around the world.

All of which accentuates the need for some real innovation around the message and the mode of corporate communications. The benefits of honest, grown-up communication are enormous—it stimulates productive debate, generates buy-in, and reduces the risk of untrue rumors spreading. And the risks are minimal, as the truth has a habit of coming out anyway. Of course there are boundaries here—especially for publicly traded companies that face strict rules on corporate disclosure—but most companies don't get anywhere near the danger zone in terms of what they talk about, or how they say it. So given the obvious limitations of a traditional top-down approach to communication, what are the alternatives?

Communication at Nationwide Insurance. Srinivas Koushik, CIO of the Nationwide Property and Casualty Company, provides a great example of effective communication in a Web 2.0 world.[10] As the manager of 2400 dispersed people (out of a total headcount of 23 000), he was faced with the challenge of how to effectively communicate with them. He and his team used the company's systems and technology infrastructure, but he was perplexed by a feeling that only 20 to 30% of the team was really engaged. A self-described "closet geek" who had spent a lot of time on the web as an early adopter of Web 2.0 technologies and social networks, Koushik began to realize that a lot of what is on the web can translate into and transform daily management practices, "if we figure out the right way to do it."

So, in late 2006, he started an internal management blog to open up lines of communication. This wasn't a decision-making forum, but an opportunity for people to have open two-way communications with Koushik. Updated every two weeks, the blog covered a variety of topics, including management from a personal standpoint. He talked, for example, about the changes he was going through in his life and career. The personal touch, which wasn't part of a conscious strategy but evolved, became very important. Explained Koushik: "It start[ed] removing the mystique around executives by making them look more human rather than faceless people sitting in their offices. It allowed people to just sign in and start adding their own thoughts to the dialogue."

Koushik's blog now receives around 2000 unique visitors every single time he posts something, with only about 1200 of them estimated to be from his own team—the others are from elsewhere in the organization. Each of his blog posts receives between 10 and 40 comments.

But Nationwide has gone further than that to communicate with its people. In 2007, the company established an employee board of managers modeled on Nationwide's board of directors, the idea being to bring 40 front-line employees together on a quarterly basis. It has a core team of five people who stay on the board for three years, with the other members serving on the board for a year.

Here's how it works, according to Koushik: "We bring them together to talk about what we're thinking about. We put a problem in front of them that the management team is facing and say, 'How would you guys solve it?' That's actually worked extremely well. We've been very open with them saying, 'OK, this is an ideas forum, there may be some ideas that we won't act on, but we'll tell you why we're not taking the idea, here are the reasons why.' You find out what's really on their minds. It also exposes them to how managers make decisions on day-to-day issues."

One of the thorny problems put in front of the employee board concerned customer satisfaction. Nationwide has a sophisticated customer enthusiasm metric that is directly tied to the salaries of front-line associates all the way up to the CEO. But what can an IT employee do to help customer enthusiasm? What is the direct connection? When this problem was put to the board, it engendered good discussions that led to the important idea of having employees set their own objectives, and stating how they can contribute to the company's success.

The Nationwide team is also championing the use of wikis to help it build community ties. The employee board has a wiki, as do the 300 or so employees who work on agile development methods. "It's the open source concept of evolving knowledge, and it's something that we've really found a lot of benefit in," Koushik noted.

With instant messaging, blogs, and wikis used extensively, Nationwide is currently implementing an IBM technology called Connections—easily understood as an internal version of Facebook. Some 200 participants have set up their own profiles, tagging themselves as experts in certain areas, such as architecture or change management. Using the search capability, people can search by name or by expertise, all of which has spawned informal communities.

Koushik has observed that Nationwide is like any other company whose traditional model for driving best practices and thought leadership is to set up a center of excellence. But he has also noted the obvious contradictions: "The whole concept of centers of excellence goes against everything that the web is about because on the web there's no center." In this new network-based environment, he said, "People determine whether you're an expert based on what you know and what you contribute and not by your title or where you belong, or any of that. The traditional model is based on command and control. We've just got to start realizing that control is an illusion in this networked world. You can join it, you can influence it, but you can't control it."

Risks in opening up communication. Koushik's experiments at Nationwide are a great advertisement for a more collaborative, and more web-savvy, model of communication in the workplace. But unfortunately he is in the minority. According to studies done in the UK, as many as two-thirds of companies had banned employees from social networking sites, such as Facebook, during the working day. In many cases, this was a knee-jerk reaction, based in large part around IT security issues. But there were also underlying risks and concerns that came out in discussions with managers involved in the research. Three in particular.

First, the perceived *loss of control*. Managers worry that by opening important issues up for discussion they will be expected to do what the "crowd" is advising them to do, even if they don't agree with that course of action. They also argue that the relevant information for making important decisions is confidential.

There is some merit to this argument. People get very upset if you seek their input and then ignore it, so you have to structure a decision process very carefully to make sure people know how much influence they will really have. And of course there is some genuinely confidential information flowing around inside companies that would jeopardize your competitive position if it were leaked. But most "confidential" information is not of that type, and more often than not the consequences of opening things up for discussion across the company would actually be beneficial (we talked about transparency in the previous chapter).

Here is Srinivas Koushik's take on this issue. "The worst thing that can happen is that you put these technologies in and you try to do the same old management practices. You need to adapt your management style to take advantage of these tools. It starts with admitting that you don't have all the answers and the only way you can get the right answers is to tap into the collective wisdom of your team. You've been trained to manage a certain way for 15 years, so unlearning some of those habits is not easy. I still find myself saying, 'I know the solution to the problem; here's the answer.' Asking, 'What do you guys think?' elicits a very different reaction and a much better solution."

A second, and related, concern is the perceived *loss of influence*. The argument goes like this: if employees have access to the same information as I do, and are weighing in on matters that I am responsible for, I risk losing my influence in the organization. While this argument is rarely articulated in so many words, it is certainly a subconscious concern for many managers.

Again, there is some truth here, but for the company as a whole such a loss of influence may be no bad thing. A high position in the hierarchy gives the manager a lot of formal power, but of course power and influence can also be gained through other, more informal, means—through vision and personal charisma, through detailed understanding of an issue, and through the network of contacts built up over the years. These informal sources of influence are the ones that make an individual worth following—that make him or her a leader. So if an individual is clinging to a formal position in the hierarchy as the only way of influencing others, then undermining that position, and letting others provide input to important decisions, may in fact be a good thing.

The third concern is simply *time wasting*. Many Generation Y employees would happily spend several hours a day on social networking sites, and managers are naturally concerned about making such sites available during the working day.

On the surface, this is of course a valid concern. But dig a little deeper, and the story gets more complicated. Recall the findings of a recent study of 1000 employees mentioned in Chapter 1:[11] more than half the respondents said they were less likely to leave a company that encouraged them to socialize. And those respondents who declared a high commitment to their employers were significantly *more* likely to spend time on social activities than those who were scouting around for another job.

There is then an important correlation between use of informal communication tools and job commitment. If you are managing a group of employees and ignore it, you do so with a certain risk. Essentially, by condoning social interaction at work, you change the psychological contract with your employees. The message is: "I trust you to do the right thing, and I will evaluate you on your outputs, not on your inputs." Your employees will appreciate the space you give them, and will likely repay your trust with more creative and more thoughtful outputs. Your employees will also likely blur the boundary between their work and home lives more—they do social stuff at work, and they do work stuff at home.

So what's next for interactive communication in the workplace? The fact is, it's here to stay. Every new technology receives the same reaction: companies were averse to putting personal computers on their employees' desks, for fear that they wouldn't get their real work done; and a hundred years ago, the same debate raged about giving employees their own telephones. So the best advice is simply to embrace the new technology, but do so experimentally, and figure out through trial and error how to make it a tool for effective management. Koushik consciously started his experiments with a technology-savvy group—his IT team. And the team, in turn, realized that they could act as a change agent for the broader Nationwide community by championing the use of technology in management. As Koushik said, "Technology can be an enabler, and it certainly is in this case."

Gaining Input from Subordinates on Decisions

Koushik's initial experiments were simply about communicating better with his dispersed team of IT employees. But over time, this one-way process became a two-way flow of information, and he began to receive useful input from his team on important decisions.

Lets look a little closer at the ways managers gain input from their subordinates. As always, the notion that employees' views should be taken into account on important decisions has been around forever. Many companies use "town hall" meetings to get feedback. Some have experimented with structured techniques such as search conferences and open space meetings for getting large numbers of people involved in setting the change agenda within their organizations. But of course the advent of Web 2.0

has made it possible to do such things on a dramatically larger scale than was ever possible before.

IBM's Values Jam. IBM was one of the first companies to experiment with a web-enabled, company-wide "jam" for getting employee input on important decisions.[12] As IBM was recovering from its near-death experience in the early 1990s, one major initiative led by CEO Sam Palmisano was to rethink the company's values. In the wake of WorldCom and Enron, Palmisano called on the company's employees to re-engage and redefine what the company stood for. This had first been articulated by Thomas Watson Sr., as the company's "Basic Beliefs," back in 1914. They were: respect for the individual, the best customer service, and the pursuit of excellence. But they had become distorted to such a degree that they were actually jeopardizing the company's stability.

For Palmisano, a lifelong IBMer, values were a powerful driver. He saw them as bringing balance between the company's culture and management system, between the short-term transaction and the long-term relationship, and between the interests of shareholders, employees, and clients.

But how do you redefine a company's values? Observed David Yaun, Vice President of Corporate Communications at IBM: "If a bunch of execs go off in a closed room someplace, smoke a bunch of cigars and then emerge with some claim that this is what our values would be, it's going to be meaningless. After all, Enron had a set of values." To be truly meaningful, the values have to come from the people.

Fortunately, IBM had been developing a technology that would allow them to get the entire employee base involved in the process. The company had first launched its intranet, a web-based internal network, in the autumn of 1996. Annual surveys of employees showed the intranet was a highly trusted information channel—by 2000 it had tied with co-workers (read: the grapevine) as a source of information, and the following year, it was rated more highly than managers and co-workers combined, opening up a whole new level of transformational intervention opportunities. On any given day about 275000 to 280000 of the 335000 IBMers access the corporate intranet.

So IBM came up with the idea of holding a live companywide conversation, or a *jam*, an activity inspired by the idea of jazz musicians coming together to riff off one another and to improvise entirely new musical experiences in real time. The first IBM jams began in the late 1990s and went digital in 2001, transported to the corporate intranet so all employees could participate.

The 2003 Values Jam was put together quickly, hosted by the corporate communications team. The groundwork for the discussion was carefully laid beforehand with four concepts tried out on focus groups and through surveys. The Values Jam discussion centered on three proposed values: commitment to the customer, excellence through innovation, and integrity that earns trust. Four forum topics provided a framework for the discussion. The first posed such questions as what would a company look like and how would it behave if it truly acted according to its beliefs. The second examined the values necessary for IBM, while the third looked more broadly at a company's impact. Finally, the fourth, a "gold standard" forum, looked at what IBM did when it was at its best.

Given such challenging questions, and the mix of old-timers and newer hires, it was no surprise that all was not plain sailing. There were cynical and negative comments aplenty, but the Jam organizers held fast to an agreement that no comments would be censored and nothing would be taken down unless it violated the company's business conduct guidelines. After the first eight hours, one senior executive was keen to call the process to a halt. But Palmisano disagreed, and decided to let it play itself out. Over the next couple of days, a broader range of perspectives came in.

The Jam lasted for 72 hours. During that time 50000 IBMers followed the online debate about the company's values. There were around 10000 comments on the intranet.

After Values Jam ended, the thousands of comments and ideas were netted down. And in November 2003, IBM's new values were unveiled—naturally via the company's intranet. The values which emerged were: dedication to every client's success; innovation that matters—for our company and for the world; and trust and personal responsibility in all relationships. Those were captured in a publication, *Our Values at Work*, which fleshed them out with multiple comments from the Jam. Along with expressions of support for the values, though, there was a pretty universal acknowledgement that IBM was not yet the company IBMers wanted it to be. "They said, 'This is the right thing to be, but we're not that'," says Wing. "But, as Sam Palmisano said, if you're a CEO who is looking to drive change, that's manna from heaven."

So to that end, a year later, another Jam was held to engage the population in bringing their values to life. IBMers in even greater numbers gave the company tens of thousands of ideas on how to close the gap between the reality and aspiration. As a result, IBM spent tens of millions of dollars putting in place different programs based on 35 specific ideas that changed major processes, procedures and policies. Important to Values Jam and its successor was that the jamming technology and approach were not a gimmicky one-off event. Indeed, jamming is now established within IBM as an important part of the company's management system, and a vehicle for change.

Other approaches to getting input into decisions. Most companies don't have to create an initiative on the scale of IBM's Values Jam to get input from their employees. But it is still important to think creatively about the process of soliciting and acting on information from different parts of the organization. Here are a couple of other examples:

- Infosys, the Indian IT services group we describe in more detail in Chapter 6, put in place a program called the "Voice of Youth" in the early 1990s. Under the leadership of the chairman Narayan Murthy, it was decided to bring five or six high-potential managers under the age of 30 into the company's leadership "council" on a rotating basis, and to have them present their thoughts and insights at the company's annual planning conference. This initiative helped the top executives stay on top of the latest thinking in the fast-moving world of IT, and to get a firmer grip on the pulse of the company.[13]

■ In the late 1990s, oil major BP started bringing in its first Generation Y employees. Rather than push them to conform and risk alienating them, BP's executives put in place a project called "Ignite" in which a group of 20- to 30-year-old employees were asked to brainstorm possible changes to the strategy and organization of the company. By giving them *carte blanche* to pursue the project on their own terms, the executives gained the trust of their Generation Y employees, and uncovered some useful new insights into the workplace of the future.[14]

Risks and benefits of gaining subordinates' input on decisions. The benefits of these sorts of processes are obvious: when they work well, the company ends up with higher-quality insight on which to base its decisions, as well as much greater commitment to the chosen course of action from employees.

So why don't we see more of this sort of thing? We talked about some of the threats to the manager in the previous section —a fear of loss of control and loss of influence, and a worry that employees will fritter away their time providing their input, and not get their real work done. All these concerns are relevant here as well. But, in addition, there are a couple of more specific points that are worth highlighting.

First, the *opportunity cost of a structured process for gaining employee input is very high.* IBM's direct investment in Values Jam ran into many millions of dollars, and of course the time spent by employees resulted in an even higher opportunity cost.

Moreover, these are not activities that top executives can delegate to others—they work *because* employees feel they are capturing the attention of the people at the top of the hierarchy. The
Infosys and BP examples were both fairly cheap to put on, but
in both cases they required the active participation of the CEO
and his management team.

Second, *the quality of feedback is directly proportional to the
clarity of the question being asked.* For the IBM team running Values
Jam, it helped enormously that they had such a well-structured
set of questions, based on all the pre-Jam work they had done.
While employees were free to say what they wanted, the process
channeled their thoughts into well-defined categories. This made
analyzing all the comments more straightforward; it also meant
that employees recognized the output, the new Values, as something that they had participated in defining. Similarly, Infosys'
Voice of Youth program gave the under-30s a voice around very
specific issues that were being debated. It was not an open-ended
process. In contrast, it is interesting to see how the Obama administration's openness to ideas from ordinary citizens has fared.
During the transition, the administration created an online
"Citizens' Briefing Book" for people to submit ideas to the
President once he arrived in office. Forty-four thousand proposals
and 1.4 million votes were received, but as the *International Herald
Tribune* reported, "the results were quietly published, but they
were embarrassing."[15] The most popular ideas—in the middle of
an economic meltdown—included legalizing marijuana and
online poker, and revoking the Church of Scientology's tax-
exempt status. Clearly, as we will elaborate on in the next section,
the crowd needed a rather more specific question than "what
ideas do you want to put in front of the President?"

Third, *it is not easy to keep the momentum going.* As we saw
with MyFootballClub earlier, the enthusiasm for participating in
decision-making tends to wane over time. BP's Ignite project was
a one-off; Infosys' Voice of Youth program only lasted for a few
years; and IBM has wisely decided not to run more than one Jam

every year. These examples highlight an interesting dynamic between manager and employee: employees want to be asked their opinion, but that doesn't mean they will always offer it. So, as a manager, you shouldn't try to get employee input on absolutely everything, because people will quickly become jaded. Rather, employee input is best sought periodically, and on matters that they really care about.[16]

Using Subordinates to Solve Problems and Innovate

The third, and most ambitious, way of applying the principle of collective wisdom in the workplace is to get employees involved in matters of real substance—solving tricky problems, coming up with new ideas, and making difficult decisions. Now, let's be clear at the outset that this is not easy to do—seeking input around well-structured issues is one thing, but opening up a mass-participation innovation process is quite another. And as we saw with MyFootballClub, the crowd is often happy to delegate *actual* decision-making to those who are best equipped to make decisions. We suggest some rules of thumb for structuring processes of these kinds later, but first let's consider a couple of examples.

Roche Diagnostics. Innovation is the lifeblood of this Swiss pharmaceutical giant, which spent 8.8 billion Swiss francs on R&D in 2008 alone. "There is no economy of scale in research—in research, it's economy of ideas," former Roche CEO Franz Humer and current chairman of the board of directors observed.

In April 2008, a cross-functional team of Roche Diagnostics managers was put together to take a fresh look at the company's innovation processes, asking whether there were smarter ways of working that would help Roche to utilize its knowledge base more effectively. The team consisted of members from the US, Switzerland, and Germany, and represented several functional areas.

As regular users of Facebook, wikis, and other Web 2.0 applications, the team knew the power of these for coordinating efforts and reaching out to colleagues anywhere. The challenge for Roche, and for many other organizations faced with similar issues, lies in actually bringing networks to life and leveraging their potential.

The team began with a survey to the R&D staff across Roche Diagnostics, which indeed showed that collaboration was desired, there were major obstacles, and people couldn't figure out how to collaborate effectively. As Tod Bedilion, one of the key members of the team, explained: "The over-riding hypothesis was that by putting more eyes on the problem, by creating virtual networks, we would be able to solve problems quickly and more efficiently. The organizing principle was that they had to be real problems, things we were actually working with right now and would have value if they were solved." Bedilion is the California-based director of technology management at the Chief Technology Office of Roche Diagnostics, a world leader in *in vitro* diagnostics.

With a faith in the power of networks, a multi-disciplinary dream team, and a range of real troublesome problems, the group's next step was to identify a suitable means of experimentation. It quickly came up with the idea of challenging two different networks of scientists to tackle the same problem, the idea being that if one group made much better progress than the other, then it should be possible to isolate the factors that made the difference. They then chose a simple compare-and-contrast framework between an internal R&D community (i.e. employees of Roche Diagnostics), and an external network of scientists.

The internal team challenged their colleagues within R&D to offer up a set of real, current problems that needed work, and they identified six challenges. The team broadcast these challenges across the Roche R&D network in June. By November, they had contacted over 2400 members of the R&D community, and around one-sixth logged onto the online system and read the challenges in detail. Some 40 proposals emerged. While many lacked detail, one real gem emerged—a novel solution to efficient power management in a portable instrument. It was actually solved by a scientist at a different site in a different function, who was unaware of the connection to the challenge. Bedilion saw that as "a beautiful example of linking people across an organization who have allied interests, [who] are working in the same field, trying to solve the same problem, [but] these people simply didn't know to ask each other."

The second part of the experiment was to take one of the challenges to the outside world. Because of the cost involved, the team chose one of the six challenges: to find a means of better measuring the quality and amount of a clinical specimen as it is passed through one of Roche's automated chemistry analyzers. This problem had, in one form or another, been wrestled with for many years by researchers throughout Roche and its external partners.

To manage the process of inviting outsiders into Roche's R&D process, the team decided to work with InnoCentive, based in Waltham, Massachusetts. Founded in 2001, InnoCentive claims to be the world's "first open innovation marketplace." It is a global web community which enables scientists, engineers, professionals, and entrepreneurs to come up with solutions to problems posed by organizations including Procter & Gamble, Eli Lilly, Solvay, and others, and boasts an average success rate of 40%. InnoCentive has around 160 000 of what it calls "solvers" in its network. Anyone can be a solver and they provide their ideas anonymously. They simply go to the network, sign up, and agree to the terms and conditions. Ideas may come from anywhere—a 20-year PhD chemist, or a graduate student, or a scientifically trained housewife, their sheer numbers increasing the chances of getting just the right solution.

InnoCentive boasts an average success rate of 40% and, as Bedilion puts it, is "very sensitive to the mechanisms for handling intellectual property. This would not have been doable without a very thoughtful approach to how you handle any kind of intellectual property that emerges. We worked with InnoCentive to refine the proposal." A $20000 award was included if a solution was produced.

Roche's challenge was posted on the InnoCentive network and had almost 1000 readers in two months. The result was 113 proposals from around the world. Their quantity and quality took Bedilion and his team by surprise. Unlike what they got from the internal network, many were multiple pages, some resulted from experiments, some included diagrams, and there were lots of drawings. And most important of all, there was a result; a solution proposed by one of the people in Innocentive's network that actually solved the problem.

IBM InnovationJam. A second example was IBM's InnovationJam, held in the summer of 2006. Building on the success of Values Jam, Sam Palmisano decided to use the same technology to kick-start a company-wide innovation project. The formula was broadened to incorporate major market trends as well as internal ideas. David Yaun described the vision: "Take the crown jewels, describe them in a simple way, put them against a backdrop of what's happening in the world, and not only invite IBMers in there but invite clients and business partners, as well. Eventually we also decided to invite IBMers' family members." The novelty of this Jam was that, for the first time, the company was seeking to build concrete, business solution innovations together, from a common base of knowledge.

InnovationJam was put together quickly, but with great care. Stage 1 in July 2006 was orchestrated around four major themes, such as "Going Places," with specific questions attached to each (How can we reduce traffic congestion? How can we make commuting more fun?). To encourage broad participation, topics were framed from the user perspective, so people would feel comfortable relating real-life experiences and talking about issues beyond their own expertise. During the 72-hour Jam a group of knowledgeable IBMers was asked to sort through the postings in real time to provide some coherence, and to give extra visibility to the most exciting ideas. Some 57 000 people logged onto the Jam, and there were 30 000 posts.

Stage 2 began as soon as the 72 hours were up. A group of 50 to 60 IBM researchers sorted through the mass of data, and pulled out 31 core ideas. For example, one was about the possible uses for a "managed personal content storage" device. Each of the ideas was sketched out with a basic business case, and then over a second 72-hour period, in September, the doors were opened again. Jammers were asked to flesh out the proposals and rate each one in terms of business impact, market readiness, and societal value. This round yielded some 9000 posts.

Stage 3 involved the internal team sorting through the 9000 posts and working up specific proposals around the key ideas in which IBM would invest. The results were announced by Palmisano at a global "town hall" meeting of 6000 IBM employees in Beijing in November 2006. They included initiatives in smart healthcare payment systems, real-time translation services, branchless banking for the masses, and partnering with others to build the "3D Internet."

Insights from these two examples. These two examples are very different, as you've seen. Roche Diagnostics used a very focused approach, asking participants to tackle specific technical problems, whereas IBM took a more discursive approach, laying out four broad themes and asking participants to suggest new ideas and build on existing ones around these themes. But obviously they were both designed as value-added ways of harnessing the collective wisdom of the crowd. So what did these two companies learn from their experiences?

First, *participants are not very good at working together in online forums.* IBM generated very high levels of participation, but a lot of it was people looking to build a platform for their own ideas, rather than pursue a collective agenda. As one of the discussion moderators observed, "In a face-to-face meeting, you'd have an easel where you could write down ideas, as reminders for a specific topic. That wasn't available here, and it was difficult to keep people on track. You came back to the Jam after eight hours of sleep, and you couldn't tell where ideas had come from."[17] The net result was that IBM received affirmation for many emerging ideas, but very little that was genuinely new. And of course the behind-the-scenes work needed to make sense of the tens of thousands of comments was enormous. Roche Diagnostics, in contrast, did not ask its participants to collaborate, and its focused questions received very focused responses.

To state this point even more starkly: online forums are not suitable for facilitating truly creative processes. Creativity typically involves divergent and convergent phases—the divergent phase is where crazy ideas are thrown out, the convergent phase is where the ideas get sorted and focused. Online forums are much better during the divergent phase. In an extreme example, a group of researchers at de Montfort University in Leicester, UK, experimented with writing a wiki novel (see www.amillionpenguins.com). They confirmed their suspicion that it would not work—the story quickly spiraled out into a series of interconnected subplots, with new characters and new locations introduced at every turn. No one took responsibility for holding it together.

Second, *there is enormous untapped potential in most large organizations for innovation.* The Roche Diagnostics experience showed just how hard it is to reach the people who have something to contribute, but also how valuable it can be when you do. "If only Roche knew what Roche knew" is the old saw, and the experiment Tod Bedilion and his team tried out proved once again how true it is. Bedilion admitted that "there's a huge amount of value in internal web-based forums. We simply don't know how to do it." Following the experiment, he and his colleagues were given the job of figuring out how to do a better job of tapping into the untapped potential of the R&D organization, including looking at incentive structures, as well as the kinds and scope of the problems that should be posed and how questions should be asked.

Finally, both cases showed that *there is enormous value in tapping into the collective wisdom outside your company's boundaries.* This was most apparent in Roche Diagnostic's experiment. As Bedilion noted: "If I had put together a brainstorming session, ten people in a room over two days, I would have got a few hundred sticky notes, and at considerable expense. At a lower cost, I ran the InnoCentive challenge, and I ended up with an entire notebook with 113 separate detailed proposals." The external networks were both highly motivated and knowledgeable. "Clearly, they had a financial incentive and it played its part here, but we think there is more going on—people also seem to get intrinsic value out of sharing their expertise through this community," observed Bedilion. IBM's experience with external participants was less definitive, but undoubtedly an important contributor to InnovationJam's success. However, it was done on a very different basis, with IBM making clear that all contributions to the Jam would be freely available for IBM, and third parties, to use as they saw fit. This raises important questions about secrecy and property rights, which we look into further in the final section of this chapter.

Making Use of External Input to Improve Decision-making

This chapter would not be complete without going deeper into the ways companies are tapping into external sources of ideas to improve their decision-making and their innovative capacity. We often call this *Open Innovation* today but, of course, this model has a long history: companies have been experimenting with ways of tapping into external expertise for decades, through such mechanisms as alliance networks, university partnerships, scouting units, venture units, and so forth. But the emergence of Web 2.0 has dramatically increased the amount of leverage companies can get from such relationships, because the number of people who can be reached online is orders of magnitude greater. The focus in this section is therefore on Web-enabled processes for making better use of external input.

Getting high-quality customer input. How can companies get better quality and more immediate feedback from their customers? As customers, we have all been asked to fill in questionnaires or we've received unsolicited phone calls asking our views about recent purchases. These are OK mechanisms for capturing customer feedback, but there is an inevitable delay in processing the data that is gathered, and success relies enormously on the ability of the survey designer to ask the right questions. More recently, companies have begun to hook themselves into social networking sites as a way of gathering information about their products and increasing customer involvement by, for example, getting customers to vote on a planned advertising campaign. But it is a risky approach: most of us have an intrinsic aversion to being bombarded with ads and survey requests when we are on Facebook or MySpace.

An interesting new model is being pioneered by 247 Customer, a California-based Customer Lifecycle services company founded by Indian entrepreneur, P.V. Kannan. Called 24/7 *Tweetview* (www.247tweetview.com), this service taps into the burgeoning social networking site Twitter. At the time of writing, some 40 million people *every day* were writing short tweets of 132 characters, about whatever was on their mind. 247 Customer takes this mountain of data, sifts through it, and pulls out all those tweets that mention a company by name. Then using advanced text mining software and sentiment analyzers, it analyzes these tweets and creates an almost-real-time report for the company that subscribes to its service. For example, AT&T

was mentioned in about 2000 tweets every day in August 2010. Most of these were negative comments ("spent two hours on the phone with AT&T this afternoon, trying to correct a billing error"), with a few positive ones shining through occasionally. By looking at the breakdown on Tweetview, AT&T managers can see what sorts of issues people are tweeting about, how they feel about their products and services, where they are located, and how and when exactly the tweets were sent.

Every source of information has its limitations, and tweets are no exception: they represent a particular style of communication, and they are predominantly sent by a younger demographic group. But notwithstanding these concerns, 24/7 Tweetview has obvious benefits as a source of real-time, unsolicited feedback about what customers think of your products and services. And for P.V. Kannan, Tweetview is just scratching at the surface of an important change in the company/customer dynamic. "The cynical approach to social networking is to say, 'How can we use this technology to market our products better?' The more honest approach is to say, 'We want to give our customers a say in everything; we want to bring them into our decision process, and we are looking for technologies that will allow us to do this.'"

Tapping into the bright ideas of non-employees. Roche Diagnostics' problem-solving experiment illustrated the power of open innovation communities such as InnoCentive, in tapping into a community of scientists all over the world. Another well-known example of the same model is Procter & Gamble's Connect and Develop initiative.[18] Building on CEO A.G. Lafley's stated objective to source 50% of the company's innovations from outside the boundaries of the company, P&G built a network of outside contacts to complement its internal R&D staff, as we describe in detail in Chapter 9. Both Connect and Develop and InnoCentive are examples of problem-driven communities, where the community gets mobilized to solve a narrowly specified problem.

IBM's InnovationJam, in contrast, was more open-ended, in that the community was asked to get involved in a very broadly defined challenge. A similar approach was used in 2007 by Cisco, the infrastructure company, when it announced an external innovation competition, the I Prize, for finding an idea that would spawn a new billion-dollar business for the company. Like IBM, Cisco put in place a very carefully structured process for documenting, evaluating, and developing the ideas that were put forward. It also established very clear rules about who owned the IP in the ideas that were put forward. The winning entry was the plan for a sensor-enabled smart-electricity grid, which was signed over to Cisco for a $250 000 prize. All other entrants were allowed to retain their own IP.[19]

Insights from these examples. There are many practical challenges involved in using external networks effectively. We will focus on a couple of the biggest ones here.

First, *the size of the community is critical.* TopCoder (see Chapter 6) and Procter & Gamble are examples of companies that have built their own communities, but in both cases it was a five-year process. And for every successful community that gets built and talked about, there are 10 that failed to generate critical mass. This is why many companies, such as Roche, choose to tap into commercially minded communities like InnoCentive rather than build their own. And this is why 247 Customer chose to partner with Twitter—because it provided ready access to a large and growing community. Building your own community, in other words, is an expensive and risky proposition.

Second, *you need a clear and consistent approach to ownership of intellectual property.* There are two coexisting worldviews out there today: most web-based start-ups, like Linux, Mozilla, and Wikipedia, subscribe to the General Public License, or copyleft, model that ensures freedoms are preserved even when the content of a product is altered. Most established companies, including Apple, P&G, and Cisco, continue to operate largely with the traditional copyright worldview that ascribes ownership of a product to an individual or a company. The challenge facing a traditional company moving into the open innovation world is that you cannot really play both games at the same time—if you claim you want the community's involvement in a new project, but you continue to hoard your own ideas, the community will quickly smell a rat.

IBM had to confront this problem when it launched its InnovationJam. While some IBMers argued for retaining owner-ship of everything said during the Jam, they quickly realized that they wouldn't get any worthwhile external input that way. So they opted to make the discussion threads public property. As Ed Bevan, vice president of communications at IBM Research, explained, "This Jam was established as an open forum, so anyone can take these ideas and use them. So we felt we were taking a few risks doing this, and perhaps it meant that our clients were quieter in the discussions than we would have liked. But it was important to make this open in every sense of the word." In fact, the third stage was the first point in the process that IBM took a proprietary perspective.

Was it a risky proposition to open their innovation process up to outsiders? Mike Wing, vice president of strategic com-munications, observed: "It is a bet that there is enough diversity and expertise in IBM that we can apply these insights for commercial ends ahead of our competitors. The fact is, no one gets to be the Roman Empire anymore. We are living in an era of open innovation." For IBM and many other companies, these types of initiatives are risky because you are exposing your ideas to others, and you are taking a bet that you can stay ahead of the competition because you are faster or more effective in implementation.

Some Final Points

It is very easy to get caught up in the exciting new worlds of crowdsourcing and social networking, and to believe the arguments that the world of work will never be the same again. My purpose here has been to find some level of balance between the opportunities that Web 2.0 affords us, and the enduring realities of managing in large organizations. This means acknowledging the pros and cons of these new ways of working, and identifying some of the conditions under which they are appropriate. To pull this chapter together, here are some summary points.

First, *hierarchy is not going away*. Large organizations will continue to be an important part of the business landscape, and large organizations need some level of hierarchy to function. The evidence for this is strongest when an organization starts out in a purely organic form, often with a great deal of anti-hierarchy rhetoric, and then over time builds up its own hierarchical structure. This is what happened with the Linux movement, which today boasts a well-functioning hierarchy. It also happened with MyFootballClub, where decision rights were quickly assigned to those best placed to make them.

Second, *collective wisdom is over-rated*. I don't mean to dispute that there is value in tapping into the views of the masses. However, given the current hyperbole surrounding the concept, I would prefer to take a skeptical view and focus on its weaknesses and limitations. These include:

- The crowd is good at providing input to well-structured problems, and providing answers to focused questions, but very bad at moving open-ended discussions along.

- The crowd likes to have an input into decision-making, but rarely does it have the skill or the will to actually make decisions.

- The crowd is fickle, and sometimes heads off in the wrong direction, at which point the wisdom of crowds becomes the foolishness of crowds.

Of course, each of these points has a flipside, suggesting that there are many circumstances where harnessing the wisdom of the crowd is a good thing. But let's just be more thoughtful about when and how we do it.

Third, *harnessing collective intelligence is going to require a significant shift in mindset among many experienced managers.* At an individual level, managers have to come to grips with the loss of control and loss of influence that comes with opening themselves up to the views of their employees. And at a corporate level, managers will have to take a more open-minded stance to the confidentiality of the information that is given to them, and to the ownership of their intellectual assets. As the examples in this chapter show, some companies are experimenting successfully with this new mentality, but many others are reluctant to take a leap.

As with the other dimensions of this framework, it is tempting to view the left-hand side, hierarchy in this case, as an old way of working that should be challenged. However, this would be an incorrect interpretation. Managers will always be required to exercise judgment and to make difficult choices. But there are important and effective ways for them to more productively tap into the collective intelligence of their employees.

Chapter 4: Key points

The traditional principle for communicating and making decisions in large companies is *hierarchy*: the idea that one individual has formal authority over another, primarily on account of his/her greater experience and breadth of perspective. The alternative principle is *collective wisdom*: the idea that under certain conditions the aggregated expertise of a large number of people can produce more accurate forecasts and better decisions than those of a small number of experts.

This chapter describes four key management tasks, and how the principles of hierarchy and collective wisdom are being used (in combination) to undertake these tasks more effectively. The four tasks are: communicating with subordinates; gaining input from subordinates on decisions; making use of subordinates to solve problems and innovate, and making use of external input to improve decision-making.

As with the previous chapter, there is an overall trend towards the collective wisdom end of the decision-making spectrum. Major reasons for this shift are the increasing availability of so-called Web 2.0 technologies for sharing ideas and evaluating each other's contributions, and the increasing numbers of Generation Y employees in the workplace. However, the evidence suggests that collective wisdom-based approaches to decision-making and innovating have significant weaknesses as well, and depending on the exact circumstances some sort of blend between the traditional and alternative models is likely to be optimal.

As with Chapter 3, your challenge as a manager is (a) to understand the relative merits of hierarchy and collective wisdom as the underlying principles by which you communicate and/or make decisions, (b) to evaluate which is the most appropriate one for the particular management task you are addressing, and (c) to envision and experiment with new practices that build on your preferred principle.

5

SETTING OBJECTIVES: FROM ALIGNMENT TO OBLIQUITY

At the beginning of Chapter 2 you met Vineet Nayar, CEO of HCL Technologies (HCL), and learned how he transformed his company's Management Model to make it more employee centric. There is more to that story, which is best recounted here because it illustrates the challenge of setting meaningful and creative corporate objectives.

The date was February 2006. Nayar had already begun many of the specific management innovations discussed earlier, including the open 360-degree feedback and service-ticket systems, and he wanted to lay out his broader vision for HCL in an open forum. So he hosted a three-day conference, "Explore and Transform," in Delhi, India, bringing together customers, analysts, and employees. It was billed as "the biggest celebration India had ever seen," and viewed as an opportunity "to showcase what India and the transformed HCL had to offer."

In the closing session Nayar introduced the concept of *Employees First, Customers Second (EFCS)*. He explained first how this philosophy would guide HCL's internal initiatives. Then he boldly made it clear that HCL was going to start making choices about which customers it wanted to do business with— even walking away from many small-time, non-strategic engagements. By creating a satisfying and empowering work environment for employees, Nayar argued, the impact would be highly positive for customers as well.

Needless to say, this was a risky approach to take in front of a large group of customers. One attendee observed, "EFCS got a good reception, but maybe it would have been safer to socialize the idea with key customers first."[1] Another recalled that some customers were unhappy and in fact walked out.[2] But the logic behind Nayar's approach was sound. He could have said employees and customers are both equally important, and the statement would have been dismissed as a platitude. Instead, by telling his customers that they were less important than his employees, he sent a very strong and positive message to the entire employee base of HCL. Four years later, EFCS is still a centerpiece of the company's Management Model. Employee satisfaction continues to improve and so, in turn, does customer satisfaction.

EFCS is a classic example of the *oblique principle—the notion that goals are often best achieved when pursued indirectly.* The oblique principle (or the principle of obliquity) is a counterintuitive way of thinking about direction setting in firms, and, as such, it helps us to resolve some of the age-old dilemmas executives face in setting direction. Unfortunately, it's also a rather peculiar and little-known word, but we shouldn't let that stand in our way.

In the pages that follow, we develop a tighter definition of obliquity, and we look at the ways managers can make use of the concept. But first, we need to explain why we need the concept at all—and what is limiting about the much-followed (and more easily understood) principle of alignment, which sits at the opposite end of the objective-setting dimension.

The Tyranny of Alignment

The principle of alignment is deeply rooted in the psyche of most business people. Many well-known business practices are built on this principle, including Managing by Objectives, Key Performance Indicators, Strategic Planning, and so on. There are also several management theories, from agency theory to contingency theory, that use alignment as a way of understanding how goals are determined in the modern business firm. And entire books are devoted to the concept, including Robert Kaplan and David Norton's latest bestseller, *Alignment: Using the Balanced Scorecard to Create Corporate Synergies.*[3]

Alignment is simply the adjustment of an object in relation to other objects. In the business context, *the principle of alignment means that all employees are working toward the same common objective.* Kaplan and Norton paint a nice picture of alignment through the metaphor of the rowing team—eight oarsmen, all pulling together in perfect harmony, moving straight as an arrow from A to B. The rowing team members share a common objective, they are skilled professionals, they work together as a team, and they know each other's strengths and weaknesses. It's easy to see why managers find the concept of alignment so attractive. But you only need think about companies in which you've worked to recognize that the metaphor, although evocative, is somewhat misleading. Here are five problems with the principle of alignment.

Individuals in companies often have very different agendas —and with good reason. Take the case of a PhD-level researcher working for a high-technology company, such as Intel, Sony, or Siemens. What gets her out of bed in the morning? I would suggest that it is the excitement of pushing the boundaries of knowledge and the possibility of creating new society-changing technologies. And I would bet that a lot of her time is directed toward *the pursuit of knowledge for its own sake* rather than toward the immediate profit-directed priorities of the company. It is therefore nonsense to say that her efforts are fully aligned with those of her employer, or indeed other employees. Big technologies companies understand and accept this, as we see later, and they know they would fail to attract top researchers if they put too many restrictions on them.

Measures and incentives are blunt instruments. The alignment model assumes that executives can set clear, quantifiable objectives to ensure that every division contributes effectively to the company's overall goals, and that these can then be cascaded down through a set of Key Performance Indicators (KPIs) for each subunit. But we all know how difficult it is to establish KPIs that really work—especially in settings requiring that employees show creativity and initiative. How would the researcher above be able to show that the new technology she's been working on for years—which may never result in a commercial product—is contributing to the company's profitability?

Short-term targets drive out long-term objectives. In the Anglo-American capitalist system, the pressure to deliver on-target quarterly earnings—largely to satisfy shareholders—is immense, and frequently such pressures lead companies to do things that are inconsistent with their long-term vision. True alignment—between the efforts of employees and the organization's ultimate objective—therefore ends up being compromised. Is it any wonder that some of the most progressive and far-sighted companies are privately held?

Shareholder demands are satisfied at the expense of other stakeholders. A broader problem with the Anglo-American capitalist system is not only that objectives tend to be short term and financially oriented, but also that they serve the interests of shareholders at the expense of other stakeholders. Here is the view of John Mackey, CEO of the fast-growing retailer Whole Foods Market:

> The best way to maximize long-term shareholder value is by managing the interdependent system [so] that all the stakeholders are linked together ... This is the best strategy to create the most value for customers, the most value for your team members, and the most value for the communities, but it is definitely the best strategy to maximize shareholder value as well.[4]

This viewpoint is gathering momentum, fueled in part by increasing concerns about sustainability, and also by the success of progressive companies like Whole Foods Market, New Balance, and Ikea.[5]

Many employees in many companies don't really know where they are or should be going. Of course, all senior executives can talk about their company's plans and objectives, but that doesn't mean the rank-and-file employees understand or buy into the plan. Without a clear sense of direction that employees can go along with, a lot of effort gets expended on irrelevant or peripheral activities.

All of which suggests the rowing team metaphor is not really a helpful way of thinking about how people work together in large organizations. If we want to use a sports metaphor, a football team is far more apposite, as it has many different types of players with different skill sets, and it requires considerable amounts of strategic thinking and individual creativity over the course of a game. But I think the football team metaphor misses the point as well, because it assumes a very clear-cut and simple measure of success, namely beating the opposition. In the business world, the measures of what constitutes success are multidimensional and dynamic.

I find it more useful to use the metaphor of the jazz ensemble. Jazz musicians work together to achieve a worthwhile outcome, blending initiative and creativity with discipline and structure. Moreover, they also have fuzzy objectives. Do jazz musicians want to make beautiful music? Do they want to have fun? Do they want to do something no one else has done before? Do they want to make a lot of money? Of course, it is some combination of all these things, and the most critically acclaimed or the happiest musicians are not necessarily the ones who earn the most money. You can easily see the parallels to the business world.

In sum, many companies find themselves suffering under the *tyranny of alignment*. Their ability to create value for their clients, employees, and other stakeholders is compromised by the obsession with short-term, quantifiable, shareholder-driven results. And their ability to generate effective collaboration between functions is compromised by their silo-driven approach to goal setting and the inadequate measurement and accountability that go along with it.

None of which suggests that alignment is a bad thing *per se.* Rather, it suggests we simply have to be more careful in deciding when an alignment-driven approach to goal setting is appropriate. My view is that there are many contexts where our existing ideas about alignment work fine, but there are many others—typically those that require greater creativity and initiative on the part of employees—where that principle gets firms into trouble.

It is therefore useful to explore the possibility of an alternative principle to alignment, what has been called obliquity. We have applied the principle of alignment to direction setting for many decades, and we have accommodated its many limitations. But these limitations and weaknesses appear to be getting more acute. Some fresh thinking is needed.

The Value of Obliquity

Obliquity is not an easy concept to come to grips with. The other "alternative" principles of management put forward in this book—emergence, collective wisdom, intrinsic motivation—are all well established, with large bodies of research to back them up. But that is not the case with obliquity, so we need to spend a little time clarifying what the term really means.

In geometry, an oblique angle is simply one that is not a multiple of 90 degrees. So the word oblique is often used in the English language to refer to any statement, or line of argument, that goes off at an angle.

The oblique principle was first put forward by British philosopher Richard Wollheim in the 1960s. He was trying to make sense of the well-known paradox of democracy: as a voter I may feel that the death penalty is wrong, but I also believe that the view of the majority should prevail, even though they might support the death penalty. Wollheim's solution to this paradox was to distinguish between direct and oblique moral principles.[6] Direct moral principles might include "the death penalty is wrong," or "birth control is permissible." Oblique moral principles would include "what is willed by the people is right," or "what is sanctioned by our legal system is acceptable."

Wollheim's point was that these two types of principles coexist in a democratic system, and sometimes lead to paradoxical outcomes. But, more generally, he was suggesting that in a social system *the pathway between our individual beliefs and a collectively acceptable outcome is often indirect or circuitous*. It would be convenient if all citizens held aligned beliefs about something as important as the death penalty, but the reality is that this will never happen. So in order to prevent anarchy from breaking out, society has created institutions that enforce the view of the majority.

The concept of obliquity was first applied to the business context by British economist John Kay. In an article in the *Financial Times* he observed:

> Strange as it may seem, overcoming geographic obstacles, winning decisive battles, or meeting global business targets are the type of goals often best achieved when pursued indirectly. This is the idea of obliquity. Oblique approaches are most effective in difficult terrain, or where outcomes depend on interactions with other people.[7]

Using examples such as Boeing, ICI, Wal-Mart, Merck, and Pfizer, Kay showed how companies with oblique goals often outperformed those with much narrower, or more financially driven, targets. And, similar to Wollheim, he argued that oblique approaches were particularly relevant in complex social systems. A small company in a predictable business environment will often succeed in pursuing its goals directly—through careful alignment of all its constituent parts. But the more unpredictable the environment, and the more complex the company, the more

Table 5.1:   Alignment versus obliquity

Management Principle	Alignment	Obliquity
Environmental context	Stable environment	Turbulent environment
Organization	Small, simple	Large, complex
Coordination challenge	Relatively easy	Relatively difficult
Consequences of your action on others	Predictable, quick feedback	Unpredictable, slow feedback
Types of goals that are most suitable	Direct	Indirect

important the oblique principle becomes. Table 5.1 summarizes this argument.

How well do companies using the oblique principle perform? It turns out there has been quite a lot of research on this issue, from a number of independent sources:

- Jim Collins and Jerry Porras' bestseller *Built to Last* compared the practices of 20 "visionary" companies with 20 long-standing competitors[8] (for example, Merck and Hewlett Packard were in the visionary group, Pfizer and Texas Instruments were in the control group). They discovered that the visionary companies put less emphasis on profitability in their stated objectives than those in the control group, but their performance over the long term was superior.

- In *Firms of Endearment*, Raj Sisodia, David Wolfe, and Jag Sheth studied the long-term performance of a group of firms, including Whole Foods Market, Harley-Davidson, and Costco, for which achieving business success is less a matter of obsessing over the financials than about focusing on how a business adds value to society. These Firms of Endearment returned an average of 1026% for their investors over a 10-year period to June 2006, compared to 122% for the S&P 500 as a whole.[9]

■ Several academic studies have looked at the long-run performance of the "100 Best Companies to Work for in America"—companies that have been voted by their employees as providing the most fulfilling and engaging work. These are companies, like HCL Technologies, that explicitly put their people first. And the evidence shows they outperform their peers consistently, and over a long period of time.[10]

We have to be careful when interpreting these sorts of findings. We know that high-performing companies in one period often revert to the average in the following period, and we know there are many subconscious biases in the methodologies used to predict superior performance.[11] Nonetheless, I think it is safe to conclude the following: *companies that consistently invest in their employees, in their relationships with external stakeholders, and in a vision that all stakeholders can subscribe to, outperform peer companies that are more narrowly focused on financial objectives.* An oblique approach to goal setting, in other words, pays off.

Three Approaches to Obliquity

So far, we have explored the potential of obliquity as an alternative principle, and we have put forward some evidence that companies with indirect or higher-order goals outperform those with narrow financial goals. But we need to be able to do more than simply argue that company executives should take a longer-term perspective, or invest more in their people. These are old arguments. Instead, we need to further unpack the principle of obliquity to make it useful. This involves first describing the three different approaches to obliquity that firms have used—pursuing an indirect goal, pursuing a creative goal, and taking a leap of faith—and looking at guidelines for pursuing each one.

As before, these different approaches to goal setting can be arrayed along a spectrum (see Figure 5.1). Pursuing a leap-of-faith goal is based primarily on the principle of obliquity, while

Figure 5.1:   The goal-setting spectrum: comparing the different approaches to goal setting

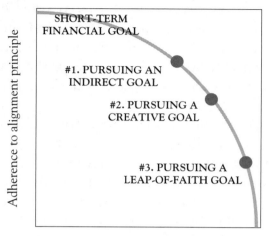

Adherence to oblique principle

pursuing an indirect goal and a creative goal are hybrid approaches that draw to some degree from both principles. In the top-left corner is the traditional short-term financial goal, which we do not discuss in detail because it is so well known.

Approach #1: Pursuing an Indirect Goal

Think back to HCL's oblique goal, Employees First, Customers Second. The logic is pretty straightforward: we will do whatever it takes to increase employee satisfaction because we believe that satisfied employees will, in turn, create satisfied customers and, ultimately, strong financial results. Of course there is no guarantee that satisfied employees will create satisfied customers (we can always imagine exceptions to this rule), but Vineet Nayar knew on the basis of his lengthy experience in the IT services industry that there was a strong likelihood these relationships would hold *and* that the risk was worth taking.

This indirect goal approach doesn't just apply in a business setting. For example, consider the Advancement[12] departments at major universities around the world. Some of these are enormously successful at raising money from their alumni and corporate partners: for example, in 2009 Harvard University had an endowment of $26 billion, and Oxford University had £3.6 billion.[13] Now, what do you think the ultimate objective of the Advancement group at a major university is? It is to grow the endowment, to ensure that the school can sustain its position in the education industry. But go to the website, or talk to one of the employees in alumni relations or corporate partnerships, and you will get a very different story: their mission is to support their school's alumni around the world, by putting on conferences and social events, by providing access to the latest thinking from faculty, and by providing career help through online postings.

The alumni people are not being disingenuous—they genuinely believe that a vibrant and well-supported alumni base is a good thing. But an engaged and growing alumni body represents an oblique goal. The financial contributions are what really matter, but everyone knows that asking for money directly (without providing the alumni with services) would be perceived as crass and ill thought-out.

And consider a personal example. We all seek to be happy in our lives, but the pursuit of happiness typically takes us on a highly circuitous route—we throw ourselves into difficult projects, we work long hours, and we attempt to surmount obstacles thrown in our path. Our happiness comes from a sense of personal achievement. Achievement is then the indirect goal, happiness is the ultimate objective. British philosopher John Stuart Mill made this same point in almost so many words 150 years ago: "Those only are happy who have their minds fixed on some object other than their own happiness ... aiming thus at something else, they find happiness by the way."[14]

These business and non-business examples share three common features. First, there is a clear and strong relationship between the indirect goal and the ultimate goal, so that by pursuing the indirect goal we can be confident of reaching the ultimate goal. Second, there are risks, and perhaps even major barriers, to pursuing the ultimate goal directly, so an indirect approach works better. Third, there is widespread agreement among stakeholders about the nature of the ultimate goal—an obvious point, perhaps, but one that needs making when this approach to obliquity is compared to the other two approaches.

Guidelines for pursuing an indirect goal. Under what circumstances should this approach be used? And what are the risks? Three points are particularly important:

- **The indirect goal has to be something people can really relate to: it has to be meaningful and measurable.** HCL's executives understand the value of building an employee-centric company, and they monitor employee satisfaction and employee turnover numbers carefully. Harvard and Oxford's Advancement teams care deeply about building an engaged and committed alumni network, and their success can be measured by looking at the numbers of alumni participating in university activities. For an indirect goal to be effective, the company's internal systems have to be directed toward helping everyone achieve it.

- **You need to be able to show how progress toward the indirect goal is leading to progress toward the end goal.** Henry Stewart, the CEO of Happy Ltd, whom we met in Chapter 2, is another executive who believes employees come first. But he is also obsessive about customer satisfaction, tracking it through questionnaires filled in after every training course the company runs. The link between the indirect and end goals is never perfect, but as long as you can demonstrate that the two are strongly correlated, the skeptics among your stakeholders won't give you a hard time.

- **Pay attention to the potential risks of actively pursuing an indirect goal.** The primary risk is simply that the indirect goal could end up being a red herring—it might not motivate employees as much as you hoped it would, it might not be as well correlated with the end goal as you thought, and this could derail the whole approach. Are Google employees spending so much time perfecting the user's search experience that they are overlooking other important things they should be working on, and this is having a deleterious effect on the company as a whole? Are HCL's managers worrying so much about making their employees happy that they are ignoring their customers or their budgets? The answer in these two cases is no, but we know from other contexts how easy it is for perverse behaviors to emerge. For example, many of the investment banks prioritized *revenue* growth in the run-up to the credit crisis, and as a result employees chased high-risk, low-margin new business. Revenue growth turned out to be a very poorly chosen indirect goal.

Approach #2: Pursuing a Creative Goal

The second approach to obliquity applies particularly to creative and science-based work, where the overall commercial objectives of a company are frequently orthogonal to the objectives of critical acclaim, peer review, and scientific progress. Management writer Bill Breen wrote a fascinating account of the drug-development process, having followed a team of diabetes-drug specialists at Pfizer who maintained their enthusiasm despite repeated failures. As one interviewee observed, "Science folk don't live for the big day when a drug makes it to market, they live for the small moments when you see exciting results in journals." For these scientists, it was the "sheer intellectual challenge of the pursuit" that they cared about. Commercial success was not irrelevant to them, but it didn't change the way they behaved on a day-to-day basis.[15]

As with approach #1, the ultimate objective in approach #2 is clear: Pfizer has to seek ways of securing a good return on its shareholders' money. And, even more so than with approach #1, pursuing this ultimate objective directly is very risky. Pfizer knows it will fail if its research scientists are told to align all their efforts around the financial objectives of the company—both because many of its experimental projects would no longer be pursued, and because its top scientists would all quit.

The distinctive feature of this approach lies in the uncertain nature of the relationship between the intermediate and end goals. Pursuing projects for their "sheer intellectual challenge" is not a recipe for commercial success. But some projects end up being successful anyway, so that the money they bring in covers a whole range of failures. Executives in pharmaceutical companies therefore play the numbers game: they allow scientists enormous degrees of freedom to pursue early-stage projects, on the basis that they can then select which ones to stop, and which to invest more money in, as their potential value becomes clearer.

In approach #1, the intermediate goal is positioned as a stepping-stone toward the end goal. In approach #2, the intermediate goal is being pursued *for its own sake*. Employees are encouraged to pursue this intermediate goal—even though its relationship to the end goal is uncertain—and it is then up to the company's executives to decide when their commercial priorities should be brought to bear.

Consider the development activities at Google as an example of how a company encourages employees to pursue creative goals. Google's engineers, like Pfizer's research scientists, want to make a real difference in the world. And Google's entire Management Model is still built largely on academic principles. CEO Eric Schmidt commented at a conference in 2008 that the model "wasn't planned. Google emerged the way it is because people acted like they were in graduate school, even though they weren't. If you take an academic culture and apply it to a business, these are the outcomes you get."[16] One employee, veteran computer science professor, Anurag Acharya, said he joined the company because he "was looking for a problem that would last me a very long time—10 years, 15 years."[17]

As we describe in greater detail in Chapter 7, Google has a highly decentralized structure with development projects done in teams of 3–4 people, and employees encouraged to spend 30% of their time on exploratory projects—20% on services that extend the core business, 10% on risky fringe ideas. This model has done wonders for Google's product development pipeline. Take a visit to Google Labs (www.googlelabs.com) to see the current range of products available for users to experiment with. At the time of writing these included Google Checkout Store Gadget, Google City Tours, and Google Mars; some with obvious commercial potential, others likely of interest only to a small niche of users.

But how does all this development effort square with the company's obligations toward its shareholders? Essentially, it's up to Google's top executives to put in place a system for prioritizing the most promising projects and downplaying others—an approach that is sometimes called *guided evolution*.[18] For example, Eric Schmidt has a vital role as CEO in ensuring that tricky decisions get made in a timely way. Every issue is debated at length, but as Schmidt observed, "if that's all you do, you end up with a University. So I have two jobs: the first is to ensure every issue is debated to find not the common outcome but the best decision. And the second is to put pressure to make it happen quick, because business is speed."[19] The company also instituted formal "innovation reviews" in June 2009, where executives present product ideas bubbling up through their divisions to Eric Schmidt and founders Larry Page and Sergey Brin. While hardly an unusual concept, such reviews "force management to focus" and help the triumvirate running the company to place their bets more confidently.[20]

Guidelines for encouraging employees to pursue creative goals. Because creative goals are typically pursued only by a sub-group of employees, the practical challenge is all about balancing the need for complete freedom in the experimental phase and tight commercial control in the production phase:

- **You need to be able to give your employees the freedom to pursue their own agenda.** R&D scientists seek peer recognition through journal publications; architects and product designers seek critical acclaim for their work. If you want these sorts of people to work in your company, you need to be attentive to their needs, otherwise they will simply move on. Consider the case of Geron, a California biotechnology company. When it bought Roslin Biomed, the Edinburgh-based spinout behind Dolly the Sheep (the first cloned animal), it had to structure the arrangement with Roslin's scientists very carefully to ensure that their needs were met. And so it gave them complete operating autonomy, co-ownership of any intellectual property created, and the right to publish their findings—all necessary elements of academic freedom.[21]

- **You need an effective way of separating out, and investing properly in, the high-potential projects.** Pharmaceutical companies like Pfizer have enormous expertise in staged investing, that is, deciding which projects to take forward to the next stage of development and which ones to kill. Other companies struggle with this process. One engineering company I know well has very relaxed procedures for deciding which projects to pursue, with the result that any seasoned engineer with a client and a project he or she wants to work on could do so—with almost no regard for its subsequent profitability. Whether it is through a process of guided evolution, as pursued by Google, or a more formalized stage-gate system, it is critical to be able to prioritize high-potential projects and kill off less-promising ones.

Approach #3: Taking a Leap of Faith

The third approach to goal setting differs markedly from the first two in one important respect—it does not involve executives taking a strong position about the company's end goal. In other words, while the first two approaches work on the basis that the company's ultimate objective is to make profits for its shareholders, the leap-of-faith approach eschews such an assumption. Rather, it assumes that every company has multiple stakeholders, without any clear hierarchical ordering of which are more or less important, and that these stakeholders are interdependent with one another.

Consider the case of Seventh Generation, a 20-year-old, privately held company that makes basic commodity products such as toilet paper, diapers, and laundry detergent. The company is committed to becoming the world's most trusted brand of authentic, safe, and environmentally responsible products for a healthy home. Its name, according to president and chief inspired protagonist Jeffrey Hollender, comes from the Great Law of the Iroquois, which says that in every deliberation it behooves us to consider the impact of that decision on us for the next seven generations. What this means, in practice, is that decisions about what products to launch, where to sell them, and how to source their materials, are made according to a dramatically different set of principles than those used by Procter & Gamble or Unilever.[22]

One such principle is transparency: when anything bad happens, the company makes sure that everyone knows about it, rather than hushing it up. It's not enough, say, for the company to be trying to eliminate a certain chemical from its laundry detergent—stakeholders have to be involved in the dialogue. So the company puts on its website anything critical that any of their stakeholders might want to know about. While such transparency may seem counter-intuitive, it has helped Seventh Generation thrive.

Another key principle is "reconciling systemic dissonance," which, in layman's terms, means avoiding the scenario where one stakeholder wins at the expense of another. For example, Wal-Mart's purpose of saving consumers money can hurt suppliers who are required to push their prices to Wal-Mart down every year, which is "the antithesis of being responsible." So Seventh Generation does not sell its products through Wal-Mart.

This goes along with a key objective of Seventh Generation—to get other companies to think more responsibly about the planet and act accordingly. According to Hollender: "A lot of what we do is to actually engage with other businesses in helping them think about these things, because the solutions aren't going to come from 7Gen. We are a little company, most of our influence is not even on our consumers; most of our influence is on other businesses who look at what we do and say wow, that's interesting, I didn't think that was possible."

Seventh Generation may be an unusual example, but it illustrates an important point. While it sells green products, its real mission is much bolder and more multi-faceted—it wants to create more conscious consumers, create justice and wellbeing through education, ensure the sustainable use of natural resources, and a number of other equally noble goals. In other words, *the company does not have a clear, unequivocal end goal.* Instead, it revels in the ambiguity of having many partly complementary and partly competing goals.

Now one might think that such an approach—nowhere among the objectives is profitability—would have a negative effect on Seventh Generation's bottom line. Not so—growth has gone from 25% per year in the late 1990s, to 45% in 2008, and even higher in 2009.

Another example of a leap-of-faith goal comes from Cargills Ceylon Plc, the biggest producer and retailer of food in Sri Lanka. Under the leadership of CEO Ranjith Page, Cargills has embarked over the last decade on an innovative approach to building up the capacity and profitability of the farming community in Sri Lanka. Traditionally, the local production process was highly inefficient: 40% of fruit and vegetable production was wasted, 20–30% of the value was paid to a middleman, and there was no investment in technology and skills in local farms. Cargills put in place a system for building relationships directly with 10000 farmers across the country, assuring them of a ready market and a better price than they were getting before, as well as technological and financial support. The model has helped the local community of farmers to develop, and has driven Cargill's rapid growth. It has been highly praised as a model for sustainable development by the World Bank and the Gates Foundation.[23]

With 6000 employees and 136 retail outlets, Cargills now expresses its mission as "serving the rural community, our customer and all other stakeholders through our core business, food with love, on the principles of enhancing youth skills, bridging regional disparity, and reducing cost of living by enhancing local and global markets." "Food with love" may not be an expression that would work in North America or Europe, but it resonates strongly with Cargill's customers and suppliers. According to Page, "We strive to ensure that these principles are foremost in every aspect of our business. We do this out of love for our country and our people. That is how our business model was born, out of love." Today, Cargills has nine collection centers island-wide to collect rice, milk, fruit, and vegetables directly from farmers, giving them a price which is consistently 20% higher than their production cost. Some 70% of its direct employee base is below the age of 25, and 80% of them hail from rural Sri Lanka.

As Sunil Jayantha Nawaratne, a senior executive at Cargills, observes, "Our company vision and mission demonstrates that we believe profit must only be generated within a business process that creates sustainable value for all stakeholders." Consistent with the philosophy of Mr Ranjit Page and in line with the traditions of Sri Lanka, the ultimate objective of Cargills is to give back to the society and, in that process, build a successful enterprise. Sunil observes that within such a culture, maximizing profit no longer becomes the end, but instead the means with which the company is able to expand and create further value for society.

Many other companies pursue their own version of the leap-of-faith approach to goal setting. As mentioned earlier, John Mackey of Whole Foods Market believes in the "holistic inter-dependence" of all stakeholders; and that profits are best pursued as a by-product of other things, including service to customers, developing employees, and improving the wellbeing of the community." Another example is Specsavers, the UK-based optical retailer, founded in 1984 by husband and wife team Doug and Dame Mary Perkins, with the goal of providing affordable fashionable eyecare for all. The founders never saw making money as their primary objective—they established the business to make it possible for everyone in the UK to have easy access to quality eyecare. They deliberately built their business model in such a way that their business partners—the store owners—took the lion's share of the profits. Now, 25 years later, Specsavers has 1400 stores in 10 countries, and the company has never closed a store.[24]

Guidelines for taking a leap of faith. In some ways this is the riskiest of the three approaches, so it's even more essential to make sure you've got the key elements in place before letting go:

- **You need to truly believe that profits aren't that important.** The difficulty here is in convincing stakeholders. Consumers, employees, and analysts are a skeptical bunch, and many of them will assume—unless you consistently prove otherwise—that financial gain is the real *raison d'être* of your company. So if you are serious about balancing the needs of all stakeholders, and about pursuing multiple ends, your actions need to reflect that belief. Seventh Generation, as we saw, runs the risk of a potential revenue loss by publicly criticizing its own products. But it does so because it is committed to transparency with its stakeholders. Cargills has a policy of paying its suppliers higher than market rate and charging lower prices than its competitors, and these commitments are visible to all. These are tangible commitments that underscore these companies' avowed objectives.

- **Your cause has to be one that consumers want to support.** Cargills is pursuing a social mission that all Sri Lankans can believe in. Doug and Dame Mary Perkins were able to transform the UK eyecare business because of a change in the law allowing deregulation and because the market was so poorly served back in 1984. Seventh Generation and Whole Foods Market have both tapped into the zeitgeist around environmental and community sustainability. And although profit cannot—by definition—be the driver of a company pursuing a leap-of-faith goal, there is nonetheless a need for a company choosing this approach to make enough profit to survive; which means offering a product or service that people really want to buy.

- **You need to track your performance on all the dimensions of performance you care about.** Well-managed companies keep track of their performance against expectations, regardless of what those expectations are. So even if your company's mission is positioned as a leap of faith, stakeholders will want to know the consequences of that leap. That is why Cargills measures the number of suppliers it has supported, the number of young people they have helped to train, and the cost savings they have passed on to consumers.

- **You must take heed of the self-apparent risks of this approach.** Obviously it's not at all easy to deliberately pursue a course of action that detracts from the short-term profitability of an enterprise, and the reality is that many leap-of-faith companies simply don't survive. It's also very hard to stay on track, particularly if new investors become involved in the company. Doug and Mary Perkins have said they will "never" sell Specsavers, as they feel their distinctive model would be quickly diluted by a new investor with different objectives. It's noteworthy, but perhaps not surprising, that most companies pursuing the leap-of-faith approach to goal setting are not publicly traded (Whole Foods Market is an exception).

In an interesting study of such companies, Marjorie Kelly identified three alternative governance models that are increasingly used by companies that shun profitability as a primary objective: *stakeholder-owned companies* that put ownership in the hands of non-financial stakeholders, such as employees or cooperatives; *mission-controlled companies*, which separate ownership and profitability from control and organizational direction; and *public-private hybrids*, where profitability and mission are combined to create unique structures.[25] It is too soon to know how all these different governance models will work out, but the enormous variety of approaches being experimented with at the moment is testament to its importance in today's society.

Some Final Points

The focus of this chapter has been on making sense of the different ways companies apply the oblique principle in their goal-setting activities, and some of the pros and cons of each approach. In this final section, let's now return to the broader discussion about the relative merits of alignment and obliquity as underlying principles for goal setting.

As a general rule, the principle of alignment works best in a stable world—where work is relatively routine and conducted in a linear manner (e.g. through a production line), where there is a reasonable degree of predictability about how things interact with each other, and where outcomes can easily be measured. It also works well in small companies where everyone knows one another, and where the objectives can therefore be quickly communicated. The principle of obliquity, on the other hand, is more appropriate in a turbulent world—where work involves a high degree of creativity and interactivity, where the system in which one operates is complex, and where outcomes are harder to predict and measure.

Clearly, aspects of our current business environment are becoming more complex—hybrid alliances, joint ventures, and outsourcing deals are increasing, and there is much greater concern today for the impact of our business activities on the social and natural environments. These and other factors are making the oblique principle for goal setting more salient. However, that doesn't mean necessarily throwing out the alignment principle.

Table 5.2 summarizes key features of our three oblique approaches plus the traditional alignment-based approach that is built around short-term financial goals. The basic assumption of the short-term financial goal approach is that everyone can work collectively and directly toward a particular target, such as profitability. The indirect goal and creative goal approaches are built on rational and linear thinking about how one goal is linked to another. The leap-of-faith approach is built on system thinking: the idea that everything is causally linked to everything else, and therefore we cannot accurately predict how our actions will play out among a diverse set of stakeholders. As always, the intention here is not to argue that one of these approaches is inherently superior to another, but rather to lay out the different options and the circumstances in which you would choose each one.

Table 5.2: Comparing four approaches to goal setting

Short-term Financial Goal	Indirect Goal	Creative Goal	Leap-of-faith Goal
People pursue narrow, financial goals because their actions lead directly to those goals	People pursue A because it is desirable and leads indirectly and eventually to B	People pursue A for its own sake, even though it is orthogonal to B	People pursue A for its own sake, with little regard for what else it might lead to, whether B, C or D
Managers align all incentives and targets around these financial goals	Managers create a scoreboard for reaching A, while also keeping an eye on how A is influencing B	Managers create a scoreboard for reaching A, and they make investment decisions, across the portfolio, to amplify the "winners" that will also lead to B	Managers create a scoreboard/vision for A, and they seek to influence B, C, D along the way. But they don't get obsessive about whether B, C or D is reached or not—it is out of their control
Aligned logic	Sequential, causal logic	Guided evolution logic	System thinking, interdependency logic

Chapter 5: Key points

The traditional principle for goal setting in large companies is *alignment*: the concept that all employees are working directly toward the same common goals. The alternative principle is *obliquity*: the concept that goals are often best achieved when pursued indirectly.

The oblique principle is not well understood in the business world, but many companies implicitly use it already, for example when establishing their long-term vision or when setting goals for R&D scientists. This chapter suggests that there are three different approaches to goal setting that draw to some degree on the oblique principle: (#1) pursuing an *indirect goal* where focusing on A leads subsequently to B; (#2) pursuing a *creative goal* where some of the efforts directed toward A are then amplified and targeted toward B; and (#3) pursuing a *leap-of-faith* goal where a higher-order vision is set with little regard for where it might subsequently lead.

As with the earlier chapters, there is increasing interest in applying the alternative principle, obliquity, to goal setting in large companies. The principle of alignment works best when the business environment is stable and predictable, and when coordination between the different functions of the company is relatively straightforward. The principle of obliquity works best when the business environment is dynamic and uncertain, and when the different functions of the company are pulling in different directions.

We describe the three oblique approaches to goal setting, and we compare them to the traditional focus on short-term financial goals. Each approach has its own pros and cons. Your challenge as a manager is (a) to understand the relative merits of each approach, (b) to evaluate which is the most appropriate one for your particular circumstances, and (c) if you believe there is scope for improvement, to envision and experiment with new ways of building on these ideas.

6

MOTIVATING EMPLOYEES: FROM EXTRINSIC TO INTRINSIC MOTIVATION

Tension is palpable as the giant screen flashes rapidly changing scores, players frantically adjust their tactics, and spectators watch in awe at the astonishing skills demonstrated by the competitors. Stakes are tantalizing—a share of the $260 000 in prize money, and acclaim for the winners. This is no sports match—though speed, ability, and strategy definitely figure in—but the TopCoder Open, a unique event in which some 120 of the world's leading software programmers gather every year at the Mirage, Las Vegas, to compete in categories including algorithms, software design, and development.[1]

TopCoder is a Hartford, CT-based software company with a very unusual business model. Founded by entrepreneur, Jack Hughes, TopCoder has built up a community of freelancers (rather than employ its own in-house programmers) who take part in mini-competitions to see who can develop the best code. The TopCoder Open is a show—it is all about who can develop the cleverest algorithms under time pressure. But TopCoder also uses the same model when it develops software for clients: the programming work is broken down into modules, and for each module the winning coder gets a prize.[2]

The TopCoder developer community is highly competitive, and the leading programmers are stars. A two-time winner of the TopCoder Open is Tomek (aka Tomasz Czajka), who won his first open when he was just 22 years old and subsequently became an American-Idol-like hero back in his native Poland, where he appeared on billboards and was heralded in a popular song.[3]

Another champion is Argolite (aka Michael Paweska), 33, who gave up a steady job at a Canadian e-business consulting firm to focus on TopCoder. Unlike Tomek, who just competes in algorithm competitions, Argolite also takes part in commericial development competitions for clients. And with enormous success: he has made more than $750 000 from TopCoder in just a few years.

None of the developers in TopCoder's community gets a steady paycheck from the company. Nor are they eligible for benefits packages or promotions, for they are all freelancers. But they are highly motivated—they work long hours on TopCoder projects, often doing it in their free time, in the evening, or on the weekend, and they show enormous loyalty and attachment to the company.

TopCoder is an unusual organization, because it relies on spontaneous coordination among self-interested individuals to get work done. It is also remarkably successful, with some 219 000 software developers in its community and a fast-growing body of software clients. It serves to illustrate a fascinating puzzle in the field of motivation studies. *Why is it that volunteers, freelancers, and temporary workers are frequently far more motivated than full-time employees?* We see this in open-source software communities, like Linux or Apache, and we also see it in volunteer-based organizations like Greenpeace and Médecins Sans Frontières. Is there something about the employment contract *per se* that drives out effort? Or are managers simply not being smart enough about the mechanisms they use to motivate their employees?

Another way of asking the same question is simply: what motivates Argolite? He isn't assured of making any money from his TopCoder work, but he ploughs all his discretionary time and energy into work that, if accepted, will help TopCoder deliver high-quality software to its clients. If we could understand what drives people like Argolite (and we will discuss his views later in the chapter), we could make significant improvements in the way we structure and allocate work.

Let's be clear—these are massively important questions. As we observed in Chapter 1, recent studies of engagement in the workplace suggest that no more than 20% of employees are actively engaged in the work they are doing. This means a whopping 80% are doing the bare minimum to keep their bosses happy. They are sitting in front of their computers planning their vacations or ordering from online catalogues, and they are applying their creative energies to their evening and weekend pursuits. Of course, there are some jobs that will never be intrinsically engaging—working in a call center and flipping hamburgers are obvious examples. But if we could just achieve a modest change in these figures, say, increasing engagement from 20% to 30%, the gains in productivity and job satisfaction would be dramatic.

In this chapter, we explore some fresh ways of thinking about motivation as a way of tackling these tricky questions. While there are some features of the traditional employment relationship that get in the way of employee motivation, the reality is that managers have many techniques at their disposal to get a higher level of discretionary effort out of their people. Some of these techniques have existed for years, but have been downplayed because they are hard to implement. Others have only gained legitimacy recently, in part through the rise of Web 2.0 technologies and the increasing presence of freelance communities.

This chapter discusses the different approaches to motivation that managers have at their disposal, and the pros and cons of each one, so that ultimately you will have a better understanding of which might be most suitable to your situation as you begin to sharpen your Management Model. But first we need to provide some historical context.

Some Historical Background

Academic theories of motivation can readily be traced back to the well-known ideas of Elton Mayo, Abraham Maslow, Douglas

McGregor, and others. But it's useful to go back even further in time to try to get a handle on the link between employment and motivation. In the book *Manufacturing the Employee*, management researcher Roy Jacques makes a persuasive case that the boss–employee relationship as we know it today emerged during the industrial revolution.[4] In the mid-nineteenth century, most people were tradesmen or craftsmen—they worked primarily for themselves, they controlled the work process from start to finish, they were multi-skilled, and they only entered wage-based work as a supplement to their primary trade. The emergence of large companies in the latter part of the nineteenth century, as described in the Introduction, led to a fundamental change in how people viewed work. Employees began to be paid for inputs rather than outputs, they committed to long-term contracts with their employers, and they accepted their role as cogs in a machine. And the language changed, with the term "employee" only coming into common usage in the early years of the twentieth century.

Jacques' analysis is important because it prevents us from taking a simplistic uni-dimensional approach to history. People have not always worked in large, industrial companies. So when we speculate that the workplace of the future will involve more self-employment and more community-based ways of interacting, we are actually predicting a partial return to the old model, rather than the creation of an entirely new one. This matters enormously to the study of motivation. Jacques made clear that tradesmen and craftsmen in the mid-nineteenth century were highly motivated. If this is the base case, then our challenge becomes one of understanding *how the traditional employment relationship in large industrial firms came to demotivate employees and drive out their discretionary effort.* We are likely to enhance employee engagement as much by overcoming the strictures of the traditional employment model as by coming up with something entirely new.

Viewed against this historical backdrop, the work of Mayo, Maslow, McGregor, and others was essentially about *rediscovering* the human side of the enterprise, while still working within the confines of the large, industrial company. Since their early work, the body of literature concerned with motivation in the workplace has grown exponentially. It's worth spending a little time in defining the particular approach to motivation that we use here.

What is motivation? Motivation is simply the internal condition that activates behavior and gives it direction.[5] In the context of business, it is what drives an individual to spend time and energy on a particular task or goal. It is obvious, when you look at the people who work for you, that motivation levels vary from person to person, and from job to job. So to understand why this is the case, researchers have taken two approaches: some have focused on employees' underlying needs and wants, while others have focused on the drivers that stimulate people to work harder.

One key insight that has emerged from this research is distinction between intrinsic and extrinsic motivation. *Intrinsic motivation* comes from the rewards inherent to a task or activity itself—for example, playing the piano, walking in the countryside, or solving a puzzle. *Extrinsic motivation* comes from outside the person—money is the most obvious example, but coercion and the threat of punishment are also common extrinsic motivators.[6] Recent research by psychologists Edward Deci and Richard Ryan has extended this thinking in a couple of useful directions.[7] One is a better understanding of the components of intrinsic motivation—the need for competence, the need for autonomy, and the need for relatedness to others. The other is the identification of a hybrid third type of motivation they labeled *internalized extrinsic motivation*. For example, when employees receive promotions, or recognition from their peers, these are externally granted but they are internalized as valuable by the individual, and therefore they become intrinsic. *The extrinsic–intrinsic dichotomy, in other words, is really a sliding scale with various levels of internalized motivators between the two end-points.*

MIT Professor Douglas McGregor's well-known distinction between Theory X and Theory Y is also highly relevant here.[8] McGregor was concerned with understanding how managers shaped the behavior of their subordinates. Theory X represented a belief that workers are inherently lazy and require extrinsic rewards to get their work done; Theory Y viewed workers as self-motivated, ambitious, and intrinsically motivated. McGregor did not view one as inherently more accurate than the other, but he observed that the system a manager puts in place tended to re-inforce itself. So Theory X managers tended to emphasize coercion and control, with their employees responding accordingly, while Theory Y managers tended to provide more autonomy and opportunities for personal development to their people.

These theoretical ideas provide the structure for the remainder of this chapter. Figure 6.1 illustrates how they fit together. On the vertical axis we have the "traditional" principles of extrinsic motivation and Theory X; on the horizontal dimension we have the "alternative" principles of intrinsic motivation and Theory Y. Now, we have to be careful here because, unlike the previous chapter, where obliquity was a new and unusual alternative to alignment, the positioning of intrinsic motivation as being either new or unusual would be simply wrong. What we are saying instead is that extrinsic motivation emerged as the *de facto* norm within large, industrial companies in the early years of the twentieth century, and intrinsic motivation is increasingly viewed as a desirable alternative as we move into the twenty-first century. Of course, the concept of intrinsic motivation has been around for decades, and its benefits are well documented. But most observers would acknowledge that few large companies are actually managed according to its principles.

Figure 6.1: The motivation spectrum: framework for comparing different approaches to motivation

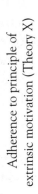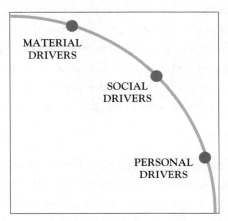

Adherence to principle of
intrinsic motivation (Theory Y)

Drivers of motivation. Positioned along the spectrum are three sets of mechanisms—the drivers of discretionary employee effort—that managers can put in place:

- *Material drivers* of discretionary effort. These are ways of providing people with material and direct rewards for their efforts. They include salary increases, promotions, bonuses, prizes. They can also include the green light given to a project, approval of a patent, or a prize for coming up with the best solution to a problem.

- *Social drivers* of discretionary effort. These are ways of providing people with a reason to belong to an organization. Most of us need to be part of a group or a community. That sense of belonging, of being a team player, of having a certain status within a peer group, can accord recognition, peer approval, and popularity.

- *Personal drivers* of discretionary effort. This refers to the ways managers structure and allocate work to make it more intrinsically appealing. This includes giving people the freedom to act, the chance to work creatively with others, the opportunity to build and demonstrate expertise, and the opportunity to contribute to a worthwhile cause. Think of artists, writers, and R&D scientists, who are often so wholly captivated by the nature of the work they do (not discounting, of course, the tortured moments of self-doubt), that the joy and satisfaction they derive is the engine that drives them.

Do managers have to choose between using material, social, and personal drivers? Can they use all three simultaneously? Alas, the answer to this question is not entirely straightforward. There is quite a lot of research showing that extrinsic rewards can drive out intrinsic ones. For example, one study of volunteer workers found that when they were paid for their efforts, they became increasingly materialistic and less inclined to work for free.[9] Studies have also shown that some motivators, particularly those concerned with working conditions and pay, only have an effect up to a certain threshold. Renowned psychologist Frederick Herzberg called these "hygiene" factors because, like washing regularly, they are best suited to preventing ill-health in the workplace rather than as a means of generating good health.[10]

These caveats apart, the three approaches suggested here are best viewed as *complements*. That is, if you as a manager can engineer a thoughtful combination of material, social, and personal drivers, it is highly likely that your employees will respond positively. In one recent academic study of R&D scientists, management researcher Henry Sauermann sought to understand why some of them chose to work much longer hours than they were required to do. The three factors that correlated with hours worked were salary, level of responsibility, and intellectual challenge—a nice combination of material, social, and personal drivers.[11] The approach taken by Indian IT services company Infosys to blend all three sets of drivers is described in Box 6.1.

Box 6.1:   How Infosys motivates its employees

Infosys, the Indian IT services company, provides a good example of how the three drivers of discretionary effort can be used in combination. Founded in 1981 by seven IT engineers, it remained a fragile start-up until the tsunami of demand for IT services hit in the 1990s. Capitalizing on a highly educated but relatively cheap Indian workforce, and committed to international expansion, it grew rapidly through the 1990s and 2000s, and is now one of the premier IT services companies in the world.

In terms of material rewards, salaries are excellent by Indian standards. In 1994 the company introduced stock options to retain the company's brightest talents rather than losing them to American competitors. Nine years later, sensing that the bar needed to be moved, it offered instead a much higher level of incentive pay, tied to individual, business-unit, and corporate performance. And in the early 1990s, the company moved from a simple model for promotion based on tenure in the company to a meritocratic model with clear definitions and competency assessments. In addition to all this, to recognize employee excellence in areas such as project management, account development, innovation, and social conscience, Infosys awards prizes each year.

In 2007 Infosys had grown to 80 000 employees, and such was the rate of growth that the median tenure was just two years; so enormous effort is put into bringing people up to speed quickly, and encouraging them to stay. There is a sophisticated on-boarding process for new recruits, a raft of initiatives for making work enjoyable (for most people, this is their first full-time job), and for matching employees to roles and for providing transparency about career progression. There are also many training programs available for employees as they rise through the ranks, and ways for employees to provide feedback on their experience and to share learning with others. Infosys has been frequently recognized for its leading HR practices. In 2007 the company won the Optimas award from Workforce Management, and in 2005 and 2006 it was named "the best company to work for in India" by BT-Mercer-TNS.

Hema Ravichandar, Infosys' former Senior VP of Human Resources, summed up the company's approach to employee engagement by saying that the company provides "Learning value-add through our training and on-the-job learning opportunities, which constantly 'stretch' employees, financial value-add through competitive pay and incentives, and emotional value-add through our strong culture." This combination has been extraordinarily successful.[12]

Ultimately, though, motivation is a highly idiosyncratic thing. Employees are individuals and respond in their own unique ways to the work they do. So while Jane may work weekends for no additional pay because she is passionate about computer programming (personal rewards), John may do the same but for a different reason—because of the status it has endowed him with, the fact that his friends and family now think he has made something of his life (social rewards). And this could change: John might need a different motivator once he has established his position with regard to friends and family—he might need rewards in the form of a promotion, with more pay (material). And Jane might need her fellow employees to acknowledge how much her work has helped them in their projects (social).

The manager's job is therefore to be thoughtful about how to get the most out of people—to enable and encourage their discretionary effort. And this means making use of these three drivers in whatever combination is appropriate. Infosys (see Box 6.1) uses these drivers in a fairly standard way to motivate its full-time employees: they get a good salary and many are also provided with share options; they give people opportunities for development and advancement; and they structure work and allocate jobs to make it as intrinsically interesting as possible. TopCoder uses an equally broad set of drivers to motivate its freelance community. Argolite's motivation for taking part in TopCoder's programming competitions is partly material (prize money of more than $750000 so far), partly intrinsic (he gets a thrill out of winning, and takes pleasure in outdoing his competitors), and partly social (he values the respect and recognition he gets from the community of elite programmers). As he says, "My office is three feet from my bed; I just get up and turn on my computer to start each morning. And meeting everyone in person at these events is a big highlight as well. There is no point in me doing anything else—I love the work, and I can make more money than I did as a regular software contractor."[13]

It's worth underlining the point that these three sets of drivers apply equally to full-time employees and to freelance community members. Many human resource managers worry about outsourcing work and using freelancers, because they feel they no longer have control over what these individuals are doing. TopCoder's experiments in building an online community of programmers suggest a very different conclusion: *you have just as many tools at your disposal for stimulating and engaging freelance workers as you do with traditional employees.*

In the remainder of this chapter, we discuss each type of driver in detail.

Material Drivers

In 1895, with just $200, John C. Lincoln founded the Lincoln Electric Company to produce electric motors he had designed. Twelve years later, having expanded into battery chargers, welding sets, and welding machines, John brought his brother James into the company, and eventually turned the management of it over to him so he could focus on scientific inventions.

James proved to be a highly progressive manager—he introduced piecework pay, established the Employee Advisory Board, which includes elected representatives from every department and to this day continues to meet every two weeks, and even provided group life insurance for all employees, a benefit practically unknown at the time. In 1923 Lincoln was one of the first companies to accord employees paid vacations and offer them stock ownership. From an employee suggestion program to the welding training school, from the annual incentive bonus offered first in 1934, to profit sharing and a no-layoff policy offered in the 1950s, Lincoln endeavored to make its employees as contented working there as possible.[14]

Fast forward to the present time, when Lincoln is not only the leading manufacturer of welding equipment in the USA, but also in the world, with net sales in 2008 of $2.49 billion and net income of $212 million. It's not just the financial success that would make John and James proud of their legacy, but also the ongoing commitment and loyalty of its employees. In the 1990s, when the company was undergoing major international expansion, employees voluntarily postponed 614 weeks of vacation to meet customer needs. And in Lincoln's centennial year, the employees assured that the company met its sales goal of $1 billion dollars. Furthermore, employee turnover is practically non-existent, except for retirement.[15]

While Lincoln uses many approaches to motivating its employees, its forte has been the creative use of material rewards to stimulate effort. The company uses clearly aligned incentives, in that the company carefully defines tasks and activities, equating them to salary scales and bonuses, and bases opportunities for promotion on a meritocratic system. This model works well because Lincoln's job descriptions are precise, and because the link between effort and output is well understood. It has also been designed with enormous attention to detail, because, as anyone who has ever been promised a bonus knows, the opportunities for "gaming" the system are manifold.

Lincoln Electric's careful use of extrinsic rewards is taught to business school students all over the world. We see extrinsic rewards emphasized in many other industries, including investment banking, auto sales, mortgage sales, and insurance, but Lincoln is one of the few cases where the financial incentive model gets a good press. It's a shame there aren't more: the intelligent use of material rewards is a key element in employee motivation, and we shouldn't throw it out just because we are shocked by investment banking bonuses, or because we find the sales tactics used by car salesmen overly aggressive.

Fortunately, the technology revolution has opened up some new possibilities in the domain of material rewards. Two models, in particular, are worth highlighting—the use of *productivity games* in the workplace, and the emergence of *prizes* as a way of stimulating collaborative effort toward a common goal.

Productivity games. Many managers intuitively know that by injecting a little bit of competition into the workplace you are likely to get people to work harder. But the increasing sophistication of gaming technology has made it possible for companies to develop productivity-improvement tools that take this notion a whole lot further.

A leading proponent of productivity games is Ross Smith, head of Windows security testing at Microsoft, whom we meet again in Chapter 8.[16] Microsoft has used simple competitions for years, such as the "bug bash" designed to squeeze out the last remaining bugs in a software product before it is shipped, but Smith decided to experiment with more elaborate models. One recent case was a "Language Quality Game" that he developed to help make sure the new version of Windows worked properly in 100 or so different languages. His team put together a community of native speakers in each language around the world, and the "game" involved each person viewing a series of screenshots, and marking up any problems. As is customary in the gaming world, the task was broken down into a series of game "levels" with 25 screenshots at each level, and they used some rudimentary animation to give it a gaming feel. Players gained access to new pen colors the more levels they covered, and they could monitor their position (in terms of levels covered and errors found) on an international leader board.

This may or may not sound like a fun way of spending a couple of hours, but it worked beautifully, and both gamers and linguists got involved. In a one-month period, several thousand Microsoft employees played the game across 36 languages, and reviewed over a half a million translated Windows dialog boxes, identifying many important issues that were then sorted out. Moreover, 29% of the participants provided additional comments that would be useful for future releases. And the game enabled the team to cut costs, improve quality and ship localized versions of Windows faster than ever before.

Ross Smith has tried out a number of related games, and he's part of a movement called *The Serious Games Initiative* that is experimenting with novel ways of bringing gaming technology into the workplace.[17] In a different context the Federal Aviation Authority has applied it to airport security testing and training. Because X-ray scanning of bags is so tedious, and because real guns and knives are so seldom found, a piece of technology called "threat-image projection" is used to plant dummy guns and bombs in the images of bags going through the X-ray machine. Operators hit the "threat" button when a suspect image is encountered, and periodically they are given scores to show how well they are doing.[18]

When do productivity games work? Ross Smith believes they work best when people are trying to expand their skill-set, and when they are taking part in extra-role activities, i.e. those beyond their immediate job description. In his experience, this is where games are the most helpful in stimulating effort that might otherwise not be forthcoming. And while the focus is on material rewards, Smith acknowledges, productivity games also tap into the social drivers of motivation (for example, through the glory and shame of the leaderboard) and the personal drivers as well (for example, the satisfaction of solving a puzzle). More broadly, productivity games have been used successfully in the following ways:

- Injecting some novelty into routine work—for example, scanning bags at the airport.
- Making a tedious project into a competition—for example, a bug bash at the end of a software project.
- Encouraging discretionary effort—for example, asking people to contribute to an online idea forum and then voting for the best ones.
- Facilitating learning—the more you learn, the higher the level you reach and the greater the functionality you get access to.

Prizes. Like productivity games, prizes are awarded for achievement in a competitive setting, but with a scale and scope that is often much grander. Prizes were often used in historical times to solve major technological problems,[19] and after a century in abeyance, their use is growing rapidly. A study by McKinsey & Company, the worldwide management consulting firm, identified 60 new prizes since 2000, and a growth in prize money from $74 million in 1997 to $315 million in 2007.[20] Many of these prizes are designed to offer societal benefits. For example, the X Prize foundation offers prizes seeking to catalyze "radical breakthroughs" in such areas as commercial space travel and low fuel-usage automobiles. Others are designed purely around commercial ends: the Netflix Prize challenged contestants to improve the accuracy of Netflix's existing algorithm for matching viewers with movies by 10%, and finally had a winner in 2009.

A prize is, by definition, an extrinsic reward. But the attraction of prizes is of course multi-faceted. As we saw with TopCoder and Argolite, prizes also motivate people to work harder toward a goal because they enjoy the thrill of the chase and they want to be recognized for solving a difficult problem. The monetary aspects, of course, certainly are part of it, too. So the burgeoning popularity of prizes is partially a reflection of these multiple benefits. It is also partly driven by technological change—the Internet has made it much easier for communities of like-minded individuals to come together and tackle important problems.

How effective are prizes in a corporate setting? The McKinsey research suggests prizes are the right strategy under certain conditions: when the goal is clear and achievable, when there are many potential problem-solvers, and when those people are prepared to assume some of the risks and costs of failure. With a little creativity, it is quite straightforward to imagine ways of making these conditions valid within an established organization. For example, the team from Roche Diagnostics who we described in Chapter 4 could easily have offered a prize to the internal R&D community for solving the narrow technological problems they posed, and it might well have increased the quality of responses they received.

Benefits of material drivers. Taken as a whole, what are the circumstances in which material drivers are most valuable?

- **They are good for rewarding outcomes.** A salary is given for inputs; bonuses, prizes, and productivity game points are all linked to specific results that the individual achieves. So to the extent that you know *exactly* what objective you are working toward, material rewards can be extremely useful.

- **They provide a direct link between effort and outcome.** When both your ends (your objectives) and your means (the management processes to be followed) are clear, material rewards can be a good way of reinforcing that link. Piecework pay is a classic example of clear ends and means, as we saw with Lincoln Electric.

- **They can spur innovation if structured appropriately.** When the ends are clear but the means are open to individual choice, a carefully structured material reward can stimulate innovation—that is the whole principle behind the X Prize and the Netflix Prize. This approach is likely to work better in a network setting to maximize the chances of different approaches being taken.

Drawbacks to material drivers. Regrettably, material drivers fail all too frequently, as we saw with the ill-conceived bonus schemes in investment banks discussed in the Introduction. Here are some other drawbacks to this kind of motivator:

- **They can drive out intrinsic interest.** Not only did the bonuses incentivize bankers to focus on the wrong things, namely low-margin, high-risk business, but they also involved such large sums of money that intrinsic interest in the job was driven out and replaced by greed.
- **Their usefulness changes as the situation does.** Think of the share options schemes of the dotcom era, which worked only when share prices were rising, and were rarely accounted for, so they had to be entirely rethought once the markets dropped.
- **They can easily fail.** The bottom line is that highly leveraged material drivers, such as bonuses and prizes, should only be used in very particular circumstances. People need to understand how their effort can lead to the required outcome, and by focusing on this one outcome they should not jeopardize or ignore other equally important outcomes. Unless these two conditions are in place, bonuses and prizes are best avoided.

Social Drivers

While material rewards focus on the individuals' needs to provide for their families and for achieving tangible outcomes, social rewards are linked to their need for affiliation and status within a social group. Social rewards cover a range of incentives, from recognition, status, and promotion through to membership and involvement in a particular community. These are all given by an employer, and gradually internalized as desirable by the individual.

Every company uses social rewards to some extent—it's part of what being a company is all about. Where do they make the biggest difference to company performance? Research suggests, not surprisingly, that they are particularly important in industries where the personal and material rewards are low, where the work is repetitive and the salary is minimum wage. Many companies, from McDonald's to Wal-Mart to Disney, have grappled with this challenge, and the answer always revolves around what we are here calling social rewards.

Consider the case of Oriflame, the natural skin care products company founded in 1967 by two Swedish brothers, Jonas and Robert af Jochnick, and their then-partner Bengt Hellsten, in their self-described "tatty two-room Stockholm office." Oriflame is a direct-selling organization, similar to Avon and Amway, where the product is sold through a multi-level structure of "consultants." Today, Oriflame has a team of some 3.1 *million* consultants, based in 61 countries (in half of which they are the market leader) on five continents. Consultants earn commissions on what they sell and are also eligible for incentive programs as they reach specific targets each year.[21]

Megha and Sunil Gandhi of Pune, India, who joined what they (and many others) call "the Oriflame family" in 2000, gave an exuberant testimonial of the rewards of their Oriflame experience: "We had just joined for quality cosmetic products, but the product which attracted us the most was the Success Plan, which made us reach our titles of Senior Manager, Director, Gold, 1st Sapphire … and now the 1st Diamond … We were rewarded with many cash awards, foreign trips, jewelry, gifts, and loads of cash, which gave us name, fame and identity." The Ghandis got more than just these generous material motivators. "To achieve all this we were supported by a great working atmosphere, top management's motivation, and world-class trainings ..."[22]

The sense of "family," of belonging, that the consultants feel toward Oriflame is one of the keys to its success. The number of Oriflame consultants is equivalent to the size of the world's 136th largest country (out of 223). They speak a multiplicity of languages, come from wholly different backgrounds, hold different values, religious beliefs, and political convictions. The secret to their sense of community, according to the brothers af Jochnick, is culture. "A common culture is an invisible bond. It has the power to unite, enthuse and lead people over borders and boundaries that might otherwise separate them. The Oriflame culture gives each person the freedom to set their own targets, income, and working hours. It is a culture that is based on respect for and belief in others."[23]

The Oriflame Management Model is designed to make it possible for people all over the world, regardless of their position in society, to start their own business, quite simply, out of their own homes. The company has three core values: togetherness, spirit, passion, which consultants embrace with remarkable zealousness. "Passionate people," the company says, "have the power to change the world. They love what they do, they believe in it. They know deep down that they can make a difference."

It should not be surprising that there are undertones of religious zealotry here. The harsh reality of direct selling is that it is tedious work, and only really profitable when you start recruiting others to sell (because you get a share of their profits). So Oriflame does its best to overcome the banalities of the work by focusing on ideals such as community and passion. They have campaigns and rallies, and they celebrate individual successes. This helps to provide focus and meaning in the lives of their consultants around the world.

Benefits of social drivers. What are the general observations that we can make about the use of social rewards in a work setting? They provide three key advantages:

- **They create a community that members can benefit from.** A community is a grouping of individuals who both share a common interest *and* derive some value from their membership in it. The role of the manager is therefore to nurture this community to ensure continued participation. In the case of Oriflame, this means reinforcing their members' belief in what they are doing and providing a steady stream of new products to sell. In the case of Eden McCallum, the consultancy we described in Chapter 3, it is about structuring the process by which work gets broken down and offered to community members.
- **They provide recognition.** Recognition for work well done is one of the most powerful motivators—it's the gold star the teacher gave us in school, the applause when we make an excellent presentation. It elevates our sense of importance, and it accords status among our peers. Oriflame puts a lot of effort into recognizing new and high-performing consultants. McDonald's corporation is also very good at promoting from within and celebrating individual success through a number of different awards.
- **They generate commitment to a cause.** It goes without saying that voluntary organizations such as Greenpeace have high levels of employee engagement. Their employees believe in the cause they have joined, and will often give up evenings, weekends, and vacation days to further it. For example, the Olympic Development Association (ODA), responsible for putting on the 2012 Olympics in London, has staggeringly high engagement levels, with 98% of employees saying they "are happy to go the extra mile at work when required."[24] Profit-making companies may not have the virtuous *raison d'être* of Greenpeace or the ODA, but they can certainly play up the higher-order value of whatever they do—for example, curing disease in the pharmaceutical industry, the pursuit of knowledge in the education industry, or "making lives better" (IKEA's mission) in the furniture industry.

Drawbacks to social drivers. Unlike the case with material drivers, an emphasis on social drivers of discretionary effort is never disastrous, but it is also not failsafe, for the following reasons:

- **Social drivers are not easy to maintain.** Building social "capital" in a network of employees or freelancers is not easy, and as we saw in both Oriflame and TopCoder it required persistent effort over many years.

- **It's hard to gauge how much to invest in them.** Every investment has an opportunity cost, and it is certainly possible to put more emphasis on social drivers than the community actually values. It remains to be seen, for example, whether MySpace or LinkedIn will ever recoup the investments they have made in their social communities.

- **They can lead to zealotry.** It's possible for a community of individuals to lose sight of the bigger picture because they become obsessed with the rituals and beliefs that those in the center are espousing. This is a common phenomenon in religious groups, less so in corporate circles. Nonetheless, it is important for managers to periodically ask themselves: is this community growing in a way that I am comfortable with?

Personal Drivers

The third way of increasing discretionary employee effort is by enhancing the intrinsic satisfaction people get from their work. Now, in certain professions it is taken for granted that work is intrinsically satisfying. It's not the money that drives academics, scientists, artists, and musicians—many persevere despite earning almost nothing, often happily working for free. So the role of the manager in overseeing such people is minimal—it involves channeling effort toward outcomes that the company values (see the discussion in the previous chapter about oblique goals) and, essentially, getting out of the way.

Most work is not *that* interesting, but it is still entirely possible for people to get personal satisfaction out of doing it. Recall the brief discussion earlier in this chapter about the drivers of intrinsic motivation: we enjoy developing personal competence, for example by achieving a difficult objective; we value the freedom to work on a task in the way we see fit; and we take satisfaction from collaborating with others on our own terms. And there are plenty of things managers can do to encourage these sorts of activities in their companies.

Consider the case of Rolls-Royce, the UK engineering company that shares the global aircraft engine industry with GE and Pratt & Whitney.[25] Back in the early 1990s Rolls-Royce was struggling with a high cost base and a somewhat calcified middle management, but rather than outsource manufacturing to Eastern Europe or Asia, the company decided to make a virtue out of its UK home, and look for creative ways of boosting productivity and quality. A target of 30% productivity improvement was set; if not met, future investment would be made outside the UK.

Through a number of related initiatives, Rolls-Royce began experimenting with high-performance working practices and in particular with the creation of *self-directed teams* in their factories. Traditional assembly lines offer no intrinsic rewards whatsoever: the worker is given a simple, repetitive job to do, and gets no sense of accomplishment. In a self-directed team, employees take responsibility for dividing up tasks and meeting targets, and they learn multiple skills. The intrinsic rewards from seeing a job through to completion are significantly higher.

During the late 1990s, Rolls-Royce established self-directed teams in its Gas Turbines and Aero Repair and Overhaul businesses. It involved a dramatic rethinking of the company's entire Management Model, and a great deal of negotiation with the unions. As Margaret Gildea, EVP, Human Resources, put it:

"The real secret for a change like this is to have a holistic underlying philosophy which has a real commitment from the senior management. It can't be achieved through piecemeal initiatives."[26]

Self-directed teams at Rolls-Royce work as follows. Teams of six people sit at a "cell" containing the machinery needed to do the processing, e.g. casting, grinding, and finishing turbine blades. There is no team leader—individuals are expected to take on specific championing roles such as delivery against target, defect prevention. Over time these roles rotate so that individuals learn multiple skills. The overall schedule is defined by supervisory management and weekly town hall meetings and then less frequent dialogue sessions are held to ensure that workers understand the broader market conditions they are facing.

The introduction of high-performance working practices helped the company hit its 30% productivity growth target. Ten years later, the factories continue to produce high-quality, cost-competitive products, and employee motivation remains high. But the process was hard work, and Rolls-Royce managers readily acknowledge that true self-direction is the ideal, not the current norm. The company remains committed to pursuing and enhancing this new way of working. As Gildea observed: "It's a simple idea—give teams clear targets, the tools and training to solve problems, and improve, coach and guide them. Prepare to be amazed at the power of what they can do."[27]

Rolls-Royce's experiments in self-directed teams illustrate a fundamental point about intrinsic motivation. If we want our employees to be more productive, if we want them to stick with us, if we want them to give freely and generously of their discretionary effort, then we must make it possible for them to derive as much job satisfaction as possible. And for that to happen, they must have a certain amount of autonomy as to what they do and how they do it. The more they define the nature of their own work and identify with it as their own responsibility, the more intrinsically motivated they will be. Our job is to encourage them to pursue their own ideas and find their own way of achieving results while giving them the freedom to do so. It's also to provide them with a supportive environment in which their ideas and energies can flourish.

Benefits of personal drivers—and how to stimulate them. Personal drivers are what make work the most intrinsically satisfying. The relevant question for managers is not just why it's important to use them, but what they can do to stimulate these drivers, as we discuss below.

- **By providing them with space, employees are spurred to assume more responsibility.** The essence of Rolls-Royce's self-directed teams' initiative was to get workers on the factory floor to take personal responsibility for their actions, and to understand how their actions fit with the broader challenges and opportunities facing the company. This approach is well understood, and it is as relevant at the level of a single boss–subordinate relationship as it is for the company as a whole. Alas, many managers still fail to provide their employees with the space they need to figure out and learn from their own errors. Charles Handy, the British management scholar, offers an interesting perspective on this point. In *The Elephant and the Flea: Reflections of a Reluctant Capitalist*[28] he recounts his experiences working for Shell Oil in Kuala Lumpur 40 years ago, and the pleasure of being so far away from the head office that he had plenty of time to correct mistakes before they were noticed. Today, he observed, he would not get that same freedom because of advances in communication technology. Technology adds value in many ways, but it also makes mistakes much more visible, which can provoke companies to restrict employees' decision-making space.

- **By providing them with support, employees are able to achieve more.** Given that personal accountability breeds intrinsic satisfaction among employees, what role should the manager play? Again, this is well-trodden ground, with a consensus that managers should act more like coaches, providing support and feedback when requested and ensuring that the direction of travel is correct. One manager recently described himself as a parasol: he shielded his employees from the harsh glare of the "sun" so that they could get on with their work uninterrupted; another saw himself as a safety net, available to provide help and respond to questions when requested. As always, there is a balance needed here. Individuals need space to get the most out of their work, but they need to know where to go for support, and they need someone to keep them on track.

- **By carefully matching employees to roles, employees are able to play to their strengths.** The idea that we are likely to get more satisfaction out of some jobs than others is an old one: "Each worker should do work for which he is preeminently fitted ... and each should be able to see and enjoy the results of his work," wrote Katherine Blackford and Arthur Newcomb in 1914, in one of the first personnel management books ever written.[29] More recently, the idea of focusing on our strengths rather than our weaknesses in the workplace has gained in popularity.[30] And it has enormous merits as a means of enhancing intrinsic motivation. Henry Stewart, CEO of Happy Ltd, says one of his key management principles is that managers should be chosen according to how good they are at managing ("our most radical principle"), and he cites the case of a marketing manager who was brilliant at the technical aspects of marketing, but terrible with people—which reduced the intrinsic satisfaction she and her team gained from their jobs. So Stewart left her as a stand-alone marketing expert, and had the team report in to someone else with strong interpersonal skills.

The drawbacks to personal drivers. Making work more fulfilling for your employees sounds like a no-brainer, but it's actually quite tricky to do well, and there are plenty of mistakes that can be made along the way:

- **It can be risky to give up some control to your employees.** In most cases, the starting point for you as a manager to enhance the personal drivers is to give your employees more control over what they do and how they do it. This can feel like a risky proposition: you are giving up some control, you may be giving away some of the interesting aspects of your job, and there is no guarantee that the outcomes will be positive. Most of the time this works out very well, but it only takes one bad experience for views to change. Consider the rogue traders gallery, from Nick Leeson (Barings) through Joseph Jett (Kidder Peabody) to Jerome Kerviel (Société Générale). They were all given enough degrees of freedom to lose billions of dollars of their employers' money. Alas, a committed rogue trader will always find ways of beating the system, but that doesn't stop banks from imposing all sorts of new controls in the wake of such scandals, to the detriment of thousands of other well-meaning employees.

- **You may not be able to satisfy your employees' expectations.** The other risk of trying to increase employees' intrinsic satisfaction in their work is that you may not be able to deliver on the promise. I was engaged in a bottom-up change program in a large US electronics retailer, and hundreds of employees got involved—entirely of their own volition—in seeking out better ways of working across the company. Toward the end of the program, a questionnaire revealed that the involved employees were significantly more engaged in their work than a random sample of uninvolved employees. However, they were also significantly *less committed to staying at the company*. Their horizons had been lifted, and many were starting to look for opportunities elsewhere, as they were not convinced the company could deliver on their new, higher expectations.

Some Final Points

The way you approach motivation in the workplace is central to your Management Model, and the primary purpose of this chapter has been to lay out the full range of ways in which individuals inside and outside the boundaries of your company can be motivated to put in discretionary effort. There is, of course, no one right way, and the approaches you have at your disposal all have pros and cons.

But it's worth making a couple of final observations. First, while the distinction between intrinsic and extrinsic approaches to motivation has been understood for at least half a century, companies continue to devote most of their effort to the extrinsic side of the equation. There continues to be enormous scope to be more creative about designing fulfilling jobs in the workplace.

Second, the emergence of community-based organizations like Eden McCallum (described in Chapter 3) and TopCoder (described in this chapter) has shown that people can become at least as motivated working on a voluntary basis as they are working through a traditional employment contract. And many of the approaches used by these community-based organizations are equally applicable in a traditional workplace environment.

Chapter 6: Key points

The traditional principle by which employees were encouraged to work hard in companies is *extrinsic motivation* such as money, coercion, and the threat of punishment. The alternative principle is *intrinsic motivation* which comes from rewards inherent to a task or activity itself. Theorists have recognized this distinction for many years and to varying degrees all companies use some combination of the two principles. However, there is still relatively speaking an emphasis on the provision of extrinsic rewards, i.e. salary and bonuses, in most large companies. This is one reason why the overall levels of employee engagement in most companies are so poor.

One important trend described earlier in the book is the emergence of network-based organizations where individuals who work for you are not actually employees. Because people working in such networks or communities cannot be coerced into working hard, it is increasingly important to focus on the intrinsic motivation they get from their work. This is perhaps one reason why such individuals are often *more* motivated to work long hours than full-time employees.

The chapter describes three sets of drivers you can put in place as a manager to stimulate higher levels of discretionary effort. Material drivers are directed toward extrinsic rewards, primarily money and prizes. Social drivers are directed toward making individuals feel part of a community, and by providing them with status, recognition, and promotion in return for doing a good job. Personal drivers are directed toward making the actual work more fulfilling, by giving individuals more freedom in how they do it, and by allowing them to develop new capabilities along the way.

As with other chapters, each set of drivers has its pros and cons. Effective managers generally use these drivers in combination, but the relative emphasis varies with the circumstances. This logic applies whether the individuals in question are full-time employees or whether they are working on a part-time or voluntary basis.

Your challenge as a manager is (a) to understand the relative benefits of each set of drivers, (b) to evaluate the combination of drivers that is most appropriate for your particular circumstances, and (c) to envision and experiment with new approaches to motivation that build on these ideas.

7

FOUR MODELS OF MANAGEMENT

We've explored quite extensively each of the four dimensions of management, looking at them in the context of the traditional and alternative principles that anchor each one. In this chapter, we pull it all together: we look at how companies apply these principles in combination to create meaningful and coherent patterns of activities. We present a simple framework that separates out the "means" and the "ends" of managing, giving us four distinctive Management Models—the Discovery Model, the Planning Model, the Quest Model, and the Science Model.[1]

By boiling down all the variables from the last four chapters into a two-dimensional matrix, we are simplifying things enormously. Nonetheless, it is a useful analytical approach because it allows us to identify patterns of activity, or *gestalts* that are obscured when we are focusing on points of detail. Once this bigger picture is properly understood, it is much easier to develop a point of view about how your own company, or unit, should change its own Management Model.

The guiding framework for this chapter is presented in Figure 7.1. The horizontal axis refers to the *means* of management (coordinating activities, making decisions); the vertical axis refers to the *ends* of management (setting objectives, motivating people). For each axis, the scale runs from *tight* to *loose*, with the traditional principles of management at the tight end and the alternative principles of management at the loose end.

How do you decide the ideal position for your company on this matrix? Recall in Chapter 2 that we talked about choosing your Management Model on the basis of certain variables, or contingencies, that were specific to your company's situation. It

Figure 7.1: Management Model framework

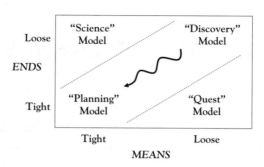

turns out that one of the key variables is the *lifecycle stage* of your company. When a new company is founded, its competitive environment usually feels highly ambiguous, and progress depends a great deal on trial and error. As a result, goals are typically vague and flexible, people work long hours for little pay, and work gets coordinated and defined through informal mechanisms. This is what we call the Discovery Model. We use Google as an example of this model, because it continues to operate much like a start-up, even though its annual revenues now exceed $20 billion.

As a company grows and becomes more successful, its positioning in the marketplace becomes established, and its positioning vis-à-vis competitors becomes clear. Internally, operations tend to become more structured, decision-making more formalized, and objectives more clearly defined. This becomes what we call the Planning Model. We use the example of McDonald's to illustrate how it works, as it has mastered the art of delivering a standardized product on a worldwide basis at a low cost.

As this description suggests, there is a natural drift over time from the Discovery Model (loose means, loose ends) towards the Planning Model (tight means, tight ends). This is not to suggest for a moment that all companies move lock-step down the same path: some, like Google, resist "growing up" for many years; some, like McDonald's, deliberately grow up quickly because it suits their business needs; and others move off away from this path toward one of the other models. It is also important to note that there are successful and unsuccessful companies in both the Discovery and Planning quadrants. Google may be a spectacular success, but plenty of earlier search companies with similar business models, like Altavista and Go.com, did not make it. Equally, some of the most successful companies on the planet—from McDonald's to Wal-Mart to Exxon—use a variant of the Planning Model. But so do many struggling corporate giants.

What about the other two models—the ones in the "off-diagonal" positions? The Quest Model is defined by tight ends and loose means. As with the Knights of the Round Table and their quest for the Holy Grail, this model gives employees enormous latitude in how they work, but very explicit instructions with regard to what they must achieve. It is an attractive model on paper, and indeed many of the examples discussed earlier, including IBM's Values Jam, Oticon's Spaghetti Organization, and TopCoder's software community, are all about freeing up the way activities are coordinated and decisions are made, without losing track of the company's overall objectives. However, it is also a challenging model to implement, because it is very difficult for executives to retain control without formal procedures and rules. We therefore use the example of the investment banking industry to illustrate the Quest Model—because it highlights the costs *and* the benefits of the model.

Finally, the Science Model is defined by tight means and loose ends. Scientific research is conducted by conforming to an established set of procedures and standards—it begins with a body of knowledge, it undertakes controlled experiments, there is open disclosure of the results, and peer reviews of the findings—but there is no predetermined direction that scientists are expected to move in. Because of the loose sense of direction this model implies, it is relatively unusual in a corporate world. The model is often used in a limited way, for example in a research laboratory or a design studio (recall the discussion of the oblique principle in Chapter 5). Many professional service organizations, from medical practices to consultancies and business schools, also use a version of it, because individuals often see the pursuit of their professional goals as more important than the goals of the organization they work for. We use the example of the engineering consultancy Arup to illustrate this model. Arup is the leading company behind such iconic landmarks as Sydney Opera House, the Beijing Bird's Nest Olympic stadium, and the Pompidou Centre in Paris, and its distinctive management philosophy makes it very appropriate for understanding the Science Model in action.

Diagnosing Your Company's Management Model

This chapter will examine each Management Model in turn, but before getting into the details, you might be curious to know where your company fits in the matrix. So go back to the questionnaire at the end of Chapter 2, and on Figure 7.2 plot your average score for questions one through four on the horizontal axis (i.e. the scores for coordinating activities and making decisions), and your average score for questions five through eight on the vertical axis (i.e. the scores for setting objectives and motivating employees). This gives you a rough fix on your current Management Model. The dots on Figure 7.2, by the way, are the positions of other companies taken from a survey I conducted in 2008. As you will see, the majority of people see their companies using the Planning Model or the Science Model.[2]

A couple of points of clarification before proceeding. First, you can use these questions at multiple levels of analysis: the company as a whole might use a Planning Model, while the R&D department uses the Science Model and the corporate incubator uses the Discovery Model. It is up to you to decide what the appropriate level of aggregation is.

Second, the value of the framework is as much about helping you to make conscious choices for *changing* your Management Model, as it is about understanding where you are today. What

Figure 7.2: Plot your company's position on the framework.

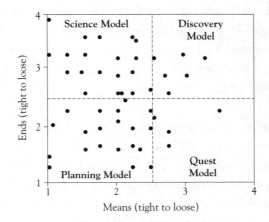

Means (tight to loose)

Note: Each dot on the matrix represents one of the companies that filled in the matrix during the research. Please contact the author for more details on the methodology and the questionnaire used.

would happen if we attempted to free up our processes for coordinating activities and making decisions? Or if we adopted a more flexible set of objectives? What would the pros and cons of this new model be? And under what circumstances would it make sense? These are the sorts of questions we will address in this chapter. But be warned—there is no simple recipe-book solution provided. The framework can help you understand the pros and cons of different approaches, but the circumstances you face are unique, and only you can figure out what the best way forward will be.

The Discovery Model: Google

Not far from where Bill Hewlett and Dave Packard made technology history in their garage, Sergey Brin and Larry Page took the Internet into the twenty-first century with their invention of an algorithm that would dramatically improve the quality of online search. In 1998, with $100 000 seed money, Brin and Page set up workspace in a garage in Menlo Park, with a view to turning their mathematical formula into a commercial venture named Google. In June of the next year, they scored $25 million in venture capital and started adding new employees. In 2001, former Novell boss, Eric Schmidt, was brought in as a commercial counterweight to the technological prowess of Brin and Page.

After experimenting with a variety of business models, they picked up on the idea of charging advertisers to place sponsored links alongside the top-ranked search results. This gave Google their much-needed source of revenue. The company went public in August 2004. The letter to potential investors stated, "Google is not a conventional company. We don't intend to become one."[3] The shares opened at $85 per share. In late 2009, they were selling at nearly five and a half times that. Full-year results for 2008 were net profits of $4.2 billion on revenues of $21.8 billion, with 20 222 full-time employees.

The environmentally friendly headquarters, Googleplex, in Mountain View, just next to Stanford, is very much like a university campus, with sports facilities, 11 restaurants offering free gourmet and often organic food, medical and dental facilities, washer and dryers, a duck pond, and a vegetable garden that helps supply the restaurants. In many other ways Brin and Page replicated their college experiences at Google. From the beginning they surrounded themselves with very smart, hard-working people eager to learn, debate, discover, collaborate, make the world a better place—and have lots of fun while doing it.

Sergey Brin and Larry Page are now part of Silicon Valley folklore. Google arrived late to the Internet party, but by the mid-2000s it had eclipsed Yahoo, Amazon, eBay, and Cisco as the most exciting dotcom company on the planet. It is worth spending some time unpicking the Google Management Model, as it is one of the key drivers of the company's runaway success. But a word of warning is also in order before we get too carried away. Fact is, Google can afford a level of experimentation on new projects that other companies can only dream of because it is phenomenally profitable. So we describe the key features of their model, but we are cautious about generalizing to other contexts.

Informal structures. In Chapter 3 we introduced the concept of managing "at the edge of chaos," a term that was put forward by Stanford graduate Shona Brown, who subsequently joined Google and helped to put her ideas into practice.[4] Work at Google is organized around small (3–6 people), autonomous, highly focused work teams whose projects last usually no more than six weeks and have limited objectives. This allows numerous projects to move forward at the same time, and it shortens the intervals between new releases because it takes only a few thousand engineers to turn out hundreds of projects.[5] Teams are self-managing, and seek feedback from other such teams.[6] Of the 10 000 employees in product development, around half work on self-directed teams, with even large projects being broken up into these smaller units.

In *The Future of Management*, Gary Hamel compares Google's organization to the Internet itself—it's highly democratic, tightly connected, and radically decentralized.[7] Employees, too, are a challenging lot, so meetings are very lively affairs with lots of toing and froing. And the meetings can drag on, because rank holds no sway as to who says what or who wins an argument. As Eric Schmidt observed recently, "I have two jobs: the first is to ensure every issue is debated to find not the common outcome but the best decision. And the second is to put pressure to make it happen quick, because business is speed."[8]

Google employees are given a lot of freedom to try out new ideas, and innovative efforts are encouraged regardless of the outcome. In one incident reported by *Fortune* magazine, a Google vice president was given a pat on the back by Larry Page after making a multi-million dollar mistake. "I'm so glad you made this mistake," Page said, "because I want to run a company where we are moving too quickly and doing too much, not being too cautious and doing too little. If we don't have any of these mistakes, we're just not taking enough risk."[9]

Coordination happens primarily through informal, lateral mechanisms. Information is shared through: MOMA, the company's intranet, where employees can discuss the hundreds of projects going on; Snippets, on which engineers post weekly progress reports; and blogs galore, whether personal ones or project ones. As management writer Bernard Girard observed: "By widely distributing information in this manner, employees adjust their behavior to suit the company's needs, and make the best use of their colleagues' capabilities."[10] And it goes without saying that communication is open and interactive. There are TGIF meetings at which Page and Brin go over the week's highlights, and then there is an open microphone. No holds barred. Managing in this situation, noted Gary Hamel, is about bringing "the collective genius of the organization to bear on decisions large and small—and this demands openness, transparency, and a lot of lateral communication."[11]

The other distinctive way of making sure Google's development efforts are focused on the right goals is from the vast army of cyberspace volunteers. Beta products are usually released via Google Labs, and engender enormous amounts of testing, suggestions for improvements, and bug identification. No focus groups, no market research, just try it and see what people think.

Google's internal labor market is also managed on emergent principles. Candidates are selected via a brutal process that may include eight interviews and Mensa-level problems they must solve then and there, with final decisions usually made by a hiring committee. Executive input to hiring decisions is important, but it's the consensus view that prevails.

Oblique and ambitious goals. Google's mission is to "organize the world's information and make it universally accessible and useful." While that may seem a good bit of hubris, it's been the perfect rallying cry for the fast-moving world Google operates in. Underlying this are the company's principles, or "Ten things Google has found to be true." Number one is "focus on the user and all else will follow," a classically oblique goal. This principle has dictated how the user interface will look, as well as the fact that advertising must be discreet and relevant. Next, is "it's best to do one thing really, really well." What Google does is of course search, and their focus on it has enabled them to branch out into unexplored territory, helping users make better use of the ever-proliferating body of information out there. Other "things" include: you can make money without doing evil, fast is better than slow, democracy on the web works, you don't need to be at your desk to need an answer, there's always more information out there, the need for information crosses all borders, and you can be serious without a suit.[12]

How do all these oblique goals square with the company's obligations toward its shareholders? Well, it helps enormously that the company is highly profitable, thanks almost solely to the margins it gets on its sponsored advertising links. But, equally importantly, Google made clear when it went public that it would not play the short-term earnings game with Wall Street. The company created a two-class stock system, with the founders and a few early executives retaining super voting control over major issues, to ensure that decisions were made with the company's long-term mission in mind. So while financial performance still matters, it doesn't have to drive short-term decision-making, thereby allowing the triumvirate at the top to push the company's oblique goals.

In terms of motivation, Google was named number 1 of the 100 best companies to work for by the Great Place to Work Institute in 2007.[13] Some 95% of employees responding to the survey said, "Taking everything into account, I'd say this is a great place to work." How was this achieved? There's the physical environment, of course, and for early employees there was the prospect of getting rich on a rapidly growing share price. In terms of lasting benefits, employees have an enormous amount of freedom in choosing and executing their projects, and having access to the technology and resources necessary to carry them through. Explains Google CEO Eric Schmidt, "We treat people as though they were the only asset. Other companies say they do, but many business people, especially in private equity, don't think of people as the asset, they think of the business with the cash flow and so forth. Whereas we understand that in an innovation model it's only about the people, and it's only about the innovation engine."[14]

Another motivator is the Innovation Time Off (ITO) policy, which encourages engineers to spend 20% of their time on adjacent business opportunities and a further 10% on wacky new ideas. This helps to invigorate employees, and gives them ownership of their projects. The company has been able to develop to great success some of the ideas created during that ITO window—Google Suggest, Google News, AdSense, and Orkut, for starters.[15]

As a young and growing company, there are also boundless opportunities for high achievers. Most of the senior executives are still under 40. There are also generous training and development activities, including tuition reimbursements, unlimited sick leave, 27 days of paid time off after one year of employment, the possibility of taking off up to five years to pursue advanced studies—and get paid $150 000 for that period. All told, it's not surprising that the company receives more than a thousand résumés a day and voluntary turnover in 2007 was at 2.6%.[16]

Evaluating Google's model. Google is probably the most informally managed $20 billion company on the planet, but it is not immune to the laws of gravity that act on all companies of a certain size. Managing "at the edge of chaos" keeps Google vibrant, but it is expensive. Without formal processes, a lot of time gets spent making and justifying *ad hoc* decisions; and without a clear decision-making hierarchy there is a risk of incoherence and duplication as people do what they see fit. So inevitably, Google's executives are beginning to impose some structure. One example is the establishment of formal "innovation reviews" in June 2009, where executives present product ideas bubbling up through their divisions to Schmidt, Page, and Brin. While hardly an unusual concept, such reviews "force management to focus" and help the triumvirate running the company to place their bets more confidently.[17] And it is safe to predict that Google will bring in more such processes in the years ahead, as its market matures and its growth slows. In the meantime, Google continues to operate with a highly distinctive Management Model that many other companies can learn from.

The pros and cons of the Discovery Model, as illustrated by Google, are pretty obvious. On the positive side, it is liberating, vibrant, fulfilling, and fun. Employees are encouraged to take initiative, and the rewards for creating successful new businesses are sizable. On the negative side, the Discovery Model is messy, and when used in large companies can create complexity and confusion for customers and employees alike.

Applying the Discovery Model in your company. So when should the Discovery Model be used? Clearly, it is the default model for a start-up venture. And for small and medium-sized companies operating in a high-velocity or uncertain environment, it is likely to be the right model. The concept of managing "on the edge of chaos" that we described in Chapter 3 is understandably popular in Silicon Valley, and it is applicable in many other fast-changing settings as well.

But the Discovery Model is also valuable in large, established companies as a way of managing a particular unit or project that is trying to do something unusual. Over the years, many companies have experimented with the concept of a *Skunkworks* or *Venturing Unit*—an informally managed team, charged with doing something difficult, uncertain, or counter-cultural, often in parallel, or even competing, with the company's formal R&D

unit. Famous examples include the original Apple Mac team, IBM's PC development team, and the Shell GameChanger team described in Chapter 3. Skunkworks are generally encouraged to adopt a Management Model that is as different as possible from the dominant corporate culture, so they typically end up with informal methods and oblique goals.

Another way for a large company to use the Discovery Model is through a particular project. For example, consider how Starwood, the global hotel chain, ran a one-day development day in Paris for 700 of its top executives. The purpose of the day, explained Robyn Pratt, Senior Director for Six Sigma and Operational Innovation, was "to get people looking at things from a different perspective, thinking how can I do this differently?" Built on the principle that the "desk is a dangerous place to view the world from," they asked the executives to roam the streets of Paris to seek new perspectives, armed only with a notebook, a camera, and a pack of Metro tickets. Each team of seven people was given one of the company's core values (e.g. beauty, luxury, style, approachability), and charged with reporting back on both traditional and unorthodox meanings of that word. On return, each of the 64 teams put together a visual representation of their findings, and there was a "fair" where each team sold their ideas and insights to their colleagues.

For the Starwood managers taking part it was an unusual experience, as they were given neither explicit objectives nor a clear modus operandi. And that, of course, was the point: the company was seeking new ways of looking at the world that might be useful for the businesses, but you don't get new perspectives without freeing people up from their traditional ways of working. So what came out of it? The 1700 ideas from the day were sorted into four categories—insights, marketing/branding ideas, inputs to ongoing projects, and "just do it"—and followed up by the appropriate people in different parts of the company. Noted Pratt: "Imagine if we all did this on an everyday basis— walking the streets and taking away things that we see and thinking about them differently. This process will be an important input to our competitive advantage."[18]

The Discovery Model, in other words, can be applied to a special unit or to a short-term project, as well as being the way an entire company is managed, and it is often more powerful as a result. Now let's turn to the opposite model, the Planning Model, where means and ends are both tightly controlled.

The Planning Model: McDonald's Corporation

This $23 billion revenue corporation whose golden arches shine from Slovakia to Suriname, Brunei to Botswana, grew out of a drive-in in San Bernadino, California, with 20 carhops and a barbecue pit. In 1948, founders Dick and Mack McDonald put in place their "Speedee Service System" to streamline food production and bring in families. A few years later, milkshake machine salesman Ray Kroc dropped in to see how it was possible that the McDonald's owned eight of his machines, far more than any of his other customers did. The answer was in the kitchen: the brothers had adapted the assembly-line production process to the restaurant business. Customers were flocking there, delighted to be served so quickly (orders were filled in 15 seconds), so uniformly (the hamburger and fries were always exactly the same), and so cheaply (burgers were 15 cents, fries 10).

Kroc knew they were on to something, and helped the brothers to expand by opening more franchises (he later bought them out). He also had the bright idea of buying up or renting space along major thoroughfares and leasing it out to franchisees at a mark-up—a move which according to some observers turned McDonald's into a real estate business, not a food business. From there, McDonald's restaurants spread across the globe like mushroom spores: in 1968 there were 1000 outlets; in 2009 there were more than 31 000, in 118 nations.

Ray Kroc remained involved until his death at age 81. Variously described as entrepreneurial, irascible, obsessive, charismatic, authoritarian, and generous, he imprinted his principles on the company: he believed in hiring people for what they could do rather than who they were, he ascribed to the importance of personal and professional development, he looked at ideas on their merits, he knew the importance of recognition, and valued trust.

A well-oiled machine. McDonald's operates as a tightly integrated system. It was the first restaurant to standardize the process of food production, and it was an early leader in automation. This integrated model has three components: the company, the franchisees, and the suppliers. Ray Kroc pushed the franchisee model to facilitate rapid growth. He put in place generous profit-sharing arrangements, but in return he insisted on absolute standardization around the stores' design and offerings, as well as the company's core values—Quality, Cleanliness, Service, and Value. Automated machinery and detailed operating manuals helped compliance, and regular and unannounced site visits were used to check up on franchisees. Business writer John Love, writing in 1995, observed, "The real secret to McDonald's successful operating system is not found in its regimen, but in the way it enforces uniform procedures without stifling the entrepreneurship of franchisees."[19]

Suppliers, likewise, are considered part of the McDonald's "family." The company works closely with them to improve the uniformity and efficiency of their production processes. Even overseas, where entire systems of agricultural production are exported,[20] so that the french fries eaten in China are made from locally grown Idaho potatoes and processed in a standardized french fry factory, and taste and look exactly like those sold in every other McDonald's store.

To enhance speed and efficiency, most company operations are centralized. Distribution is managed through massive regional centers; stock management is done via the Restaurant Supply Planning Department; the McCommunications Network is used to get instant approval from all regions for ad campaigns. Corporate and crew are governed by a four-pound, 750-page training and operations manual,[21] referred to as "The Bible," that spells out absolutely everything, from procedures to job descriptions to roles—in excruciating minutiae.

To ensure standardization and reduce training (turnover is high, with the average crew member lasting less than two months), processes are automated as much as possible, and crew are given as little decision-making autonomy as possible. Franchisees, for their part, face exacting targets in terms of sales volume, profitability, and adherence to the company's values, with store managers expected to do everything to reach those targets. The company keeps tabs on the restaurants via the Field Service Consultants who give letter grades based on Quality, Service and Cleanliness (QSC) that becomes part of the Full Operating Report. Not only are the grades the basis for renewal of the 20-year license or approval to purchase another franchise, but they also indicate areas where the owners need to improve, and targets to which they can strive.[22]

So it is clear that McDonald's operates a tight system for getting the work done. But the system has some flexibility built into it. First, it's based on respect. Since Ray Kroc's day, managers were encouraged to show the utmost respect in dealing with employees, most having risen up through the ranks. Most people, regardless of level, are on a first-name basis, and regional managers have been known to get behind the counter when visiting a store, signaling not just that they have no problem getting grease on their pants, but also how important the crew jobs are. Second, some players in the McDonald's system get authority over certain areas. Regional managers get to decide on real estate matters and licensing, often working with boards of operators comprised of people from marketing, public relations, and operations. And while franchisees are bound by the covenants of "The Bible," they are also encouraged to come up with new ideas. In fact, some of the most successful products—Big Mac, Filet-o-Fish, McMuffin, Chicken McNuggets, as well as Ronald McDonald—were proposed by franchisees.

So while McDonald's is structured hierarchically, it tempers it with flexibility. A tree, even a very large one, will break if it doesn't bend in a strong wind. And the experience of the last few years is that listening more carefully to customers is important.

Clear goals and objectives. Ray Kroc had a pretty basic mission: "All I wanted was to make McDonald's the winner in the hamburger business."[23] To do this, he knew he had to offer customers pleasant, affordable experiences, and he knew he had to get his employees, franchisees, and crew all aligned behind it.

In 2002, however, when the stock had declined 60% over three years, franchisees were losing money, and surveys had come out putting McDonald's last in terms of food quality among all the other hamburger chains,[24] a turnaround plan was put in place to get the arches shining again. This global strategy, called the Plan to Win, included a revised mission—to "be our customers' favorite place and way to eat"—and centered on "the five basics of an exceptional customer experience—people, products, place, price, and promotion."[25]

How does McDonald's motivate its employees? The word McJob entered *Webster's Dictionary* in 1991, a testament to the menial, often stressful, and poorly paid work that McDonald's crew perform. Employees often feel they are disposable, with neither talent nor skill. And turnover is extraordinarily high—not just because the work is tedious and hard—and generally offers no benefits—but also because it's a high-school job or fill-in work. So the challenge of motivating hundreds of thousands of crew around the world to get out of bed every morning, and put in a decent day's work, is far from straightforward.

McDonald's motivates its employees through what we earlier called social drivers: recognition, opportunities for advancement, and the feeling of belonging to a "family." Its approach bears some similarities to the Oriflame model we described in Chapter 6.

The company puts a lot of emphasis on awards and celebrations. Walk into any McDonald's restaurant in the world, and you will see a line of "employee of the month" pictures. There is also a vigorous awards system for such things as putting customers first, years of service, or jobs done particularly well, and may include money, trips, plaques, paperweights, certificates. These are often celebrated with much festivity and jubilation. According to Paul Facella, who started behind the grill at McDonald's and ended as a regional vice president, recipients got hooked on that sort of recognition, because it was given in "sincere, heartfelt appreciation."[26] One former employee, a recipient of The President's Award (given each year to the top 1% of all corporate employees), said, "McDonald's has made more folks than I can possibly imagine millionaires, and yet those millionaires get teary-eyed and turned on when they are given a plaque— the handshake is the most prestigious."

Opportunities for promotion and development are also plentiful. Promising crew are promoted quickly (a large percentage of senior executives worked their way up through the stores), although it's difficult to move from assistant manager to store manager because of the limited number of those positions. At the higher levels of the McDonald's hierarchy, pay and bonuses are generous. For those seeking to move up in the McDonald's hierarchy, or improve their management skills, there is the possibility to take courses in-store via e-learning, at one of the 22 regional training centers in the USA, at Hamburger University in Oak Brook, Illinois, or at campuses in six other countries. More than 5000 people from all over the world attend the university each year, taking classes on topics specific to their level, with interpretation available in 28 different languages. At the end they can receive a degree in Hamburgerology, the possibility of gaining up to 46 college credits, and the chance to advance.

There are also intangible benefits, as management professor Jerry Newman discovered when he took 14 months off to study fast-food jobs by working undercover behind the counter and then writing about his discoveries.[27] He found crew jobs offer flexibility—crew could take time off for vacations (usually unpaid), to be available for a child. Employees who were most valued were those who could do the most different things, who performed fast and well, which often resulted in their being given more hours. Conversely, those who performed poorly could have their hours reduced drastically. Surprisingly, there is also job security, for those who can tolerate the grueling, mindless work—because of the heavy turnover, managers need to keep as many staff as possible.

Evaluating McDonald's model. It has not all been plain sailing for McDonald's in recent years, and this illustrates the pros and cons of the Planning Model. During the 1990s, the company was condemned for its employment practices, its slaughterhouse methods, its gobbling up of agricultural land, its expansion into foreign countries and cultures, its non-recyclable packaging—to say nothing of its fatty, sugary, chemically enhanced products. The company fought back, and over the years it replaced Styrofoam with paper for its packaging, made its slaughterhouse processes more humane, and added healthier options, such as salads, to the menu. In 1999 the company experienced its first-ever quarterly loss but, guided by its Plan to Win strategy, it made the necessary adjustments so that by mid-2000 it began posting consistent market share and profit gains.

The Planning Model has given McDonald's a position of dominance in the fast-food industry, but of course the flip side of creating such a tightly coupled system is that it cannot adapt quickly to changing market conditions. So when faced with these problems in the late 1990s, the company took quite a time to react, and even with the changes it has made, the actual differences in terms of the company's products and processes have been pretty incremental. Much the same, by the way, appears to have happened to Dell Computer: it was a finely tuned machine selling low-cost, direct-to-the-home computers, but it proved difficult for it to make even relatively minor adjustments in the face of changes in the marketplace.

Applying the Planning Model inside your company. The Planning Model works in a stable world—where work is relatively routine and conducted in a linear manner, and where there is a reasonable degree of predictability about how market conditions will evolve. Many mature industries fit this description, but the trouble is that sooner or later every industry faces some sort of disruptive shock—social changes in the case of McDonald's, technological changes for Dell, economic changes for Exxon—that require adaptation. So as we described in Chapter 3, many companies have developed flexible bureaucracies to give themselves additional degrees of freedom, and many blend intrinsic and extrinsic approaches to motivation.

As with the Discovery Model, the Planning Model can be applied at multiple levels of analysis. Even a discovery-based company like Google has occasional projects that are managed on short time scales with very clear targets and pre-defined roles. Arup, discussed below, is managed as a whole by the Science Model, but its public-sector infrastructure work conforms more to the Planning Model.

The Quest Model: Investment Banking

Rather than focus on a single company, we look at the investment banking industry as a whole, as an interesting example of the Quest Model in action. During the credit crisis, there were winners (Goldman Sachs, JP Morgan) and losers (Lehman Brothers, Bear Stearns, Citibank), and by looking at both side by side we can draw out the strengths and weaknesses of the Quest Model.

We saw in Chapter 1 how Lehman Brothers developed a distinctive Management Model around certain core themes: an emphasis on bringing good people in, and rewarding them generously if they performed well; ambitious growth targets, aimed at taking Lehman to the top of the investment banking leader-board; and an informal, meritocratic style of working that en-couraged people to take initiative and seek out new business opportunities. It was a classic example of what in Chapter 3 we called an "internal market" model, in that it blended certain market-like principles (highly leveraged rewards for successful entrepreneurs, short-term profit orientation) with certain fea-tures of the traditional firm (a single brand, encouragement of teamwork and collaboration).

There is little more to say about the emphasis on alignment and extrinsic rewards. Investment bank employees are motivated by many things—the thrill of bringing in a major client, the status and reputation that comes with success—but everyone knows what the unstated, underlying motivator is. In Michael Lewis' now-classic book *Liar's Poker*, he explains the golden rule of interviewing for a job: "never, ever mention the money." Equally, the objective of the investment bank as a whole, its *raison d'être*, is all about financial returns: "Achieving a high return is considered so important, so fundamental to their exist-ence, that challenging it would be greeted with incredulity."[28]

But it is in the relatively loose approach to coordinating activities and making decisions that the story gets interesting. We must be careful in generalizing here, because many parts of an investment bank—its transaction processing functions, its information technology group, its risk-management teams—are highly formalized and tightly regulated. It is the front office, the client-facing teams, where the principles of emergent behavior and collective wisdom are put into practice; where traders and investment bankers are encouraged to take responsibility, act quickly, and try out new ideas.

A closer look at the way decisions get made in investment banking reveals an interesting tension between control and freedom. On the one hand, banks rely on *formalization*, which involves using system-wide procedures and rules to evaluate and adjudicate on what risks are worth taking. On the other hand, they also value *personalization,* which involves pushing the responsibility for evaluating and making a judgment to those individuals on the front line, and requiring them to live with the consequences of those decisions.[29]

Most big banks have become advocates of formalization over the years, often with hundreds of employees working in their risk management activities. But the evidence of widespread poor risk management in 2007 and 2008 showed that even well-intentioned managers could no longer see the forest for the trees. As noted in Chapter 3, "the risk governance failings [of the banks] resulted from an over-reliance on low-level risk decisions in siloed businesses, product lines, and trading desks that ignored how these exposures contributed to a firm's overall risk profile."[30]

The banks that did best through the credit crisis were the ones that blended formalization with personalization. Goldman Sachs, as a former partnership, emphasizes a greater degree of personal accountability and ownership than in most other banks. As the *Financial Times* reported, "Employees [at Goldman] typically view themselves as being affiliated to the bank, not the business line, and there is a strong ethos of shared accountability."[31] JP Morgan Chase, another bank to have thrived through the credit crisis, also emphasizes personalization. CEO Jamie Dimon is known to have taken an active personal role in risk briefings.[32] And Dimon and his team saw early warning signals, back in 2006, of the credit risk on mortgages and the market risk on CDOs, and as a result, they reduced the bank's level of exposure to mortgage backed securities.

Investment banking is an example of the Quest Model because it encourages a high degree of informality in *how* work gets done. But as this discussion indicates, the mechanisms for doing so are not straightforward, and require a delicate balance between both personal accountability and formal systems. Like the checks and balances in the US Constitution, companies need the two to exist side by side to make smart risk management decisions.

Evaluating investment banking's Management Model. The enormous profits and spectacular losses made by the investment banking industry in recent years highlight the pros and cons of the Quest Model. On the positive side, this model helps to free up the entrepreneurial spirit of employees, it encourages innovation, and it helps a company adapt to changing market conditions. But on the negative side, it runs the risk of creating complexity and disorder. Employees are prone to push their autonomy too far, and to push into business areas that are out of the scope of the company's strategy, or too risky. Both Lehman Brothers and Enron Corporation adopted versions of the Quest Model, and in rather different ways, and it was the informal, entrepreneurial culture created in both companies that got them into trouble.

Under what conditions is the Quest Model most useful? It is most relevant for established companies in well-defined and mature markets that are seeking to do something a little bit different. Perhaps the industry is being threatened with change; perhaps the company is seeking to grow its market share or profitability in an aggressive way. In such cases, the objectives of the company are usually self-apparent, but the means by which those objectives might be reached are not.

Applying the Quest Model in your company. In contrast to the Discovery and Planning Models, it is hard to find companies that conform closely to the Quest Model (Figure 6.2, which plots the positions of companies that responded to my questionnaire, confirms this). But, paradoxically, the Quest Model is the one that many companies currently using the Planning Model aspire to. The idea that we know where we want to go to, and we are open to ideas about how we get there, is enormously attractive.

This model is not easy to deliver on, in large part because it's really hard to take people out of the routines of behavior that have become ingrained over the years. Nonetheless, there are some interesting examples of companies that have, in part, adopted the Quest Model. We discussed BP's use of a peer-review process as a key element of its transformation in the 1990s. Another element was the concept of a performance contract between each business unit head and the top executive team. As explained by former deputy CEO Rodney Chase, "We [the executive team] negotiate a performance contract within the scope of the strategy and then get out of the way. The business unit heads are free to deliver that however they wish, with no interference from anyone outside their enterprise."[33] This combination of clear objectives and autonomy in delivery is exactly what the Quest Model is about.

Another example is UBS's Private Bank (nowadays called "Wealth Management"), which in 2000 was looking for ways of accelerating its organic growth, and decided to eliminate its formal budgeting system because it was getting in the way. The CFO at the time, Toni Stadelmann, explained: "Why do we do the budgeting process when we are looking for growth? Budgeting is highly defensive. It is not just cumbersome, it is fundamentally *against* growth. It is about negotiating down the targets that are proposed by the centre. And it causes people to talk about numbers not about clients and market opportunities." Instead of a traditional budgeting system, UBS Wealth Management built a new system based on giving client advisors around the world freedom to invest as much or as little in their business as they saw fit. Then, rather than comparing the performance of client advisors with a budget number, Stadelmann and his team evaluated them against themselves (their previous year's results) and against their peers. Performance league tables were created, and then fed into the annual bonus process. This change was part of a broader shift in the culture of UBS Wealth Management, toward greater levels of personal accountability and entrepreneurial leadership across the bank, and it helped to generate several years of impressive growth.[34]

This same model can be applied at any level of analysis. Recall the discussion in Chapter 6 about personal drivers of motivation. As a manager, your ability to get the most out of your team often comes down to the personal space you provide them in meeting their goals. By giving employees or teams miniature "quests" you make work more satisfying, and you will often be surprised by the quality of the results people deliver.

The Science Model: Arup

"The Anti-Gravity Men" is the title of an extensive profile of Arup star Cecil Balmond, largely in reference to the seemingly gravity-defying nature of some of the international engineering consultancy's designs.[35] But it is equally apt in defining the company itself (though "and women" would need to be appended), whose ways of thinking and doing have been released from the weight of convention and status quo. For starters, the company is owned by a trust on behalf of its staff, so it is not in thrall to the short-term demands of shareholders. Second, employees are encouraged to think beyond the constraints of their individual disciplines and cultures, and collaborate with thousands of their diverse colleagues around the world. Third, and equally uplifting, is the company's dedication to reinventing the built environment, designing the tools and techniques necessary to do so when the firm is breaking new ground—as it usually is. Arup states its approach quite simply: "We shape a better world."

The visionary behind this unusual enterprise was an Anglo-Danish engineer Ove Arup who was, self-avowedly, inclined to gaze at stars. And a little peculiar. He was reported as carrying chopsticks in his pocket to help himself to food from others' plates[36]—perhaps a reflection of his belief in sharing (information, knowledge, expertise, profits) and challenging employees to do things differently. In 1946, at the age of 51, Ove set up his consulting engineering business in London, which expanded rapidly because of its ability to come up with advanced and economical solutions to buildings. It first gained world recognition with its design for the Sydney Opera House, which was a triumph in the use of precast concrete and structural design.

More recently, its Bird's Nest and Water Cube for the Beijing Olympics gained the attention of more than 4 billion people around the world. Perhaps only the Word Trade Center has gotten more attention—and there's a link: Arup was the design firm called in to investigate its collapse. In addition to major buildings and infrastructures (including the Channel Tunnel Rail Link and the Second Avenue subway line in New York), Arup has expanded horizontally, working on everything from the superlight energy-efficient car to solutions for MRSA superbugs to an eco-village near Shanghai to offshore engineering, acoustics, and security management tools.[37]

When Ove reached retirement age, the company board awarded him the permanent age of 64 so he could continue working.[38] He died at 92, and, like Ray Kroc, he left behind a set of principles, delivered in his now-legendary 1970 Key Speech,[39] that still inform the company today. These include sustainability, humanitarianism, quality, and the notion that work should be interesting and rewarding. He also felt strongly that the organization should be "human and friendly," and that it "act honorably in [its] dealings with its own and other people." One word that reverberates throughout the Key Speech is "holistic," a notion that applies not only to Arup's designs and the firm's adherence to the concept of "Total Architecture," but also to their thinking and working—the end being sustainable solutions.

Ove's inspiring philosophy coupled with the brilliance of the firm's employees and its distinctive Management Model have enabled the company to become a world leader in engineering, design, and planning, with total profits in 2007–2008 of £81.4 million.[40]

A reinforced structure. On any given day Arup designers are working on thousands of major projects out of their 90 offices in more than 30 countries in Europe, South East Asia, Africa,

Australasia, and North America. Thanks to an elaborate intranet, people can readily collaborate on the same project with colleagues on the other side of the planet.

Highly skilled teams of anywhere from half a dozen to 100 people come together on a project basis, with team leaders shifting according to particular expertise and need. "That's something that amazed me when I was younger in Arup's, how one week I'd be working for somebody and the next week he'd be working for me," former chairman Terry Hill commented in an interview.[41] Local leaders have a great deal of freedom in determining ways of working, and this makes for an adaptable and innovative environment responsive to the particular market needs.[42] Assisting the 10 000 employees in their varied endeavors is a network of "knowledge activists" who serve as resources, mentors, and facilitators.

But while the structure of teams is flexible and dynamic, the work gets done according to very clear rules and procedures. Remember, many of Arup's professional employees are qualified engineers, and they are used to working with formal procedures at all stages of a project. There are external professional bodies and regulatory agencies overseeing all engineering projects, whether public or private sector. And within Arup there are numerous tools and technologies to bring people together, support project practices, enable strategic knowledge management throughout the company, and foster collaboration and communication globally.[43]

In his Key Speech Ove spoke about the need for "some sort of hierarchy which should, as far as possible, be based on function," adding that "there will always be a need for a strong coordinating body."[44] But it doesn't get in the way. Hill noted in another interview that he was "initially struck by … the ability of people to get on with the job without worrying about hierarchy."[45] Structures for decision-making at Arup cross regions and disciplines. Policy is set by the group board, whose chair and members rotate. The board reports to the company's trustees, and to the company itself, represented by the global college of directors and principals. The five regions are each responsible for geographic strategy and management. Four markets (Property, Social Infrastructure, Transport and Energy, Resources and Industry) develop appropriate strategies for the client sector. Arup operates 18 businesses, with regional and global leaders working together to develop them.[46]

So you can see that Arup uses relatively tight means for coordinating work. Many of the formal procedures it uses are externally driven, from building codes to procurement policies. But there is also something in the engineer's mindset that encourages Arup employees to conform to accepted norms of conduct even in the absence of a deep hierarchical structure.

Sustainable ends. Ove's Key Speech makes it very clear how people in the company think about objectives. Here are his thoughts about why people go to work:

> There are two ways of looking at the work you do to earn a living. One is [that] work is a necessary evil. Your life is your leisure lived in your "free" time. The other is: To make your work interesting and rewarding. You enjoy both your work and your leisure. We opt uncompromisingly for the second way.

And here are his views on motivation and happiness:

> There are also two ways of looking at the pursuit of happiness: One is to go straight for the things you fancy, without considering anybody else beside yourself. The other is: to recognize that no man is an island, that our lives are inextricably mixed up with those of our fellow human beings. Which leads to an attitude which would accord to others the rights claimed for oneself. We, again, opt for the second way.

Ove's words are uncannily close to the principles of obliquity and intrinsic motivation as described in this book. Employees, in his view, enjoy their work and pursue projects because they are interesting and important, not because of their potential for making money. Arup's five-year plan set out in 2005 is a good reflection of this philosophy. In preparing it, the company looked carefully at drivers of change and accordingly identified areas where it should concentrate—the effects of climate change and urbanization, universal access to clean water, renewable sources of energy. It further defined its aims as being to use its influence with clients to shape a better world, to be sustainable in its own operations and projects, and to be a leading player in its chosen fields.[47]

In addition to providing intrinsically interesting work, Arup also provides other ways to charge up and recharge its people. The company firmly believes in developing its employees. Much happens on the job, as employees work alongside and learn from experts in many fields. On top of that, the company has all kinds of networks, personnel, and programs for training and career development. The Arup Cause, for example, provides structured opportunities for its people to develop personally, make use of their professional skills, and contribute to development globally. Arup employees who have proven themselves in terms of talent and effort have the opportunity—and encouragement—to work on humanitarian projects, whether through a three-month sabbatical, a one-year leave of absence, or emergency deployment to a disaster area.[48]

And it works. Arup's 2008 employee survey revealed job satisfaction levels at 85%.[49] Employees feel highly engaged and secure in their jobs, they are able to use and build on their skills, and they feel the firm cares about employee wellbeing, has an open and friendly culture with low bureaucracy, and encourages innovation, sharing of ideas, and learning from one's mistakes.[50]

Evaluating Arup's model. Arup is a highly successful company. Its employees have high levels of satisfaction, often working very long hours because they enjoy the work, and clients value their innovative designs and solutions. The company's "loose" objectives make Arup an interesting and inspiring place to work. Client-facing employees are encouraged to take the initiative in developing new services and pursuing new markets. But there is also a great deal of debate inside the company about its Management Model. Most of Arup's competitors are publicly traded companies, and over the last decade several of them, notably AECOM, have grown much faster. Arup very rarely makes acquisitions—there would be concerns about cultural fit, and there would be concerns about borrowing large amounts of money. Some observers have also suggested that the company's oblique goals and its emphasis on intrinsic motivation mean that it lacks the decisiveness and discipline of some publicly traded competitors.

In recent years, the company has made some incremental changes in its Management Model. Greater financial discipline has been imposed, and greater focus has been placed on prioritizing projects that yield an acceptable profit margin, but all within a structure that is consistent with the values and the management philosophy laid down by Ove Arup 40 years ago.

Applying the Science Model in your company. The data from Figure 6.1 shows that many companies use a version of the Science Model—a relatively tight set of systems and procedures, but a relatively loose set of goals and objectives. It is commonly seen in a number of professional service contexts—engineers like Arup, and also certain law firms, accountancy practices, and management consultancies. It is also seen in many knowledge-based industries. For example, the R&D laboratories in many large companies operate with the creative goals we described in Chapter 5. Creative groups in advertising agencies, design studios, and media organizations also use a variant of this model.

The crux of the Science Model is, again, the tension between freedom and control. But in contrast to the Quest Model where people are encouraged to seek new ways of delivering on narrow objectives, the Science Model is all about using the existing tools and methods of the profession to colonize new territory. Walt Disney's mantra was "I don't make movies to make money—I make money to make movies." So Disney creative teams are given incredible freedom to come up with new concepts for movies, but at the same time they operate within a clearly-defined structure to ensure that movies still get made on budget and on time.

While the Science Model can certainly be applied at a company-wide level, it can also be thought of as a way of structuring a specific project or activity. It works best when individuals have clearly defined roles and skills, and you are trying to combine their talents, or their ideas, to create something entirely original. For obvious reasons, management writer Eddie Obeng refers to this type of project as "Making a Movie."

Some Final Points

The four basic Management Models described in this chapter help to show how the various pieces of the management puzzle fit together. But they are also perhaps *too* simple, in that all the different elements of management are collapsed down into just two dimensions. So, using this framework to diagnose your Management Model is a bit like using a personality test to understand your inner self—it tells you how you compare to others on a couple of important dimensions, but it reveals nothing at all about what makes you unique. And of course uniqueness is what ultimately matters in the world of business, because you are seeking to differentiate your company, and its offerings, from those of your competitors.

So this chapter should not be viewed in isolation. If your big-picture Management Model is the focus of this chapter, then the four preceding chapters provided the detailed ideas for what you might do to fine-tune or adjust your Management Model in response to changing opportunities and threats in the business environment. We turn next to the question of *how* you make changes to your Management Model—the steps you can take as an individual to make conscious and explicit changes in how work gets done in your company.

Chapter 7: Key points

This chapter pulls together the ideas from the previous four chapters to create a single unifying framework. We make a conceptual distinction between means and ends: means refers to coordinating activities and making decisions; ends refers to setting objectives and motivating employees. By mapping means and ends on a two-dimensional matrix, we end up with four generic Management Models.

The Discovery Model has loose ends and loose means, and it is most commonly seen in start-up companies and in entrepreneurial environments. Google continues to exhibit most of the key characteristics of the Discovery Model.

The Planning Model has tight ends and tight means, and it is the default model in large, established companies that have a clear set of strategic objectives and a routinized set of processes for getting work done. There is nothing wrong with the Planning Model, as it can be highly efficient and profitable in a stable and predictable business environment. McDonald's is a good example of the Planning Model.

The Quest Model is one in which the company has very clear objectives, and motivates people primarily through extrinsic means, but gives its people enormous degrees of freedom in *how* they reach those objectives. It is a difficult model to manage well. We consider the investment banking industry as an interesting example of this model, because it includes both consistent high performers like Goldman Sachs as well as companies that got into deep trouble during the financial crisis, like Lehman Brothers.

The Science Model uses fairly tight and standardized procedures, but it encourages employees to seek out and address opportunities wherever they arise. We use the example of Arup, the engineering consultancy, to illustrate the Science Model. Arup is unusual because it was founded explicitly on the principles of obliquity and intrinsic rewards while at the same time, because it is staffed almost entirely by engineers, it operates according to formal rules and procedures.

8

THE CHANGE AGENT'S AGENDA

In the summer of 1987, Art Schneiderman faced a dilemma. As Quality Improvement Director at Analog Devices, he had been asked by CEO Ray Stata to develop a new annual planning process that focused on the non-financial drivers of quality improvement. Stata was interested in innovation and how the organization and its people worked. But alongside him, COO Jerry Fishman was more focused on financial performance and the bottom-line. Insiders referred to the Stata-Fishman partnership as "the two-headed monster." As Schneiderman noted, "Opposites work very well together." Except when you're in the middle. And it became very apparent to me early on that I was in the middle. I had to not only manage Ray, but Jerry as well."

The differing approaches of the company's two top executives were abundantly clear at the monthly business meetings, which were chaired by Schneiderman. He always put the non-financial performance measures first on the agenda, followed by the financial measures, and Fishman would switch them around.

Fishman challenged Schneiderman to find a way to make them both happy. A few days later, while at home in the evening, Schneiderman saw a television commercial that emphasized how Reese's Peanut Butter Cups were a combination of two different products: peanut butter and chocolate. As he recalled, "Suddenly the light bulb lit: combine the financial and non-financial metrics as a single agenda item. So I added a small number of key financials at the top of the scorecard, and the problem was solved to everyone's satisfaction."

Schneiderman's new reporting system became known as the Corporate Scorecard inside Analog Devices. A few years later,

Harvard Professor Robert Kaplan wrote about Schneiderman's endeavors in a 1993 Harvard Business Review article titled "The Balanced Scorecard"[1] (though Analog Devices was not actually named), leading to the popularization and widespread implementation of the concept. Today the Balanced Scorecard is one of the most widely-used management tools in existence.[2]

This story of the origin of the Balanced Scorecard is typical of how innovations in management practice happen—a combination of conducive circumstances, personal initiative, and serendipity. There is no standard formula for making management innovation happen, but there are certainly things you can do to increase the likelihood that you will succeed in making changes to your Management Model. And that is the focus of this second part of the book. If Chapters 3–7 were primarily about *what* Management Model innovation is all about, then the next two focus on *how* it can be implemented.

It goes without saying that change in an established organization is slow and difficult. It is hard enough to introduce new products and services that represent a departure from the way things have traditionally been done. It is even harder to introduce new management practices where their potential benefits are so subjective and unmeasurable. It takes an enormous amount of effort and personal conviction to move an organization out of the deep grooves of established practice and onto a new track.

Who are the *dramatis personae* in this play? We have the CEO, of course, who carries ultimate responsibility for the long-term success of the company. Ray Stata at Analog Devices was not the originator of the Balanced Scorecard, but he gave Schneiderman the space to experiment, and he endorsed the idea when it was put forward. The CEO's perspective is the focus of Chapter 9. But there are also hundreds of mid-level executives in any medium- to large-sized company who, like Schneiderman, have a point of view on the future direction of the company and useful insights into what should be changed to achieve success. This chapter is written for such individuals. I call them "Change

Agents" because of their vital role in making things happen.[3] There is also a third set of actors, the external consultants and experts like Robert Kaplan, who often play a useful supporting role in helping Change Agents like Art Schneiderman.

Change Agents are *entrepreneurial* by nature: they don't have the formal authority to act, but they see an opportunity and they choose to proceed anyway, perhaps by doing something within their sphere of immediate influence, perhaps by building a coalition of like-minded people, perhaps by pushing their boss to do something new. Recall the famous words of the American cultural anthropologist Margaret Mead: "Never doubt that a small group of thoughtful, committed citizens can change the world; indeed, it is the only thing that ever has." This is true in the domain of social change, through the efforts of such individuals as Aung San Suu Kyi, Mohammad Yunus, and Bono. It is also true in the domain of corporate change, where successful business ideas often emerge through the championing efforts of mid-level managers who succeed *despite* the formal system, not because of it. Well-known examples of products that have emerged through the efforts of bottom-up innovators include Sony's Playstation, HP's Laserjet Printer, Ericsson's mobile handset business, and Microsoft's Internet Explorer.

The purpose of this chapter, then, is to focus on your role as a Change Agent, in envisioning and promoting Management Model innovation inside your company. What changes in management practice would you like to see? Where should you start? Whom should you work with? You may not have the formal authority, budget, or breadth of perspective of a Chief Executive Officer, but you have a very practical understanding of what is preventing your company from realizing its potential, and you typically have more degrees of freedom in enacting change than you might realize. We take an in-depth look at two cases of individuals pursuing their own Management Model innovations in large, established companies: a divisional manager at Microsoft seeking to enhance the intrinsic motivation of his team by developing a less bureaucratic way of working; and a team of mid-level managers in UBS Investment Bank seeking to tap into the collective wisdom of the organization to develop new and better ways of working. We then consider the key lessons that can be drawn from their experiences.

Microsoft and the 42Projects Experiment

Ross Smith is not your typical corporate executive. He is happier with a snowboard or X-Box console in his hand than a computer mouse, and he does not own a business suit, but he has been with Microsoft for 18 years, and is now leading a fascinating experiment in innovative management techniques.[4]

Smith leads an 85-person test team in the company's Windows division. The team works to ensure the quality of Windows security-related features. It may not sound sexy, but it is high-pressure, high-status work within Microsoft. Marc McDonald, the very first Microsoft employee, is part of the team. Others have chosen to join the team after successful development manager jobs elsewhere. Expectations are high as hundreds of millions of people trust—and demand—that features work correctly and Windows is trustworthy.

After Windows Vista shipped in 2007, Smith took over the Windows Security Test Team effort. As part of his preparation, he met individually with everyone on the team—all 85 people. "As I was doing these meetings, I began to realize the depth of talent in this group. Over a third of the team had a master's degree or higher, which is very unusual. And from the annual employee survey, I knew people were feeling underutilized. The nature of our work is unusual—it is intense and painstaking, but it ebbs and flows, which means sometimes there's spare capacity in terms of brainpower, and even effort. So it got me thinking about what we could offer these people in terms of figuring out how to apply that talent."

The testing team members live online, love competition, devour technology in any form and, perhaps surprisingly, are avid readers. Smith observed: "Generation Y wants to work on cool, cutting-edge projects, and Generation Y wants to be recognized for its work by peers, family and friends." And if such projects aren't provided in the workplace, many will choose to find them in online communities and work on them—for free— in their spare time.

As Smith got to know his new team and started to understand what made them tick, he saw an opportunity to do things differently. "We wondered if we could bring that extra effort inside Microsoft's walls and share our human and corporate resources to encourage some of that innovation to happen right here. We wanted to create an environment where the team could have more freedom with the 'how' rather than be relentlessly preoccupied with the 'what.'"

Starting Points. In early 2007, Robert Musson, a developer on the team, stumbled on a paper by John Helliwell and Haifang Huang at the University of British Columbia that examined the relationship among trust, pay, and job satisfaction.[5] Musson reflected: "Trust in management is, by far, the biggest component to consider. Say you get a new boss and your trust in management goes up a bit at your job—say, up one point on a 10-point scale. That's like getting a 36 percent pay raise, Helliwell and Huang calculate."

The team began to think about how trust worked in the Microsoft environment. Trust is a large and abstract issue—but one that lies at the heart of working life and working relationships. To Smith, "It's like freedom and air. You know when you don't have it, but it's really hard to measure it and to know when you do have it."

The first step, therefore, was to brainstorm to identify the behaviors affecting trust that people saw in their day-to-day work. As this progressed, the team created some games and experiments with voting to try to prioritize the lengthening list and to learn more about what could be done to increase trust. At http://www.defectprevention.org/trust, you can view one of the games the Microsoft team used to develop its trust model. Users are asked, "Which trust factor is more important to you?" and then given a series of two-option responses such as "Don't skirt real issues" and "Don't bury your head in the sand." Users can select from as many pairs as they like, then view the compiled results from all who participated.

The result was a better-ordered list of trust factors. The trouble with this approach was that it was situational—the ordered list might apply to me, but it might not apply to you, or, it might apply to me on Tuesdays but not on Fridays. More research led to the creation of a playbook for people to reference and use. Things like "Be more transparent" or "Demonstrate integrity" were highlighted. The challenge was to link these notions to tangible activities. Members of the team then worked to write up a paragraph on each trust behavior. This information was then opened up as a wiki to generate community participation and build understanding. Around 40 percent of the Windows Security Test Team actively contributed to this process.

Pizza With Everything. To keep the dialogue open, the team started a weekly "free pizza" meeting in the autumn of 2007. It proved to be a powerful forum. As Smith explained, "These meetings started with trust and have evolved along with the program. They can range from people presenting their ideas to brainstorming, but really, the main goal is to keep the program alive and build relationships around the team. The structure is really flat—everybody's ideas get equal billing, and everybody's comments are valid. It gives people a forum to share their ideas and to share the projects they're working on."

One conversation led to another. Some Web-based tools for sharing information about project status, submitting calls for help, and promoting new ideas were introduced. As Smith explained: "The hope is that people will vote with their feet for good ideas. There's no community rating system or voting for each idea. Ideas are like children—everyone loves their own. And we wanted the program to support that. If you see an idea you like, you can just talk to the person who's listed on the site. This gave people another platform for promoting their ideas."

Giving it a name. The spirit of learning, trust, and respect for new ways of working was coming alive in the Windows Security Test Team, but it needed a name. They settled on 42Projects. For the uninitiated, the number 42 is the answer to life, the universe, and everything in Douglas Adams' cult classic *The Hitchhiker's Guide to the Galaxy*. In the book, the Deep Thought computer takes more than 7 million years to figure this out—"'I checked it thoroughly,' says the computer, 'and that quite definitely is the answer. I think the problem, to be quite honest with you, is that you've never actually known what the question is.'"

The number 42 helped to capture the quirkiness of the team's approach and the broad objectives of the program itself. It also tapped into the Generation Y spirit. During 2007 and 2008, the program grew organically, and tentative steps led to a profound cultural shift within the team. As Jonathan Ng, a recent computer science graduate and software development engineer in Test observed, "The best thing about 42Projects is the fact that you can just jump right in and define your own role. Self-role definition in the context of a work career isn't really something that happened until recently."

What's more, it appealed to senior members as well. McDonald was Microsoft's first employee, a friend of Bill Gates in high school, and a key member of the Windows Security Test Team. As he noted, "42Projects tries to recapture the feeling and passion you have at a small startup or at the beginning of an industry by breaking down the stratification of a large organization." The team also has a dozen senior Microsoft employees on the team with more than 10 years at the firm. The program appeals to them as much as it does to their Generation Y colleagues.

Another important step forward was to capture raw feedback from new employees, via what became known as the 42New program. This initiative targeted employees with fewer than two years' experience and encouraged them to share their ideas in a separate forum. As Program Manager Lori Ada Kilty explained: "We hire really intelligent people and when they first start, they are left to figure things out on their own. Many feel we don't necessarily take the time to hear what they have to say because they don't have a lot of experience. So we started a group called 42New. It's a forum where there are no managers, and new hires can get their voices heard. They get together, get their ideas out and talk about things that are bothering them or things that they would like to see."

Playing games. The spirit of gaming is fundamental to Generation Y, as we saw in Chapter 6, and so Smith naturally utilized game playing as a means of learning. When a product needed to be pushed toward a certain behavior, the team built a productivity game around it. Recall how the test team organized "bug bashes" in which the participant who found the most bugs was given a prize. But Smith and his team have taken this a step further: "Using games is a powerful method to influence changes in organizational behavior, though it requires care in the design and use."

So the team looked for ways to build the principles of gaming into its work. For example, one team member had a desire to learn a new development technology and built a prototype of a customer feedback game. He was able to connect with another employee who was developing an idea to use native language speakers to help verify international versions of Windows (we described this game in Chapter 6). Explained Mark Hanson, test manager: "Our culture is competitive. People by nature love to compete and play games and want to see themselves at the top of the leader board."

Even before Smith took the helm, one of the sources of inspiration for the team was the written word. The team started a book group called 42Books, which encourages reading and discussion on various texts, and blew their book budget, mostly centered on books about innovation, leadership, and trust. The team had a visit from Mike Armour, author of *Trust-Centered Leadership*, and recently hosted a discussion with Adrian Gostick, one of the authors of *The Levity Effect*.

All of this is linked to an evolving process of change. Commented Smith: "We have had a few cases where someone has an interest in learning something and instead of going home and working on it, they have brought it inside. Whether it's a book, an idea, a project, a course—doing it here exposes them to more resources, people who've done that, used that technology before, as well as potential 'customers' for their end result."

Trust, too, is constantly evolving. As Hanson explained, "We're giving people the latitude to go off and do their own thing. We trust them to do their regular jobs and to experiment, innovate, and have fun. We're developing a level of trust where there's no required accountability that you need to log your time or provide an example of what you did during that day when you worked from home."

Spreading the Word. Success has not come easy for the team. Dramatic change doesn't normally bubble up from the bottom. But there is now solid evidence that the change program kicked off by Smith in early 2007 is paying dividends. Employee retention rates within the team are higher than they have ever been—an important factor in a specialist activity such as testing. The level of engagement within the team is extremely high. As Mike Tholfsen, a test manager in the Office Division, says: "Finding 42Projects was like walking into a haven of all the things I hold dear—building trust, experimenting with new ideas in management and group dynamics, trying out new innovation concepts, and a little bit of rule breaking."[6] And most important of all, productivity and quality indicators indicate that Smith's team is one of the highest performing across the Microsoft group.

What's next for Smith's cultural revolution? How can the engagement he has created in his division be leveraged and scaled across other parts of Microsoft? In September 2008, Smith was given the chance to post his views on the Microsoft internal blog site, which is open to Microsoft's 60 000 employees around the world. His post focused on the spirit of 42Projects: "It was basically, think back to the day you started at Microsoft and the energy you had, the feeling that you were there to change the world. I asked, 'Do you still feel that way today?' And then I touched on some of the themes of 42Projects, like trust and empowerment, things can start with anybody." The blog got a lot of responses from people across Microsoft. More recently, in 2009, Smith was asked to head up Test in the Office Communicator and Design group, and he is already "working his magic" with a new team of 85 people.[7]

Ross Smith may not be a typical corporate executive, but the challenge he faced on taking charge of his 85-person team was no different to the one faced by many mid-level managers: how to get the most out of his people so that they would be engaged and productive in the workplace, and how to do his bit to improve the organization. And while his approach was highly individualistic, the key point is that he did it without getting anyone else involved. He set the ball rolling, and then just kept it going.

Christian Doll and the Service Sourcing Project

For a rather different story of change from within, consider the case of Christian Doll, a mid-ranking manager in Siemens IT Solutions and Services (SIS). In 2007, he was assigned to a large bid where the client was asking Siemens to provide on-site services (for handling technical problems) in 100 countries. And as he recalled, "we did not have these technicians in our organisation." While the bid team eventually made this project a success, Doll felt it was a complex and high-risk game they were playing.

"I wanted to do something about this, to avoid the situation occurring again."

How might Siemens have done things differently? "Developing a proposal for new business can be complex. It's vital to engage with potential third party service partners as early as possible, and to get input from internal providers such as procurement, key customer account teams, legal support, and risk management. Our business wasn't set up to do this efficiently. The bid development process was thus far more complicated than it should have been. This was the challenge that I wanted to address."

Consider, for a moment, the magnitude of this challenge: Doll wanted to get eight internal divisions of Siemens to collectively rethink the way they would work with external providers. There may be tougher management challenges out there, but this is just about as tricky as it gets. And of course this was not Doll's official responsibility, it was simply something he felt was sufficiently important that it needed to be done anyway. "It was not my job to think about processes across the organisation; it was my job to design services for customer needs," he recalls.

Building a Team. Doll began canvassing his colleagues, beginning with his boss. He approached some 20 people in different roles below Board level. All of them agreed that the sourcing and management of third party service providers needed to become more professional, and they offered help. "This buy-in ensured that both the project team and steering/advisory boards were defined. Managers allocated employees to the project team and volunteered to be members of the boards."

While sanctioned at corporate level, the project team members also had to continue with their day jobs. Much of the work was undertaken "out of hours" because local legislation prohibited employees working more than 40 hours a week. "It had to be designed in such a way that everyone really liked what they were being tasked to do. Without this enthusiasm, why would they give up their spare time?" At around the same time, a new team was set up to manage the operational or "delivery" aspects of working with external partners. The focus of Doll's project was thus sharpened: to propose a new model for the sourcing of services from the external market. The team agreed to come up with a vision and strategy, with a specific focus on field services.

Prototyping the future. Using ideas from his MBA, Doll used a standard process with six key steps: Knowledge exchange using mood boards and storytelling; Ideas generation; Modelling and discussion; Prototyping; Feedback (road shows); and Finalisation of the prototype.

But he also decided to push some slightly unusual ideas, especially in the area of visualizing and prototyping new ideas. "I decided to use Lego™ building blocks to help model the service processes in 3D. Often it is hard to express something abstract or complex in words, so I asked the team members to build a model, a prototype, out of Lego. While it's not a new idea, it was certainly something that provoked a reaction in the team members. "The first time the Lego bricks came on the table, people were really confused—we are playing with Lego, is that leading to anything? So I came up with a very small Lego model, where I showed how the top-level process might look; and with that they understood and it became an important part of our work.

"Everybody was buying in except one person. He couldn't get beyond the idea of Lego as a children's toy, preferring instead to illustrate our business concepts in PowerPoint. His was the only real dissenting voice. I had a tough discussion with him, in front of the others, and at the end the others felt trust in my approach and they wanted to try it out. The guy who was not happy to work with Lego never again showed up in the project."

Doll has no doubt about the value of using prototypes. "Working with prototypes in a trial and error-mode and involving stakeholders along the whole project lifecycle can help to reduce uncertainty. As a result the risk of failure can be significantly reduced. Nowadays there are several tools available to generate prototypes. Lego is just one of them."

Selling the concept. While the value of using the Lego prototypes was clear to the team, they didn't know how it would look to the steering and advisory boards. As Doll recalls, "Everybody was worried: how would management react if they see a big Lego town on the meeting table? Doll sensibly got some early buy-in: he showed the Lego town to one senior member of the steering board. "At first this executive was shocked, but I took him through the logic and he liked the idea. He gave me the backing I needed to sell it to the others". In fact, during one board meeting, the Lego prototype helped to push things forward: "I remember one board meeting where they were first confused, but then the most senior guy on the board said, thank you for using Lego, now I understand better what your ideas are about, but I am encouraging you to be more crazy; it's too soft, too conventional at the moment." So in further workshops the team developed the service concepts still further: for example, a Global On-Site Services (GOSS) structure was put forward for managing service contracts with service providers in the delivery phase.

But the Lego prototype also proved to be something of a distraction when Doll presented the final project findings to the steering board. He was given an hour to convey the project findings. He worked up a PowerPoint presentation and, to help clarify things, he brought the prototype with him to the meeting. "I wanted to explain the main ideas using the sophisticated Lego prototype, but there was one person on the Board who I was not able to brief up front. She raised an issue that was not part of my presentation and that killed the whole presentation. I spoke to one of them afterwards, asking where I had gone wrong, and he said, the prototype is good for fostering discussions, but that is not what you want in a Board presentation. That was a lesson."

What were the outcomes? Despite the problems at the final Board meeting, many of the ideas were implemented. The details are confidential, but they included novel ways of pre-selecting service providers and defining a "best and final offer" to the customer, as well as clarity around who should start an engagement. Some of the more ambitious ideas did not work out – for example one idea to use open-source principles for delivering field services was deemed too radical.

Responsibility for implementing these ideas was handed over to the manager responsible for service delivery to external providers. Some members of the project team joined that group, which by 2011 numbered 50 people. Doll himself moved out of Siemens IT Solutions and Services in 2010 and joined Siemens Corporate Technologies, an internal consulting group helping the company to be more innovative.

Five Lessons for Change Agents

I chose these two examples in large part *because* they are partial successes. Ross Smith has had enormous impact on the productivity and engagement of his team, but he has had limited impact on the rest of Microsoft. Christian Doll was ultimately successful in getting his new service model accepted, but not without problems along the way. Over the course of this book we have talked about a number of other bottom-up initiatives, including Roche Diagnostics' experiment in using internal and external experts for problem-solving, and Srinivas Koushik's novel use of Web 2.0 technology for communication at Nationwide, all of which are best classified as works-in-progress.

But this shouldn't be seen as a cause for pessimism. For starters, the teams in both Microsoft and Siemens were more engaged working on these initiatives than when simply doing their jobs, which is good for them and good for their employers. And second, their efforts have the potential to make a real difference—to productivity improvement and enhanced trust in Microsoft, to service model innovation in Siemens, and indeed as inspiration to others reading this book.

What then are the key issues for Change Agents to think about as they start experimenting with new management ideas? Here are five important themes that should be borne in mind.

Figure out your own degrees of freedom—and use them to the fullest. While you may not have a multi-million dollar budget, you probably have more room to maneuver than you realize. Ross Smith had his own team of 85 people, and took it upon himself to redefine how they thought and behaved, while still delivering on all the performance targets handed to him from above. Christian Doll and his team were more constrained because they were doing this work over-and-above their "day jobs," but some had budgets to put costs against, while others were able to influence their colleagues in the various operating businesses of Siemens. Both of these teams chose to act innovatively *within* the rules. But the history of corporate innovation also includes many examples of individuals who overstepped the official boundaries, some of whom got away with it (and sought forgiveness, rather than permission), while others did not and got into trouble. Our discussion of Enron's highly entrepreneurial internal market system in Chapter 6 illustrates the point: individuals were encouraged to break the rules, and the entire organization and its shareholders paid the price. The challenge is best encapsulated in the so-called Serenity Prayer: Grant me the serenity to accept the things I cannot change, the courage to change the things I can, and the wisdom to know the difference. The best Change Agent is a wise one.

Build a team of allies inside and outside the company. The Siemens team was a group of volunteers from across the company, all of whom took part with the permission of their respective bosses. In addition, they had support from some senior executives, as well as occasional outside help to ensure that they were going about their activities in the most thoughtful way. Ross Smith took a different approach: he got very little support from the rest of Microsoft, but he invested a great deal of energy in reaching out to like-minded people in other companies, and to academics and thought-leaders writing about issues of trust, engagement, and innovation in large companies.

Allies and mentors provide Change Agents with a vital resource called legitimacy. A legitimate innovation project is one that conforms to people's expectations about what is good and proper. Legitimacy gets conferred in part by the nature of the project itself, but also in part by the words used to describe it and by the people supporting it. So smart Change Agents spend a lot of time thinking about getting the right levels of mentorship from the right quarters.

But there is an interesting wrinkle here. By bringing in external experts and making the innovation legitimate and widely known outside the company, there is a risk that its internal legitimacy will be lost. For example, management writer Art Kleiner recounts the story of Kraft's experiments in improving the quality of working life in its Topeka, Kansas, factory in the 1970s. By any objective measures those experiments were a success, but paradoxically they had a bigger impact in the world of management thinking than in the actual management methods used by Kraft in the ensuing years. And the two key individuals behind the program ended up leaving the company, frustrated that their innovations had not made more impact. This is not to suggest that external success always comes at the expense of internal success—Schneiderman's corporate scorecard had a positive outcome on both dimensions—but there is certainly an ongoing tension in managing both internal and external allies.

Take an experimental approach. The big battle facing anyone seeking to change his or her company's Management Model is that you never really know if the change was a success. There are so many interacting parts in a management system that you can not disentangle cause and effect in a definitive way, nor can you anticipate the potential knock-on effects when you make significant changes to, say, the compensation and bonus system in a bank. And as a result, the default approach in most large companies is to leave things as they are.

Experimentation represents a sensible way of overcoming such intrinsic resistance. This doesn't mean experimentation in the manner of a fully-controlled laboratory experiment. Rather, it means trying out an idea in a low-risk, self-contained setting where the outcomes can be carefully monitored. In Chapter 4 you saw Roche Diagnostics' carefully controlled study of the problem-solving capacity of internal and external experts. Christian Doll's service sourcing project at Siemens represents an alternative model, using the logic of prototyping to flesh out an idea and then refine it gradually over several iterations. Ross Smith's 42projects is also a form of experiment, in that he is doing it entirely within the scope of his 85-person team, rather than rethinking Microsoft's entire Management Model. As he said, "One of our guiding premises is that we're learning, we're experimenting, we're humble, we're open to feedback—and this is all opt in. We didn't send a big memo out that says, 'OK, everybody, start trusting each other.' So it's been very important to retain that theme throughout."

Alas, the language of experimentation is not popular in large corporate settings (except in R&D labs). Executives prefer to talk about prototypes or pilots, on the basis that they think they know where they are heading, while still leaving open the possible need for mid-course adjustments. However, this thinking is starting to change. There is evidence of companies taking a more experimental approach to product and service innovation. I would like to see this same approach applied to management innovation. We discuss these themes further in the next chapter.

Give it a name. You may not be entirely aware, but there are word games going on in companies all the time. Try telling your colleagues you want to do a re-engineering project, and see what sort of reaction you get. Re-engineering was the hot label for making dramatic improvements in business processes in the 1980s, but by the mid-1990s it was entirely passé, overtaken by such concepts as Six Sigma and Knowledge Management. So while many companies still make improvements in their business processes, they find another way of talking about it, to avoid appearing out-of-touch.

So it is useful to give your activity or project a name, in order that people have something to hold onto, but it has to be a carefully chosen name. Ross Smith's 42projects is a bit quirky, but it works for his target audience of computer geeks and Generation Y employees. Christian Doll opted for a more conventional name—the Service Sourcing Project—that was a better fit with Siemens more conventional culture. Along the lines we discussed earlier, the name you choose is partially about building legitimacy within your target audience. For example, we discuss Procter & Gamble's open innovation program called Connect + Develop in detail in the next chapter. This name was chosen in part to help the Research & Development employees in the company realize that they weren't being outsourced: Connect and Develop was designed to turbo-charge the existing R&D capability, not replace it.

Seek out support from above as it takes shape. The biggest challenge in pushing a bottom-up initiative is knowing when and how to "hand it over" to the folks at the top. Sometimes you don't want to hand over your baby. Other times, you would like to hand it over but the key executives have their hands full with other initiatives.

For Christian Doll, the handover time was straightforward— it was at the end of the project. For Ross Smith, the handover has yet to happen: he continues to push his initiative, with a great deal of support from below and from outside the company, but without any impetus from above. As he said, "The feeling is that that this will snowball. People take a step to improve one thing, and they see that one improvement makes a difference or saves them time, and they follow up with a bit more, and it just continues to grow. It is a grassroots, organic movement."

Robin Mouer, a retired Microsoft director who's acting as a consultant to the team, provided the context: "It's important to remember that rather than this being a conventional approach to change inside an organization, this is from Ross, his peer group and entire team taking the initiative. It is not the consequence of the CEO or executive leadership team issuing a mandate or direction. Can it scale beyond 85? Can it be cloned? Can other groups be given some guidance and some of our key learning? We believe that it could be. It's very organic. It has common denominators in it that people are looking for almost regardless of their level in the company, their time at the company, or the kind of work that they're doing. People do want to know that trust exists. They do want to know that they can achieve great things and that they're going to be supported in doing so."

A team of Change Agents can go a long way toward changing a company's Management Model, but they cannot do it alone. Ultimately, the process needs CEO and executive team support if it is going to make a long-lasting difference to the fortunes of the company. In the next chapter we address the CEO agenda.

Chapter 8: Key Points

This chapter and the next focus on how companies develop the new ideas and practices that form part of their distinctive Management Model. My research suggests that Management Model innovation is typically driven by the efforts of three sets of actors: mid-level change agents, top-level executives, and external partners such as consultants and academics. This chapter describes the agenda of the mid-level change agent who seeks to do something innovative without formal permission. Using examples from Microsoft, Siemens and Analog Devices, five lessons are put forward.

1. Figure out your degrees of freedom and use them. Most managers have far more space to try new things than they realize. As the old saw says, it's often easier to ask forgiveness than permission.

2. Build a team of allies inside and outside the company. One approach is to build a group of colleagues inside the company who can collectively get things done. Another approach is to tap into external sources of insight to help build legitimacy for what you are doing.

3. Take an experimental approach. Experimentation is a good way of overcoming internal resistance, because it gives your colleagues and your boss the right to say no.

4. Give it a name. Your project needs a name that your colleagues can hold onto, to help them understand why they are taking part in it. A great name makes people curious to know more and will help it to rise above the noise.

5. Seek out support from above when it takes shape. The biggest challenge you face is to sell your project to those above you in the organization. As always, the best advice is to build on small successes and to use your allies inside and outside the company to create some momentum behind the project, so that your boss has no choice but to endorse it.

9

THE LEADER'S AGENDA

In 2000 Procter & Gamble (P&G) was at a crucial point in its long history. Its CEO Dirk Jager had left after a mere 18 months in the job. In March, the company announced it would not meet its projected first quarter earnings. The stock price was spiraling downward—falling from $116 in January to $60 per share by March. *Ad Age* headlined its front-page story: "Does P&G still matter?"

P&G's new CEO, A.G. Lafley, provided an instant dose of reality: "We weren't delivering on goals and commitments to analysts and investors. P&G brands were not delivering good consumer value: we weren't consistently leading innovation, and prices were too high. Our costs were also too high. We had frayed relations with important customers. We were too internally-focused." Lafley's prescription for the ailing corporate patient was wide-reaching. He focused the company on four core businesses, the big, leading brands, and the top ten countries. Nearly 10 000 jobs were lost around the world as underperforming activities were closed.

And, perhaps most boldly of all, Lafley announced an entirely new approach to innovation. In the future, instead of relying on its internal research and development, P&G expected that 50% of its innovation would come from outside the company. The logic was simple. For every one of the company's researchers, P&G calculated there were 200 people—scientists and engineers—outside the company who had talents the company could utilize. Instead of 7500 people in corporate R&D, P&G recalculated that there were 1.5 million worldwide whose knowledge they needed to tap into. R&D was reincarnated as

Connect + Develop, and a set of new initiatives was put in place to help the company tap into the enormous knowledge base beyond its boundaries. For example:

- P&G's leading 15 suppliers have around 50 000 people employed in R&D. P&G built an IT platform to share technology briefs with suppliers.

- P&G created a network of "technology entrepreneurs"—70 senior technologists who act as the eyes and ears of Connect + Develop, making contacts within industry, with suppliers, and with local markets. By 2008, the technology entrepreneurs had brought over 10 000 products, ideas, and technologies to the attention of P&G.

- P&G taps into a number of open networks. It is involved with NineSigma, which connects companies with researchers worldwide, with InnoCentive, which deals with more specific technical problems, and with Yet2.com, an online intellectual property marketplace.

The Connect + Develop story is now well known in terms of *what* it set out to accomplish, as well as how successful it has been, with the number of new products coming from outside the company rising from 15% in 2000 to 35% eight years later. But less well known is *how* P&G created its Connect + Develop model. Unsurprisingly, it did not emerge fully formed, like Venus from the sea. Rather, it took many years of hard work from a team of P&Gers led by Larry Huston, Vice President for Innovation and Knowledge.

How Connect + Develop came about. The idea that became Connect + Develop started percolating back in the mid-1990s. Huston described the process this way: "It's just like the way people develop lots of prototypes when they develop products, or how artist[s] will develop sketches before they commit to putting the paint down and creating the final painting." He cites how American Regionalist painter and muralist Thomas

Hart Benton worked as an example of this process. "He would create clay models and then more models of what he was eventually going to paint, and then he would start working on the perspectives with all kinds of sketches. He would work on the concept for a long, long time before he ever actually created a successful painting. And, in the case of this new innovation model, I worked, probably, five or six, seven years on creating the studies that led to it coming together, ultimately, in the year 2000."

Huston was initially interested in how to develop a new organizational model combining chaos and order. As he explained: "I wanted to create an organization where people would be fluid and move around and could swarm to the good projects, yet protect the base business and have rules in place where you just can't go and leave." So he talked extensively with thought leaders such as complexity theorist Stuart Kauffman and Dee Hock, the founder of the VISA group. He also explored a number of different strategies, including working with a web-based company in which people were rewarded for participation. Then came the major breakthrough: by studying initiatives that had been undertaken outside P&G, they realized that these had created about twice as much value as internal initiatives. Huston extrapolated from this revelation potential new ways for driving P&G's business and its productivity.

Following A.G. Lafley's appointment as CEO, Gilbert Cloyd, P&G's chief technology officer, approached Huston with a challenge: could he create a new R&D model for the company? This was in essence an opportunity to develop an entirely new operating method. Huston had spent six years doing the groundwork. Then he created the conceptual positioning for Connect + Develop, around turbocharging. The imprimatur for the endeavor came when Lafley announced, very publicly, that the company would henceforth get half of its innovation from outside. Commented Huston: "That was a major intervention, and so we were off and running."

Reactions were decidedly mixed. According to Huston, "Some people's first reaction was, 'Wow, P&G is getting rid of its R&D. This is an R&D or science-driven company, what are they doing, have they lost their minds?' They didn't realize that what we were doing was substantially strengthening our R&D capability."

The positioning of Connect + Develop was important. First, it was made clear that it was not a matter of outsourcing P&G's research and development capability; rather it was about finding good ideas and bringing them in to enhance and capitalize on internal capabilities. The second point was that Connect + Develop was not a "transformation" program. Noted Huston: "I think transformation is a dirty word. In the case of Connect + Develop we were careful not to position it as trans-formation—even though now it is. We said, we have a strong, powerful, global organization, we've built the capability all over the world, we have world-class people, what we're going to do is take this already strong capability and turbo charge it. And so the core idea is based upon how do we turbo charge."

Procter & Gamble's experience in launching Connect + Develop offers useful insight into the process of management innovation. For starters, Lafley's public commitment to changing the company's innovation model was critical, because it gave Huston and his team the authority to try out their experimental ideas. Unlike the teams from Microsoft and Siemens we talked about in the previous chapter, Huston was operating with the full backing of the company's chief executive. Huston readily acknowledged the importance of that: "This is all about leader-ship, number one, being clear about where to play, how you're going to win and where you want to grow. That's the job of the CEO and the top management to really figure this thing out."

The second point is that Connect + Develop didn't just happen: it was based on many years of capability building by Huston and his team. Huston points out the parallels between the development of new products and the development of new

Management Models: "The one thing that is really important is to get the concept right. P&G is a concept-driven company. The concept is how the product's going to make your life better. So we practice concept development here every day, because we have to move hearts and minds." For one of the precursors to Connect + Develop, Huston created a storyboard for the concept and then took it to 21 different targeted companies. They commented on and critiqued the idea before he ran financial models to see if the concept was capable of making money. And only at that point did P&G put any money into the project.

Four Steps to Innovating Your Management Model

Here is a summary of the key steps that led to the introduction of Connect + Develop. From a top-down perspective, there were essentially four steps:

1. **Understanding:** P&G realized it needed to dramatically enhance its innovation pipeline to achieve higher levels of organic growth.
2. **Evaluating:** A key blocker of innovation was found to be the internally focused and siloed R&D organization.
3. **Envisioning:** The company looked into alternative collective-wisdom-based innovation models, involving networks and communities of external people.
4. **Experimenting:** With Lafley's approval, Huston and his team tried out different elements that eventually became Connect + Develop.

This is a fairly obvious set of steps that could apply to many situations, and hopefully they are familiar to you. As you may recall, we put these forward in Chapter 1 as a guiding structure for the book. We now use them again in this chapter to provide you with a specific framework as to how to innovate your Management Model.

One point worth bearing in mind, before proceeding, is that the four steps do not always take place entirely in sequence. For example, in P&G some of the envisioning and experimentation took place during the late 1990s, whereas Lafley's evaluation of the situation only took place in 2000. So while it is useful to think of these steps in a linear sequence, you need to bear in mind the possibility that there will often be a modification to this chronology.[1] We turn now to a closer look at each of those four steps.

1. Understanding: Framing the Challenge

It is tempting to look at the success P&G has had with Connect + Develop, and to leap to the conclusion that your company might want to do something similar. But that is not necessarily what I am trying to suggest. One of the key objectives of the book is to help you understand better how you manage your company—to make you aware of the subconscious choices you have made about your Management Model over the years, and to help you assess the costs and benefits of these choices. And, in some cases, you will conclude that your Management Model is basically fine, and simply needs a little fine-tuning.

But in many other cases, a deeper understanding of your Management Model and the situation you face in your business environment will reveal some underlying problems or challenges. And this dissatisfaction with the status quo is the lever you need to get people in your organization thinking creatively about new ways of working. Typically we see companies thinking about Management Model innovation when they are challenged by the following sets of circumstances:

Responding to a crisis. For a company with its back to the wall, there is a real opportunity to try something unusual. We saw in Chapter 3 how the Danish hearing aid company Oticon developed its spaghetti organization as a response to the competitive threat the company faced from Siemens and Philips. A less well-known example is Litton Interconnection Products, a Scottish factory engaged in the assembly of backplane systems for computers. In 1991 George Black was brought in by the US parent company to turn the factory around. As he explained, "We were a company going nowhere, doing assembly work no different from the work of dozens of larger, more efficient competitors. So we thought: what should we do? And the answer we came up with was to be different—to provide a new service to our customers, and a new way of working. It was deliberately contrarian, and somewhat risky, but we did not have much to lose."

This analysis led Black to put in place a radical new design: a business-cell structure with each cell of employees dedicated to meeting the entire needs of a single customer. Employees were trained in a broad range of skills, from manufacturing to sales to service, resulting in a dramatic improvement in customer responsiveness, reduced cycle time, and lower staff turnover.

Facing a new strategic threat. A more common scenario is when a company recognizes changes in its business environment that it is ill equipped to deal with, and which require new thinking. For example, recall the brief discussion in Chapter 3 of GlaxoSmithKline (GSK). During the late 1990s, big pharma players like GSK were suffering from declining productivity in their R&D activities, while at the same time many biotechnology companies, with a fraction of the resources of GSK, were becoming remarkably successful. Under the guidance of Tachi Yamada, the global head of R&D, the company responded with a radical restructuring of GSK's drug development operations into seven Centers of Excellence with biotech-like levels of flexibility and autonomy while still benefiting from the scale of GSK's global presence.

Overcoming a nagging operational problem. An even less dramatic situation is where the company realizes it needs to address a nagging operational problem that hinders its perform-ance. This is best exemplified by Motorola's development of the Six Sigma methodology for controlling the quality of a manu-facturing operation. This innovation can be traced back to the concept of zero defects proposed by quality manager Bill Smith in 1985 and "the Six Sigma Quality Program" that CEO Bob Galvin subsequently initiated in January 1987. But the inspir-ation for Smith's idea was not a specific problem facing the company; rather it was part of an ongoing drive for excellence in manufacturing quality that had been in place since Galvin's arrival in 1981. Six Sigma was revolutionary in its consequences for Motorola and for many other companies, but it was evo-lutionary in its origins.

Addressing an unprecedented challenge. Finally, there are occasionally situations where a company is faced with a genu-inely unprecedented challenge that cannot be addressed using standard solutions. For example, in Chapters 3 and 6 we dis-cussed the community-based organizational models that Eden McCallum and TopCoder put in place, both of which required them to develop new ways of motivating and coordinating their networks of freelancers. Another example is Infosys, the Indian IT services company that by 2006 was receiving more than 1 million job applications per year. It was simply impossible for the company to process that many job applications through tra-ditional means, so they had to become very thoughtful about defining the key things they were looking for in potential hires. Ultimately they put in place an automated front-end process for identifying the 100000 or so who would be taken forward for interviews. This is a classic case of necessity being the mother of invention.

These four different scenarios highlight the multifaceted nature of dissatisfaction with the status quo in established companies. Of course, the process of articulating the need for change doesn't necessarily mean that the solution is a new Management Model—sometimes the best way forward might involve strategic changes (e.g. refocusing the product portfolio, selling off underperforming businesses), sometimes it might simply involve improving operational efficiency. But whichever route you end up going, a clear articulation of the problem you face is a good starting point. And the more narrowly and precisely you can define the problem, the better.

As an aside, the challenge facing a start-up venture is very different to the challenge facing an established company. Recall the example of Happy Ltd in Chapter 2, a start-up that was built on novel management principles from its inception. Start-up companies always have the luxury of defining their own unique Management Model, and when they do so it often becomes an important element in their success. But, interestingly, most end up defaulting to fairly standard ways of working that they have experienced elsewhere. In my view this is a wasted opportunity: I would like to see start-up companies becoming as innovative in their management practices as they are in the products and services they offer.

2. Evaluating: Defining the Blockers

The next step in motivating change in an established company is to look at the "blockers" that prevent people from doing what they want to do. Blockers, in our language, are simply those aspects of the Management Model that get in the way of innovation, collaboration, and change. The list of blockers includes such things as a silo mentality, risk-aversion, short-term thinking, ambiguous reporting structures, and too many layers of hierarchy. We see this especially in large, established companies that have traditional Management Models that were built to deliver efficiency but are less well equipped to deliver innovation, collaboration, or change.

It is remarkably easy to get managers in a large company to list off the blockers they face. With little prompting, they will draw up a list rather like the one above. But for this analysis to be useful, it has to go deeper. First, it needs to be much more specific than the list above. For example, short-term thinking is a generic blocker, whereas a bonus system designed to reward people for short-term sales growth is a specific blocker. Second, the blocker has to be relevant to the strategic challenge identified in step one. For example, if the strategic challenge facing the company is organic growth, the key blockers are likely to be such things as risk aversion and short-term thinking, rather than ambiguous reporting structures or a silo mentality.

Let's consider a couple of examples of companies that were very thoughtful about identifying their blockers:

UBS Wealth Management. We discussed in Chapter 7 how UBS Wealth Management (UBS) eliminated its traditional budgeting system in favor of a quest-based model, in which individual client advisors were encouraged to shoot for the highest possible return on investment in a given year, rather than work toward an agreed target. But it's worth describing how this new model came about.

UBS emerged as the world market leader in private banking following the merger of Swiss Bank Corporation and Union Bank of Switzerland. But with only 4% of a highly fragmented market, the potential for growth was enormous. So in 2003, the executive team led by Marcel Rohner began to shift the emphasis away from cost control. As Toni Stadelmann, CFO at the time, recalled: "Our strategic challenge at that point was to shift the focus on costs to a focus on growth and efficiency. And that required a different culture, a different attitude."

The 20 most senior executives of the business group held an off-site in a "windowless room" in London at the end of 2003, during which they developed a clear agenda for growing the business. They started looking at the things that were standing in the way of the growth agenda, including centralized structures and processes, and lack of scope for initiative taking. But the biggest single obstacle they identified was the company's budgeting process. As Stadelmann observed, "Budgeting is highly defensive. It is not just cumbersome. It is fundamentally *against* growth." Following the off-site, a working group was set up to "enable and drive growth," with the abolition of the budgeting process as a key topic on the agenda. And as described in Chapter 7, the budgeting process was duly eliminated and replaced with a model that encouraged client advisors to think and act more entrepreneurially.[2]

Irdeto. A very different process was followed by Irdeto, a leader in content security products and services for digital entertainment content operators. Irdeto is a mid-sized company of 900 employees, incorporated in the Netherlands, but the global scope of its business—meant it needed a strong presence in both the Western and Eastern Hemispheres. In 2007, Graham Kill, the chief executive, began thinking deeply about the exciting global prospects for Irdeto, and about the things that might get in the way of its growth. At the top of his list was what he called the firm's "dominant mothership" syndrome—the tendency for people at HQ to implicitly assume that they should be the sole custodians of new directions and technologies, and a corresponding tendency on the part of its overseas operations to defer back to HQ in a more subservient fashion. According to Graham Kill's analysis, this problem would constrain growth in the very geographical areas that had the greatest long-term growth potential—those largely away from the Netherlands HQ. It was causing dynamics ranging from investment to be less aligned with the future growth areas to causing promising employees in those other geographies to leave the company because of their perceived lack of career development outside the mothership. Looking at all these dynamics together, he felt they were putting Irdeto at a competitive disadvantage vis-à-vis its emerging Asian competitors, and potentially retarding growth where the opportunities were the greatest.

The change Graham Kill came up with was to replace the Amsterdam HQ with a dual-core HQ split between Amsterdam

(Western Hemisphere) and Beijing (Eastern Hemisphere). Decision-making and traditional HQ functions would be shared across the two locations, and he himself would move with his family to Beijing, with two more executive team members following shortly thereafter.[3] By 2010, the "dual-core" HQ for Irdeto was fully-functioning, the company was performing well, and Graham Kill was pondering the creation of a third core to its HQ, located in North America.

In sum, for UBS, the key blocker to organic growth was the budgeting system; for Irdeto, the key blocker for building a global presence was its dominant mothership—its Amsterdam-based corporate headquarters. We cannot judge whether these were the "correct" blockers to identify, because in reality there are always many interlinked factors at work in large, complex organizations. But the point is that by focusing on one specific blocker in each case, Rohner and Kill were able to mobilize their respective teams to make changes. If the analysis had stayed at a high level of abstraction, it would have been much more difficult to move forward.

What can *you* do to identify the blockers that are preventing you from achieving your strategic objectives? Sometimes they are obvious, and sometimes you can get inspiration by looking at the approaches taken by companies like UBS and Irdeto. But there are also more structured approaches out there. For example, one well-known approach often goes under the name "root cause analysis:" it involves taking a generic or superficial problem, and repeatedly asking "why," to expose the underlying problems that cause the superficial one to exist. Figure 9.1 is one example, taken from analysis done by Ross Smith at Microsoft within his 42Projects initiative (see Chapter 8). Looking for ways Microsoft could become more innovative, Smith and his group acknowledged that "human imagination is constrained in the company today,"[4] a big generic blocker to innovation. By asking "why" repeatedly, Smith and his team realized that this problem was driven, in part, by the way employees were assigned roles and by the lack of group-wide incentives for working together. While

Figure 9.1: Exposing the underlying blockers of innovation

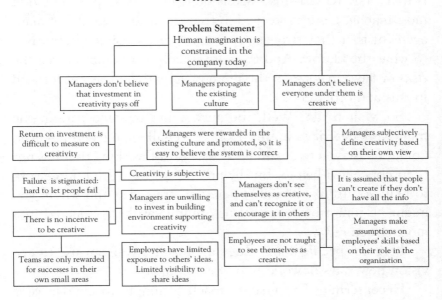

not quite as neat an analysis as those that enabled UBS and Irdeto to come up with their solutions, it nevertheless provided very important input into Microsoft's subsequent discussions about changes to its Management Model.

3. Envisioning: Identifying New Ways of Working

Steps one and two are all about clarifying and narrowing down the problem that needs to be solved, and when this is done well, the solution will often leap out at you. Once Graham Kill had reached the conclusion that a sole reliance on an Amsterdam-based HQ was the problem, it was pretty straightforward for him to come up with the idea of a dual-core HQ as the solution. Similarly, UBS Wealth Management's view that budgeting was blocking growth helped them to jump quickly to a narrow range of possible alternatives.

But often the way forward is far from obvious. I have led many workshops designed to help managers innovate their

Management Models, and the place where they usually get stuck is here. The reason this stage is difficult is, unsurprisingly, that most managers are so steeped in their traditional model of management that they struggle to imagine any sensible alternatives to what they know. And they are usually very quick to see the risks or flaws in some of the more imaginative ideas put forward in this and other books.

So what to do? Well, the answer lies in large part in the framework described in this book. It is challenging, perhaps even unfair, to ask you to dream up a new way of working that has not been conceived before. But by providing you with a framework to help you think through where you are today and where you might be tomorrow, your brainstorming can be conducted in a more structured way.

Let's be specific about three approaches you can use to envision new ways of working in your company.

Decentering. The first approach is simply to change your perspective, by looking at the company through the eyes of your employees. Psychologists call this decentering—seeing the world from the subject's perspective, in order to understand what inspires them and what demotivates them. It's a curious fact that most books on management are written from the perspective of the manager—the person doing the managing. The result is that we have limited insights into what makes employees tick, and what they really think of the various approaches to management that are used "on" them.

For example, I believe some level of *fear* is endemic in the workplace, even in organizations that are reasonably well managed. In a recent survey conducted by management writer Gary Hamel, the need to "reduce fear and increase trust" was identified as the single most important challenge facing large companies today.[5] Fear is multifaceted—we worry about looking foolish in a meeting, we worry about not living up to expectations, and we are concerned that we may lose our job. And fear is not the only hidden emotion in the workplace. Many employees are confused—they simply don't understand why they have been asked to do a particular piece of work. Others disagree with the direction their managers are pushing them in. Collectively, these emotions breed cynicism and disengagement—and all because managers have failed to put themselves in the position of those who work for them.

How do you come to grips with your employees' hidden emotions? Well, for starters, try walking a mile in their shoes. Here is a personal anecdote that might help make the point. Not too long ago my wife asked me to help clean house because a realtor was coming over to give an appraisal of our property. I was confused, because I didn't see the importance of making the house spic and span for the realtor. And I didn't know what to do, because my standards of what passes as "clean" are rather looser than those of my wife. So I started behaving like a recalcitrant employee—I worked whenever she was watching, played with my Blackberry when she wasn't, and did the bare minimum while she got the bulk of the work done. For two hours I was a confused, cynical, largely unproductive employee. The next day I was back at work—in my position as manager of others. But I had a much greater sense of empathy for my employees' fears and their needs.

A more structured approach is the one used by Henry Stewart, CEO of the computer-training firm, Happy Ltd, whom we have already met. In seminars, Stewart likes to ask people the following: think back to the last time you were really productive and engaged at work, and describe the experience. He shows, perhaps unsurprisingly, that people will typically describe a project where they were in control, where they were able to bring their personal strengths to bear, and where there was a sense of personal achievement at the end. Projects, in other words, that relied primarily on intrinsic motivation. Of course, there is no mention of a manager anywhere in this description, and that is Stewart's point. But there is still a role for the manager in structuring such projects so that employees have a license to do their best work.

Some of these approaches were described in Chapter 6 when we looked at the personal drivers of discretionary effort.

An even more dramatic approach to decentering was the one pursued by Stephen Martin, CEO of a UK construction company called Clugston. He dressed himself up as a casual laborer and worked for a week—incognito—on his company's construction sites. This gave him insights into what his employees thought of the company that he could never have received through the formal lines of communication (see Box 9.1 for details).

Box 9.1:   Going underground

For a really innovative approach to decentering, consider the case of Stephen Martin, CEO of UK construction company Clugston.[6] Martin knew when he took over as CEO in 2007 that the company had been managed on very traditional lines with a "them-and-us sort of culture." Clear evidence of that was the fact that he was isolated at one end of the building, where it was almost impossible for anyone to get near him. He wanted to improve the quality of information coming to him, and to push responsibility down to those closest to the action, but he was acutely aware that his knowledge of the day-to-day work in Clugston was filtered through many layers.

When Channel 4, a UK TV production company, approached him to participate in a program called *Undercover Boss*, where the CEO of a company spends a fortnight working incognito with front-line employees, Martin leapt at the opportunity to learn what his employees were thinking that he didn't know about.

And so he spent two weeks working as a laborer on Clugston building sites, followed around by a TV crew, which the other workers thought was filming a documentary on a regular guy trying out a new trade. What did Martin learn as an undercover

CEO? "The camaraderie on the site was just absolutely amazing. If somebody had a better way of doing something they would describe and explain it and help, support, and question. You don't get that in an office." More troubling, though, Martin discovered that no one read the regular stream of emails and newsletters the company used to communicate, either because they didn't have time, or because they just wanted to know the absolute essentials. He also became aware of the looming skills gap that was widening as experienced workers were retiring, and high-quality contractors were getting laid off.

On returning to his normal duties, Martin made some major changes. The emails and bulletins stopped and were replaced with twice-weekly meetings where supervisors gave employees a 10–15 minute update on what was happening. Short monthly newsletters were mailed out with everyone's pay slips. Skip-level meetings were introduced, where people were encouraged to meet with their boss's boss to discuss things that were concerning them. Martin instituted weekly lunch meetings in his office with front-line employees—no agenda, just sandwiches and a general chat to find out what was on their minds.

Martin's experiences as an undercover executive are highly instructive. He simply could not have had those conversations with his front-line employees any other way. And Clugston is far from unusual in this regard. Many managers regard themselves as open-minded and good listeners, but to some extent every message they receive is filtered or biased by what the messenger thinks they want to hear. While you can't call Channel 4 to come film you going underground in your own company, you can probably adapt some of the changes Martin made at Clugston to be able to get upfront and personal with his employees. Decentering, then, is difficult but not impossible, and it's an important starting point for you as a manager if you want to understand what motivates your team.

Learning from other contexts. One of the great myths of innovation is the idea that it takes place through the work of the lone creative genius who toils away in his or her laboratory or garage for years before eventually making a breakthrough. The reality is usually far more mundane. As management researcher Andrew Hargadon showed in his book, *How Breakthroughs Happen*, most innovations are actually ideas that were taken out of one setting and brought into a new one. Henry Ford didn't invent the assembly line, he simply took the production process he saw in a local abattoir, and transplanted it into automobile manufacturing. Thomas Edison wasn't a lone creative genius; he was a "technology broker" par excellence who "combined existing ideas in new ways."[7]

In this book we have described many innovative approaches to management, and in the vast majority of cases these were inspired by experiences or insights gleaned from other places. For example:

- Vladas Lasas, the Lithuanian executive who invited his employees to set their own salaries (Chapter 3), got the idea for doing this from reading *Maverick*, the best-selling book by Brazilian executive Ricardo Semler.

- Lars Kolind, CEO of Oticon (Chapter 3), got his inspiration for his new Management Model from his deep involvement in the Boy Scouts movement. As he explained: "The Scouting movement has a strong volunteer aspect, and whenever Scouts come together, they cooperate effectively together without hierarchy. There is no game playing, no intrigue. My experiences in Scouting led me to build a system that encouraged volunteerism and self-motivation."

- Larry Huston, architect of P&G's Connect + Develop program, which we discussed earlier in this chapter, was inspired by the collaborative organizational model developed by the founder of the VISA organization, Dee Hock, as well as by the ideas of complexity theorists like Stuart Kaufmann.

These examples suggest some fairly straightforward tips you might consider: read a wide variety of business and non-business books; look at the innovative ways of working that are being tried out in other industries and other parts of the economy; and talk to experts and thought leaders from different fields. These approaches do not require enormous creativity—just a high level of curiosity and a willingness to open your mind to new possibilities.

But you can also take a more structured approach to learning from other contexts. According to Hargadon, Thomas Edison was a "broker" who went out of his way to connect and combine technologies that had previously been operating in isolation. Edison and his team divided their time between clients in the telegraph, electric light, and railroad and mining industries, and used his work "to bridge these different worlds when he and his team saw ideas in one that showed promise elsewhere."[8] Much the same approach can be used in the field of management practice. It's often the management consultants and business school professors who find themselves performing the brokering function, but there is no reason why you cannot do it yourself—by sharing ideas at cross-industry events, by putting together collaborative forums, or by arranging job swapping opportunities with peers in other companies.[9]

Inverting your traditional principles. A third approach to envisioning new ways of working is to operate at the level of the underlying management principle, rather than the visible management practice. Again, it's useful to think about how innovation happens in other settings. Gary Hamel has argued that successful innovators are typically those who take a contrarian view and challenge the *orthodoxies* about how a particular industry works. For example, Ikea's development of flat-packed furniture and Dell's direct-sales model deliberately went against the prevailing orthodoxies of the furniture and computer industries of the time, and resulted in long-term competitive advantage for both companies. It's possible to apply a similar logic here by substituting the concept of an industry orthodoxy with the concept of a deeply held management principle. For example:

- For Oticon, the principle of allocating people to project teams was ineffective, so the company experimented with allowing project teams to form in an emergent way, as we saw in Chapter 3.
- For BP, the principle of reviewing performance on a top-down basis was limiting, so it experimented with a peer-review based model, which we discussed in Chapter 3.
- For P&G, the principle of controlling the innovation process was resulting in too many missed opportunities, so it experimented with an open and collaborative model, discussed earlier in this chapter.

I am not trying to suggest that the executives in these companies went through the thought process described here—their thinking was typically a great deal more intuitive, and involved a great deal of trial and error. However, the point is that a better understanding of traditional and alternative management principles can provide a useful structure as you seek to broaden the range of possible ways forward. And of course a discussion of such principles is one of the key features of this book.

Table 9.1 provides a summary of how these three steps fit together. For six of the companies that we have talked about in the book, it lists the major strategic objective, the key blockers, the innovative solution that was put in place, and the management principle that the solution was built on.

4. Experimenting: Trying It Out and Monitoring Progress

One of the consistent themes throughout this book has been the need for more experimentation in management. We saw it in the work done by Larry Huston in preparation for what became

Table 9.1:   Summary of six Management Model innovations

Company	Strategic Objective	Blocker	Innovation Solution	Management Principle(s)
P&G	Innovation	Lack of access to best ideas	Connect + Develop	Collective wisdom
UBS	Organic growth	Budgeting process	Elimination of budgeting	Emergence
Irdeto	Global presence	Dominant single HQ	Dual-core HQ	Collective wisdom
Oticon	Agility	Traditional resource allocation system	Spaghetti organization	Emergence, intrinsic motivation
HCL	Service innovation, decommoditization	Ineffectual and controlling management style	Open 360° feedback, service tickets, etc.	Obliquity, intrinsic motivation
BP	Collaboration	Silo mentality	Peer review	Emergence

Procter & Gamble's Connect + Develop initiative; we saw it in the design used by the Roche Diagnostics team when they sought to tap into the collective wisdom of their organization (see Chapter 4); and we saw it in the step-by-step approach used by the Innovation Exchange team within UBS Investment Bank (see Chapter 7).

Some Management Model innovations lend themselves to proper experimentation. When the hypothesis can be clearly defined and tested (as in the Roche Diagnostics case), and when the activity is self-contained (as with the UBS Innovation Exchange case), the experimental approach works very well and is entirely sensible. But you may have noticed that a few of the cases described in this book were of the "big bang" variety. For example, Oticon's spaghetti organization was put in place very quickly by CEO Lars Kolind. He took the view that a radical change was the only way to get people thinking and acting differently. He accepted that there was some risk in putting in place an unproven Management Model, but he felt that risk was smaller than the risk of doing nothing.

Whether the implementation of the new Management Model is done quickly or slowly, it makes good sense to monitor progress carefully. Because of the interconnected nature of management systems it is not always possible to isolate the specific dimensions of success, but it is a useful discipline to think through in advance exactly what you are hoping to achieve so that you can identify the most suitable measures possible.

Irdeto provides a nice example of how to monitor progress. Graham Kill, you will recall, decided to create a dual-core head-quarters with his moving to Beijing in September 2007, with two more executives moving out there afterward. Rather like Lars Kolind at Oticon, he decided that he needed to act decisively to get the message across that things had changed. On moving to Beijing, he located his desk in the middle of an open-plan suite, rather than taking any kind of office, let alone the large corner office people had expected him to choose. As he explained: "This is shock therapy. By making these changes I am creating a deliberately extreme message for the management team. There is some risk in doing this, but the only way to break a norm is to cut through it, and then to manage the consequences." For the managers in Beijing, Graham's open-plan office layout was not what they were expecting, but it allowed them to build stronger personal relationships with him than they had before. It was a tangible way of decreasing the hierarchical distance between executives and employees, in an office that had been used to being largely subservient to the Amsterdam HQ. And the managers in Amsterdam, who had deferred to Graham on many issues, began to make more decisions themselves.

But in order to get a real fix on what had happened, Graham was careful to measure the changes in attitudes and behavior over time. Before moving to Beijing, he developed some clear hypotheses about what he expected to happen (e.g. awareness of opportunities in China would increase, levels of integration between China-based and Europe-based managers would increase). He surveyed the 30 senior and middle managers before he left for Beijing, and then surveyed them again nine months and 18 months afterward. And he was able, as a result of this process, to get some very clear insights into the impact of creating a dual-core HQ. And of course the management challenge of integrating the two regions and creating a global mindset in Irdeto is still ongoing. Irdeto is not the first company to try to cure the "dominant mothership" syndrome, but it may well be the first to know whether it has succeeded.

Some Final Points

Before closing this chapter, it is useful to circle back to the original framework put forward in Chapter 2, in which we identified the four key dimensions of management and the spectrum of choices companies have to make on each one, anchored by a "traditional" principle on the left and an "alternative" principle on the right.

Because most large companies have Management Models that are built around the traditional principles, the opportunity to make a model distinctive usually comes from developing new ways of working that employ one or more of the alternative principles. Indeed, the vast majority of the examples we have talked about here involve some combination of emergent coordination, collective decision-making, oblique thinking, and intrinsic motivation.

But it would be wrong, as we have explained, to suggest there is an inexorable trend to the right side of the framework. Part of the discussion in each chapter has been about the risks and limitations associated with new practices, and hopefully these cautions will allow you to be selective about when and where you employ them. And one of the themes in Chapter 7, in particular, was that it's how the choices on the four dimensions *fit together* that matters most. A Management Model built on tight ends and loose means has certain attractive aspects, in terms of freeing people up to experiment with new ideas, but it also runs the risk—as we saw with Lehman Brothers and Enron—of creating a materialistic and amoral culture.

Does it ever pay for a company to move further toward the left side of the framework, towards a more "traditional" set of choices? What the left side gives you as an executive is control— control through hierarchical monitoring, formal rules, aligned goals, and extrinsic rewards. As we saw in Chapter 7, most companies gravitate toward a more controlling Management Model over time to cope with the increasing size and complexity of their operations. It is also very common in times of crisis to see companies shift their Management Model to the left side. Whenever a new CEO is brought in to turn a company around, he or she starts by taking tight control: discretionary spending is stopped, numbers are monitored on a weekly basis, formal procedures are imposed, and so on. This approach often makes good sense during a genuine crisis, but the trouble is that it usually takes a long time for the company's systems and procedures to be freed up again afterward. This is certainly one of the reasons why many companies find themselves stuck on the left side of the framework.

In sum, the traditional side of the management spectrum is not necessarily a bad place to be, but the nature of the threats and opportunities in the business environment today makes it increasingly less attractive. The challenge for most executives is to be creative in identifying opportunities for embracing these alternative principles on the right side of the framework, while also being realistic about the risks and limitations of the new methods and techniques they come up with. A good Management Model is one that involves making *smarter choices* about how you work, rather than just adopting the latest ideas for their own sake.

Chapter 9: Key points

This final chapter describes the four key steps leaders should follow to implement a new Management Model in their company. These steps are presented in a linear fashion, but often companies take a more iterative approach, going back and forth between steps.

1. **Understanding.** A thoughtful discussion of the strategic imperatives your company faces is the starting point for a discussion about whether changes to your Management Model are necessary.
2. **Evaluating.** The second step is to evaluate the "blockers" in your current model that prevent people from doing what they need to. The sharper the definition of these blockers, the easier it will be to come up with innovative solutions that unblock them.
3. **Envisioning.** The third step is the creative one: it requires you to come up with some ideas about novel ways of overcoming the blockers that are preventing you from delivering on your strategic imperatives. We look at three ways of doing this: decentering, learning from other contexts, and inverting traditional management principles.
4. **Experimenting.** Finally, once a possible way ahead has been selected, it is advisable to start small and in as experimental a way as possible. Once you have started, it is also advisable to monitor progress carefully.

EPILOGUE

BROADENING THE DEBATE ON REINVENTING MANAGEMENT

As I write this in the Autumn of 2011, the global economy continues to be in a state of great turbulence. Many important industries, from healthcare to banking to automobiles, face a bleak or uncertain future. The recession has created high levels of unemployment and even higher levels of debt in the large developed countries of the world. Businesspeople, especially bankers, are no longer trusted. When faced with problems of such magnitude, our natural inclination is to take stock. Where did we go wrong? And are there better ways of doing things that would allow us to avoid these problems next time round?

This book argues that one way of tackling these big problems is by rethinking and reinventing management. Of course policymakers and central bankers are still the best equipped to take decisive action, and we continue to rely on them to tackle pressing short-term problems. But economic resurgence and enduring change has to come from below—from the companies and other institutions that make up the economy, and from the efforts made by individuals to make these organizations productive and engaging. If we can make genuine improvements in the way work gets done, then the consequences for individual quality of life, for company performance, and for productivity as a whole, will be profound.

The first step forward is to recognize the specific problem that needs addressing. Henry Mintzberg has said that companies these days are "overled and undermanaged" and I believe he has a point. Leadership, we are told, is all about creating and articulating a vision, and inspiring people to pursue it; management is about getting work done. For many companies, the managerial ability to get work done has been in short supply in recent years. Too many executives have assumed that as leaders they don't have to get involved in the nitty-gritty work of implementation. They have abrogated their responsibilities as *managers*, and this has resulted in such problems as flawed execution, poor customer responsiveness, and occasional (but serious) cases of rogue behavior.

So the key purpose of this book is to get you to think seriously about management again. Management is the act of getting people together to accomplish desired goals and objectives. Expressed in such a way, management sounds prosaic. But I believe the simplicity of this definition is what makes it profound and useful. There are many ways of getting people together to accomplish goals, so there is scope for creativity and innovation in how discipline of management is enacted. And this scope exists at two levels.

First, there is scope for innovation at the **company level**. The collective set of choices you make about how you manage is what I am calling your Management Model. And as we have seen, a distinctive Management Model can be a source of competitive advantage for your company. Some big companies are *serial management innovators*, always on the lookout for ways of sharpening or improving their Management Model. Examples include: GE, always on the forefront of the latest management practices; and Procter & Gamble, the originator of brand management in the 1920s and now a leading proponent of open innovation. Another group of companies were *founded on unique management principles* and work very hard to sustain their uniqueness. Examples here would include W.L. Gore, Wholefoods Market, Seventh Generation, and Google. A third group of companies are what I call the *quiet management innovators* who, unlike the GEs and P&Gs of this world, prefer to keep out of the spotlight and just plug away with their own distinctive approach to management. By definition, these companies are not well-known, but I would include the French food group Danone, The Swedish tooling company Sandvik, and the UK engineering consultancy Arup. There are other companies out there who have also invested in management as a source of competitive advantage, but collectively these companies are still in the minority. The majority find themselves playing catch-up: they look at the leading practices of the companies highlighted here and attempt to copy them; but they give little thought to how those practices might work together to create competitive advantage, nor how they might push them forward in distinctive ways. Such companies are admitting, implicitly, that they will never derive any advantage from their Management Model.

Second, there is scope for innovation at the **individual level**. The practice of management is like a Russian Doll—the same principles apply at nested levels, all the way from the overall Management Model of the company as a whole down to the style of management practiced by one individual. So regardless of how effective your company's Management Model is, you can take responsibility for improving the quality of management in your own team, through how you coordinate work and make decisions, through the objectives you set and the way you motivate people. There is nothing to stop you trying out something innovative in your corner of the organization you work for. Just recall the examples of Ross Smith of Microsoft (Chapter 8) and Srinivas Koushik of Nationwide (Chapter 4), both of whom—in their own distinctive ways—did things differently and achieved tangible benefits. Ideally such initiatives become the seeds of change on a wider scale but, whether that happens or not, the initiative is still worth pursuing.

A Broader Discussion

The primary audience for this book is managers—people with responsibility for getting work done through others, regardless of whether their organization is private or public sector, large or small. But in this Epilogue I would like to broaden the discussion to consider some of the other audiences that might find the idea of reinventing management important.

Recall the arguments in Chapters 1 and 2 that management, as we know it today, was a social innovation that took shape during the late nineteenth century. Since then, it has played a massive role in facilitating productivity growth and economic progress. But the emergence of modern management could not have happened without a whole range of institutional changes that facilitated its emergence. One key institutional innovation was the joint-stock company that allowed investors to put their money into a legal entity with limited personal liability if it lost money. Other important institutional innovations were the protection of intangible assets through patents and trademarks; the emergence of anti-trust policy; and the creation of professions such as accountancy and law. The details of how these policy-led innovations came together and shaped the modern company do not really matter here. The key point is simply that management innovation did not happen in a vacuum—it happened because the circumstances in the broader legal and economic environment made it possible.

So looking to the future, I believe many parties share responsibility for helping to move management forward. While one company can (and should) strive to gain competitive advantage from developing an innovative Management Model, there is a bigger prize, at a societal level, in ensuring that the improvements made by that company diffuse across the entire economy. Indeed, when we look at the major management innovations of the past century, we see exactly this happening. Toyota was the pace-setter in Total Quality Management in the 1960s, and today it still produces automobiles more efficiently, and at a higher quality, than its major competitors. But its innovative work practices have also spilled over into the rest of the auto sector and beyond, raising productivity and quality levels for all.

Management Model innovation, in other words, is too important just to be left to companies and individual managers to figure out. It needs to be supported and facilitated by a range of cross-industry bodies, and by the worlds of policy and education as well. Let's take each of these in turn.

The Business Community Agenda

The form of benchmarking that many companies practice is tyranny. If you keep track of how you are doing using narrow indicators of performance against your immediate competitors, and if your competitors do the same, you will end up running round in circles. Your management practices will converge, and your customers will no longer be able to tell you apart. Benchmarking is useful for companies that are a long way behind the curve, but if you are doing well it is a dangerously self-referential exercise.

On the other hand, there is enormous value in learning from organizations in different settings—other industry sectors, and indeed other contexts altogether. Recall the discussion in Chapter 9 about how breakthrough innovations happen; it is typically the boundary-spanners, the brokers, who have the knowledge and the perspective to take a practice from one context and bring it into another.

So one important point that the business community as a whole needs to think about is: how can we facilitate the sharing of ideas across traditional sectoral boundaries? Almost by definition, strong personal relationships tend to exist *within* these sectors, but my view is that the greatest potential for improvements in management occur when relationships cut *across* sectors. There are plenty of third parties out there, including business school academics, journalists, and consultants, who see their job as helping to bridge these sectoral gaps, but the reality is that the gaps are still very large. The "marketplace" for new management practices is highly inefficient.

I would like to see a business-led approach to the development and sharing of new management practices. While there will always be a role for third parties such as consultants, it is in the interests of the business community that they learn to talk directly with one another, so that the message doesn't get diluted or lost in translation. Of course there are plenty of *fora* out there for facilitating such conversations. One example is the Beyond Budgeting Round Table, a cross-industry group that meets up to explore cutting-edge ideas about alternatives to the traditional budgeting model used by most large organizations. But I cannot help thinking that the game-changing opportunity here is online. One of the themes of this book has been that Web 2.0 is making it possible for groups of people to share ideas and collaborate online in ways that would have been impossible before. Such communities exist in many other spheres of social and economic interest. There is no reason why the management community shouldn't do likewise.

The Policy Agenda

I argued earlier that one of the drivers of management innovation in the late nineteenth century was the institutional innovations—in such things as corporate governance and property rights—that preceded it. Today, we can see similar things going on, though perhaps on a less dramatic scale. For example:

- New governance models. Twenty years ago, most observers would have argued that the joint-stock public corporation was the most advanced and most effective model for overseeing a profit-making enterprise. But since then, a number of different governance models have risen to prominence—private equity took off; family-controlled and trust-controlled companies came back into favor; public-private partnerships grew in popularity; and a plethora of social enterprise models started to emerge, each with its own distinctive approach to governance. It is beyond the scope of this book to evaluate all these different models, but the sheer variety out there today is important for two reasons. First, we know from Charles Darwin that variety is the lifeblood of progress: competition between different governance models spurs them all to improve and to increase their odds of survival. Second, new models of corporate governance are likely to spawn new models of management. If for example an organization is run primarily for its employees or its trustees, rather than for the benefit of disinterested shareholders, it makes new approaches to goal setting and motivation much more feasible. So to the extent that governments can encourage the proliferation of new models of governance, there are likely to be significant benefits to the practice of management.

- New rules around the ownership of Intellectual Property. The creation of the General Public Licence (GPL) for software development in 1989 was a massively important piece of legislation, because it created a mechanism for encouraging open innovation. The GPL essentially ensures that once a piece of software is created under its rules, then derivative works (e.g enhancements to it) are also protected under the same rules. Again, the implications for management innovation are substantial, because old assumptions about controlling ideas and employing people to do proprietary work can now be challenged. It is no coincidence that some of the most creative approaches to collective wisdom and emergent coordination are happening in the high-technology companies that are affected by this and related pieces of legislation.

Other changes in legislation and policy are also emerging. The rules on privacy, especially in the online world, are under enormous scrutiny at the moment. Social policy in many countries is making it easier for people to work from home or from offsite locations. Some countries, including Norway and South Africa, have put in place explicit policies of positive discrimination to increase the percentage of female and black workers, respectively, in senior management positions. This is by no means a complete list, but the point is that these are changes that will directly influence the practice of management in the workplace in the near future.

I am not arguing that the tail should wag the dog. Changes in policy have to be made with regard to the interests of a broad range of stakeholders, so it is important to keep a sense of perspective. But it is certainly true that the types of institutional innovations I am describing here will always have consequences for the practice of management. So it is important for policy-makers to think through the consequences of their policies, and where possible to take actions that will help management move forward.

The Education Agenda

I would like to end on a more personal note. As a Professor in a leading business school, I know how difficult it is for us to make dramatic changes in what we teach, and how important it is that we try. My late former colleague, Sumantra Ghoshal, used to say that business schools are both less influential and more influential than we would like to think we are. We have relatively little *direct* influence on the decisions made by senior executives in major companies. Our research is often ignored by the business world and our relationships with top executives are weaker than those of comparable professions such as banking, law, and accountancy. On the other hand, we have enormous *indirect* influence through the way we shape the minds of the next generation of business leaders. Our ideas and models find their way, often subconsciously, into the attitudes and belief systems of hundreds of thousands of MBA students every year. These students quickly move into positions of real influence in the business world, and what we have taught them ends up having a significant impact on the way they behave.

So what do we teach our students? Business schools received their share of criticism during the financial crisis for giving the students an unduly narrow set of tools and techniques, and for failing to provide the breadth of perspective or the ethical grounding needed for a successful business career. I don't believe these criticisms are entirely accurate. All the business schools I am familiar with provide a good breadth of perspectives (including a grounding in ethics), and spend a lot of time helping students to improve their self-awareness and their interpersonal skills. Moreover, business schools are also very conscious of the need to move with the times. They take feedback from students very seriously, and they are highly competitive, and as a result we see significant innovations in curriculum content all the time—both in terms of specific classes that address the latest contemporary issues, and in terms of entirely new core and elective courses.

But I believe there is a problem, and it is the following. We spend a lot of time teaching our students the standard canon of business and management thinking, but we spend very little time asking them to evaluate and critique it. For example, most courses in economics and finance build on the so-called Efficient Market Hypothesis, and most courses in strategy start from the principles of Competitive Strategy, but it is rare for students to be exposed to the academic debates that lie behind these theories. So rather than getting a chance to evaluate for themselves the pros and cons of these theories, students are asked to accept and apply them as if they were basic laws of nature.

This is a problem because, as I have said many times during this book, the "laws" of management were created over the last century without any evidence that they were necessarily the best ways of doing things. At engineering school, students are asked to make use of the basic laws of physics to help them in their work, safe in the assumption that those laws are immutable. But the "laws" of management are of a different form altogether: they will never be definitive and immutable because they deal with human behavior, and human behavior is not entirely rational or predictable.

I would like to see our students given much more opportunity to evaluate and critique our theories of human behavior, and to help us reinvent management. Now, some care is needed here because if we give our students the right to challenge the existing practice of management before they have understood it, we run the risk of creating complete chaos. My proposal is slightly more cautious: I would like to see MBA students spend the first half to two-thirds of their program learning the canons of management, and then invite them to spend the latter part of their time at business school seeking to reinvent management. They should learn the skills of critical thinking; they should be exposed to the academic debates that question the validity of the very theories we have just taught them; and they should take courses or write assignments that allow them to dream up entirely new management practices.

In a small way, I have tried some of these ideas out. With my colleague Gary Hamel, I have twice taught a course, *Adventures in Management Innovation*, at London Business School, in which we asked our students to work in groups to dream up radical new management practices. Using some of the techniques described in the previous chapter, the students were asked to identify a major strategic imperative that companies were concerned about, identify the biggest blockers preventing them from delivering on it, and then propose a radical remedy. Executives were brought in to judge the best proposals and to pick a winner. Our experience of doing this suggested that it works best in two settings. For full-time MBA students it works well at the tail-end of a two-year program, as a way of challenging and reviewing some of the materials they have been taught up to that point. For experienced "executive" MBA students it works well early on in the program, because they have enough diverse experiences that they understand immediately how to apply the tools in a useful way.

I don't believe business schools should be radically overhauling their curricula, because there is a body of knowledge that every business professional needs and which they expect to get when they go to business school. But we have a responsibility to arm our students with a much richer perspective on the ideas that we teach them—the theoretical assumptions on which they are based, the era in which they were created, and the difference between an underlying principle and a visible management practice.

***

If I have a single objective with this book, it is to put the discipline of management back on the agenda as an important area for businesspeople, policy people, and educators to take seriously; and for them to consider the consequences of what they are doing to improve the practice of management in the years ahead.

Notes

Chapter 1

1 National Commission on the BP Deepwater Horizon Oil Spill and Offshore Drilling, Chief Counsel's Report, Chapter 5.

2 www.newscorpwatch.org. Two Leading American Shareholder Advisory Groups Urge Shareholders To Vote Against Murdoch And Other Directors. October 11, 2011.

3 www.portfolio.com. You, Too, Can Be a Rogue Trader, by Kirsten Grind, September 19, 2011.

4 See the full report on the FSA website: www.fsa.gov.uk

5 This quote and all others about Lehman and Dick Fuld are taken from Andrew Gowers, "Lehman: Consumed by the Death Spiral," *Sunday Times*, December 14 and 21, 2008.

6 Special report on investment banks, "The Price of Atonement," *The Economist*, November 14, 2002.

7 This quote is taken from Sarah Kaplan, "The CEO as organizational architect: A case study of John Reed, Citibank, and the commercial real estate crisis of the 1990s." Rotman School, University of Toronto, Working Paper.

8 Alfred Sloan, *My Years with General Motors* (New York: Doubleday, 1964); Peter Drucker, *The Concept of the Corporation* (New York: The John Day Company, 1946).

9 John Kenneth Galbraith, *The New Industrial State* (London: Hamish Hamilton, 1967).

10 Taken from a January 21, 1988, memo from Elmer W. Johnson to his Executive Committee headed "Strengthening GM's Organizational Capability," http://s.wsj.net/public/resources/documents/BA_gm_memo.pdf.

11 Thomas Moore, "The GM System Is Like a Blanket of Fog," *Fortune* magazine, February 15, 1988.

12 Lydia Saad, "Nurses Shine, Bankers Slump in Ethics Ratings," Gallup, November 24, 2008.

13 Emma de Vita, "Do You Trust Your Boss?" *Management Today*, September 2009, Page 44.

14 Richard Layard, *Happiness* (London: Penguin Books, 2005).

15 Ronald Purser and Steven Cabana, *The Self Managing Organization* (New York: The Free Press, 1998), Page 3.

16 Roy Jacques, *Manufacturing the Employee* (Thousand Oaks, CA: Sage Publications, 1996); Peter Drucker, *Management*, fourth edition (New York: Collins Business, 2008).

17 Peter Drucker has gone so far as to state that "Management may be the most important innovation of the twentieth century" (*Management*, fourth edition, op cit).

18 Books by Mary Parker Follett include *Creative Experience* (New York: Longmans, Green and Co., 1924); *Freedom and Coordination: Lectures in Business Organization* (London: Management Publications, 1984); *Prophet of Management: A Celebration of Writings from the 1920s*, with Pauline Graham (Boston: Harvard Business School Press, 1995).

19 Charles Sabel and Jonathan Zeitlin, "Historical Alternatives to Mass Production: Politics, Markets and Technology in Nineteenth-century Industrialization," *Past & Present*, 1985, 108: 133–176.

20 Michael Brocklehurst, Chris Grey, and Andrew Sturdy, "Management: The work that dares not speak its name," *Management Learning*, 2010, 41: 7–19.

21 This table is drawn from the writings of John Kotter and Warren Bennis. See in particular: John Kotter, *Force for Change: How Leadership Differs from Management* (New York: The Free Press, 1990); Warren Bennis, *On Becoming a Leader* (New York: Addison-Wesley Publishing Co, 1989).

22 Nicholas Carr, *The Big Switch* (New York: Norton & Co., 2008).

23 Harold Leavitt, *Top Down* (Boston, MA: Harvard Business School Press, 2005), page 1.

24 Henry Mintzberg, *Managing* (San Francisco: Berrett Koehler, 2009).

25 Thomas Malone, *The Future of Work: How the New Order Will Shape Your Organization, Your Management Style, and Your Life* (Boston, MA: Harvard Business School Press, 2004).

26 Howard Rheingold, *Smart Mobs* (Cambridge, MA: Perseus Publishing, 2003), page xii.

27 Jeff Howe, *Crowdsourcing* (New York: Crown Books, 2008), page 18.

28 Robert G. Eccles and Nitin Nohria, *Beyond the Hype: Rediscovering the Essence of Management* (Cambridge, MA: Harvard Business School Press, 1992), page 19.

29 Jeff Howe, *Crowdsourcing* (New York: Crown Books, 2008); James Surowiecki, *The Wisdom of Crowds* (New York: Doubleday, 2004).

30 Michael Porter, "What is Strategy," *Harvard Business Review*, 1996, 75(6): 61–70; Patrick Barwise and Sean Meehan, *Simply Better* (Boston, MA: Harvard Business School Press, 2004).

31 Letter from Cecily Drucker, "Will GM Ever Take Peter Drucker's Advice,?" *BusinessWeek*, June 22, 2009.

Chapter 2

1 Information for the case study on Happy Ltd came from: Julian Birkinshaw and Stuart Crainer, "Management by the (new) book," *Business Strategy Review*, 2008, 19: 18–22. See also the company website www.happy.co.uk.

2 The Happy Ltd management model is described in a recently-published book by Henry Stewart called "The Happy Manifesto". http://www.happy.co.uk/about/free-publications/.

3 Information for the case study on HCL technologies came from: Julian Birkinshaw, "Employees first," Labnotes, May

2007, 4: 1–5, http://www.managementlab.org/publications/casestudies/hcl-technologies. See also Linda Hill, Tarun Khanna and Emily Stecker, "HCL technologies," Harvard Business School case study 408004; and the company website http://www.hcl.in/vineet-nayar.asp.

4 HCL's model is described in Vineet Nayar's book, *Employees First Customers Second*, (Boston, MA: Harvard Business School Press, 2009).

5 Peter Drucker, "The theory of the business," *Harvard Business Review*, 1994, Sept–Oct: 95–104.

6 Some readers may wonder whether "Management Model" is another expression for "organizational culture." There is some overlap of course between the two concepts, but there are some key differences as well: organization culture is the shared belief system of individuals in the organization, and the behaviors emanating from those beliefs; Management Model refers to active choices made by those leading the organizations about how work gets done; that is, the belief system is instantiated in actual structures, processes, and systems.

7 These lists of management activities were taken from: Henri Fayol, *General and Industrial Management* (London: Pitman, 1967); Luther Gulick and Lyndall Urwick, *Papers on the Science of Administration* (New York: Institute of Public Administration, 1937); Peter Drucker, *Management*, 4th edition (New York: Collins Business, 2008); Henry Mintzberg, *Managing* (San Francisco, CA: Berret Koehler, 2009).

8 For example, GE developed a distinctive practice called "Work Out" in the 1980s that was unique to GE; other companies adapted the practice to their own context, often with a very different name.

9 Ozco is a disguised name. Specific details have been altered to preserve anonymity.

10 Gary Hamel, *The Future of Management* (Boston, MA: Harvard Business School Press, 2008), Chapter 1.

11 Jeff Howe, *Crowdsourcing: Why the Power of the Crowd is Driving the Future of Business* (New York: Random House, 2008); Nicholas G. Carr, *The Big Switch: Rewiring the World, from Edison to Google* (New York: W.W. Norton & Co., 2008); Gary Hamel, *The Future of Management*, op. cit.

12 Don Tapscott, *Grown up Digital* (New York: McGraw Hill, 2009), page 35.

13 This research was conducted by You at Work, a leading player in the market for flexible benefits consulting (corporate. youatwork.co.uk). It was reported in: Julian Birkinshaw, "Play hard, work hard," *People Management*, October 30, 2008: 46.

14 David Edery and Ethan Mollick, *Changing the Game* (London: FT Press, 2009); John Beck and Mitchell Wade, *Got Game* (Boston, MA: Harvard Business School Press, 2004).

15 See the website: www.Amillionpenguins.com.

16 Gary Hamel, "Bringing Silicon Valley inside," *Harvard Business Review*, 1999, Sept–Oct: 70–84.

Chapter 3

1 Quote taken from Tom McNichol, "Roads gone wild," *Wired*, December 2004.

2 Formal evaluation by NHL, University of Applied Sciences, http://www.fietsberaad.nl/library/repository/bestanden/ Evaluation%20Laweiplein.pdf.

3 Most observers would see a blurred line between hierarchy and bureaucracy. Hierarchy is often seen as an element of bureaucracy; and decision-making typically takes place through a formalized bureaucratic process as much as through hierarchical control. I find it useful to separate the two out because one is focused primarily on managing across and the other is focused primarily on managing down; but I acknowledge that this is not a clear-cut distinction.

4 Max Weber, *The Theory of Social and Economic Organization* (London: Hodge, 1947).

5 Paul S. Adler and Bryan Borys, "Two types of bureaucracy: enabling and coercive," *Administrative Science Quarterly*, 1996, 41: 61–89.

6 These quotes are taken from interviews with Professor Sue White at Lancaster University, based on research in the following paper: K. Broadhurst, D. Wastell, S. White, C. Hall, S. Peckover, K. Thompson, A. Pithouse and D. Davey, "Performing 'initial assessment': identifying the latent conditions for error at the front-door of local authority children's services," *British Journal of Social Work*, 2009: 1–19.

7 *Emergence* is the title of a book by Steven Johnson (New York: Scribners, 2001). This form of coordination is also referred to as self-organization, and there is a large, multidisciplinary body of research on the phenomenon. See for example: Stafford Beer, *Brain of the Firm* (New York: J. Wiley, 1981); Stuart A. Kaufmann, *Origins of Order* (New York: Oxford University Press, 1993); John H. Holland, *Emergence: From Chaos to Order* (Reading, MA: Addison-Wesley, 1998).

8 A useful and comprehensive discussion of this body of work can be found in: Eric Beinhocker, *The Origin of Wealth: Evolution, Complexity, and the Radical Remaking of Economics* (Boston, MA: Harvard Business School Press, 2006).

9 Margaret Wheatley, © 2007, "The unplanned organization: learning from nature's emergent creativity," *Noetic Sciences Review #37*, Spring 1996.

10 Shona L. Brown and Kathleen M. Eisenhardt, *Competing on the Edge* (Boston, MA: Harvard Business School Press, 1998), page 28.

11 This discussion was based on: J. Kao, "Oticon," Harvard Business School teaching case 395144 (1995); R. Morgan Gould and Michael Stanford, "Revolution at Oticon: acquiring change competence in a 'spaghetti' organization," IMD teaching case IMD081 (1994); Julian Birkinshaw and Stuart Crainer, "Spaghetti organisation," *Labnotes* 1, October 2006: 7–8.

12 These changes are documented in N.J. Foss, "Selective intervention and internal hybrids: interpreting and learning from the rise and decline of the Oticon spaghetti organization," *Organization Science*, 2003, 14(3): 331–349.
13 Quote from Foss article, ibid.
14 Phanish Puranam and Ranjay Gulati, "Renewal through reorganization: the value of inconsistencies between formal and informal organization," *Organization Science*, 2009, 20: 422–440.
15 This basic distinction goes back to Ronald Coase's 1937 article "The nature of the firm," *Economica*, 1937, 4: 386–405, and Oliver Williamson's book *Markets and Hierarchies* (New York: Free Press, 1975). It is worth noting that the established academic literature sees hierarchy as the alternative organizing principle to the market. I have gone against conventional academic wisdom here to separate out the lateral task of coordination (bureaucracy) with the vertical tasks of decision-making and communication (hierarchy). So in my schema, the bureaucratic mode of coordination is the antithesis of the market-based mode of coordination.
16 Jeremy Hope and Robin Fraser, *Beyond Budgeting* (Boston, MA: Harvard Business School Press, 2003).
17 For a detailed discussion of how BP moved away from its peer review processes towards a more centralized model, see: Michael Goold, "Making peer groups effective: lessons from BP's experiences," *Long Range Planning*, October 2005, Vol. 38: 429–443.
18 Michael Phillips and Salli Rasberry, *Honest Business* (New York: Random House, 1981) and John Case, *Open-Book Management: The Coming Business Revolution* (New York: HarperBusiness, 1995).
19 These initiatives were announced by Asda in a press release on October 1, 2009. Website: your.asda.com.
20 www.guardian.co.uk/socialaudit.

21 Andrew Kuritzkes, "Risk governance: seeing the forest for the trees," MMC Knowledge Center, January 2009, http://www.mmc.com/knowledgecenter/viewpoint/Risk_Governance.php.

22 David Demortain, "Credit rating agencies and the faulty marketing authorization of toxic products," *Risk & Regulation*, January 2009, LSE/CARR publication.

23 Elinor Ostrom, *Governing the Commons: The Evolution of Institutions for Collective Action* (Cambridge: Cambridge University Press, 2002).

24 Thomas Malone, *The Future of Work: How the New Order Will Shape Your Organization, Your Management Style, and Your Life* (Boston, MA: Harvard Business School Press, 2004).

25 Morten T. Hansen and Julian Birkinshaw, "The innovation value chain," *Harvard Business Review*, 2007, 85: 121–130.

26 Harvard Business School case study: Robert S. Huckman and Eli Peter Strick, "GlaxoSmithKline: reorganizing drug discovery," Harvard Business School Press, May 17, 2005, ref. 9–605–074.

27 Gary Hamel, *The Future of Management* (Boston, MA: Harvard Business School Press, 2008), page 89.

28 The arguments and quote about Enron Corporation are taken from: Julian Birkinshaw, "The paradox of corporate entrepreneurship," *Strategy + Business Magazine*, Spring 2003, Issue 30: 46–58.

29 This example was taken from: Julian Birkinshaw, John Bessant and Rick Delbridge, "Finding, forming and performing," *California Management Review*, 2007, 49: 67–84.

30 Quote taken from Julian Birkinshaw and Michael Mol, "How management innovation happens," *Sloan Management Review*, 2007, 47: 81–88.

Chapter 4

1 This story is based on data and quotes from the MyFootballClub entry in wikipedia and and an article: S. Macaskill, "Ebbsfleet

United's online owners may be forced to sell," *The Daily Telegraph*, February 19, 2009.

2 http://www.ciao.co.uk/myfootballclub_co_uk__6838432.

3 Ebbsfleet Chairman Holt hopes fans will aid finances. BBC Sport website, March 5, 2010.

4 Gunnar Hedlund, "Assumptions of hierarchy and heterarchy, with applications to the management of the multinational corporation," in Sumantra Ghoshal and D. Eleanor Westney (eds), *Organization Theory and the Multinational Corporation* (London: St Martin's Press, 1993), pages 211–236.

5 Harold Leavitt, *Top Down* (Boston, MA: Harvard Business School Press, 2005), page 49.

6 Quote from Elliott Jaques, "In praise of hierarchy," *Harvard Business Review*, January 1, 1990, ref. 90107.

7 See, for example, James Surowiecki, *The Wisdom of Crowds* (New York: Doubleday, 2004); Thomas Malone, *The Future of Work: How the New Order Will Shape Your Organization, Your Management Style, and Your Life* (Boston, MA: Harvard Business School Press, 2004).

8 James Surowiecki, ibid.; Jeff Howe, *Crowdsourcing* (New York: Crown Books, 2008); Howard Rheingold, "Smart mobs," *Demos Collection*, 2004, No. 20: 189–204; Don Tapscott and Anthony D. Williams, *Wikinomics: How Mass Collaboration Changes Everything* (London: Atlantic, 2008).

9 Gary Hamel, *The Future of Management* (Boston, MA: Harvard Business School Press, 2008), page 250.

10 Julian Birkinshaw and Stuart Crainer, "Using Web 2.0 to create Management 2.0," *Business Strategy Review*, 2009, 20: 20–23.

11 This was a study, "Social colleagues", conducted by You at Work, a UK flexible benefits provider. The survey was based on responses from 1183 UK workers, June/July 2008. Contact James Keen at www.youatwork.com for more information.

12 Julian Birkinshaw and Stuart Crainer, "E-Jamming," *Business Strategy Review*, 2007, 18: 23–27.

13 Julian Birkinshaw, "Infosys: growing gains," *Labnotes*, May 2008, 8: 8–11.

14 See: Lynda Gratton and Sumantra Ghoshal, "Improving the quality of conversations," *Organizational Dynamics*, 2002, 31: 209–224.

15 Anand Giridharadas, "Democracy 2.0 awaits an upgrade," *International Herald Tribune*, Saturday–Sunday, September 12–13, 2009, page 2.

16 Interestingly, this is the same conclusion that proponents of direct democracy have reached. Certain countries, like Switzerland, make frequent use of referendums to get citizens' input on important decisions, but they have discovered that citizens have limited enthusiasm for taking part in referendums, and are generally most keen on the idea when their government refuses to offer them this right (witness the UK government's refusal to grant the public a referendum on the EU constitution).

17 Osvald Bjelland and Robert Chapman Wood, "An inside view of IBM's 'Innovation Jam,'" *Sloan Management Review*, 2008, 48, Fall: 27–30.

18 The P&G Connect + Develop program is described by its founders in: Larry Huston and Nabil Sakkab, "Connect and Develop: inside Procter and Gamble's new model for innovation," *Harvard Business Review*, 2006, 84, May: 58–66. For an academic treatment, see: Mark Dodgson, David Gann and Ammon Salter, "The role of technology in the shift to open innovation: the case of Procter & Gamble," *R&D Management*, 2006, 36: 333–346.

19 This example is taken from Guido Jouret, "Inside Cisco's search for the next big idea," *Harvard Business Review*, 2009, 87, September: 43–44.

Chapter 5

1 Quote taken from: Linda A. Hill, Tarun Khanna and Emily Stecker, HCL Technologies (B), Harvard Business School teaching case, 9–408–006, July 2008.

2 Quote taken from blog: http://blog.nasscom.in/emerge/2009/
   01/hcl-technologies-%E2%80%93-employee-first-customer-
   second/.
3 George Labovitz and Victor Rosansky, *The Power of Align-*
   ment: How Great Companies Stay Centered and Accomplish
   Extraordinary Things (New York: Wiley & Sons, 1977). Also,
   Robert S. Kaplan and David P. Norton, *Alignment: Using the*
   Balanced Scorecard to Create Corporate Synergies (Boston,
   MA: Harvard Business School Press, 2006).
4 Quote taken from: Simon Caulkin, "No half measures,"
   Labnotes, December 2008, 10: 14–15, www.management.org/
   publications.
5 Rajendra S. Sisodia, David B. Wolfe and Jaddish N. Seth,
   Firms of Endearment: How World-Class Companies Profit from
   Passion and Purpose (Pennsylvania: Wharton School of
   ·Publishing, 2007).
6 Richard Wollheim, "A paradox in the theory of democracy,"
   in Peter Laslett and W.G. Runciman (eds), *Essay in Philosophy,*
   Politics and Society (New York: Barnes and Noble, 1962),
   pages 71–87.
7 John Kay, "Forget how the crow flies," *The Financial Times*,
   January 16, 2004.
8 James C. Collins and Jerry I. Porras, *Built to Last: Successful*
   Habits of Visionary Companies (New York: HarperBusiness,
   1994).
9 Sisodia, Wolfe, Seth, op. cit., page 132.
10 Alex Edmans, "Does the stock market fully value intangibles?
   Employee satisfaction and equity prices" (August 12, 2009).
   Available at SSRN: http://ssrn.com/abstract=985735. See
   also: Ingrid S. Fulmer, Barry Gerhard and Kimberly S. Scott,
   "Are the 100 best better?: an empirical investigation of the
   relationship between being a 'great place to work' and firm
   performance," *Personnel Psychology*, 2003, 56: 965–994.
11 Philip Rosenzweig, *The Halo Effect: And the Eight other*
   Business Delusions That Deceive (New York: Free Press, 2007).
   One of the key issues here is termed "survivor bias" because

we only see those companies that survived, rather than the ones that got into trouble. Hypothetically, the companies pursuing the oblique principle might have a higher risk profile, and therefore be more prone to failure.

12 Advancement is a relatively new term for what many universities call "development" and "alumni relations."

13 The Harvard figure of $26 billion was taken from a press release on September 8, 2009, down from $37 billion a year earlier. The Oxford figure includes the endowments of all its constituent colleges, based on public source information from 2009.

14 John S. Mill, 1861, Geraint Williams (ed.), *Utilitarianism, on Liberty, Considerations on Representative Government, Remarks on Bentham's Philosophy*, Everyman's Library series (New York: Alfred A. Knopf, 1993 edition).

15 Bill Breen, "The thrill of defeat," *Fast Company*, June 2004, Issue 83.

16 Speaking at the Future of Management conference, Half Moon Bay, CA, 2008. Speech written up in: *Labnotes*, September 2008, 9, www.managementlab.org/publications/labnotes.

17 Gary Hamel, *The Future of Management* (Boston, MA: Harvard Business School Press, 2007), page 107.

18 Sumantra Ghoshal and Bjorn Lovas, "Strategy as guided evolution," *Strategic Management Journal*, September 2000, 21: 875–896.

19 Speaking at the Future of Management conference, op. cit.

20 Jessica E. Vascellaro, "Google searches for ways to keep big ideas at home," *Wall Street Journal*, June 18, 2009: B1–B5.

21 Robert H. Tansley, Gordon Murray and Julian Birkinshaw, "Roslin Biomed (A)" and "Roslin Biomed (B)," London Business School case study, 2002, ref. 302–062–1 and 302–063–1.

22 The quotes and ideas on Seventh Generation were taken from: Simon Caulkin, "Renegades in chief," *Labnotes*, March 2009, 11, www.managementlab.org/publications.
23 Taken from company website plus personal interviews with Sunil Jayantha Narawatne.
24 Taken from company websites plus: Angus Jenkinson and Branko Sain, "Specsavers, an innovative, integrated marketing business model," Centre for Integrated Marketing, University of Luton, 2003.
25 Marjorie Kelly, "Not just for profit," *Strategy + Business*, February 26, 2009.

Chapter 6

1 The TopCoder material is taken from: Stuart Crainer and Julian Birkinshaw, "Who needs employees?" *Business Strategy Review*, 2008, 19, Issue 3: 18–21.
2 While the winner gets the biggest prize, TopCoder also pays second place (usually half the amount of the first place prize), and all submitters who pass a certain level of quality are awarded points that give them a percentage of a prize pool that is distributed every month.
3 Information about Thomas Czajka is taken entirely from Internet sources, including: www.cs.purdue.edu/people/czajkat and http://www.cs.purdue.edu/homes/czajkat/.
4 Roy Jacques, *Manufacturing the Employee* (London: Sage Publications, 1996).
5 Definition taken from Wikipedia.
6 These definitions are taken directly from Wikipedia.
7 Deci and Ryan's work is known as Self-Determination Theory. Key publications include: Richard M. Ryan and Edward L. Deci, "Self-Determination Theory and the facilitation of intrinsic motivation, social development, and well-being," *American Psychologist*, 2000, 55(1): 68–87; Edward L. Deci and Richard M. Ryan, "The what and why of goal pursuits:

human needs and the self-determination of behaviour," *Psychological Inquiry*, 2000, 11(4): 227–268.

8 Douglas McGregor, *The Human Side of Enterprise* (1960), 25th Anniversary Printing (New York: Irwin/McGraw-Hill Companies, 1985).

9 Described in: Edward L. Deci and Richard M. Ryan, "The what and why of goal pursuits: human needs and the self-determination of behaviour," *Psychological Inquiry*, 2000, 11(4): 227–268.

10 Frederik Herzberg, *The Motivation to Work* (New York: J. Wiley, 1959).

11 Henry Sauermann and Wesley M. Cohen, "What makes them tick? Employee motives and industrial innovation," working paper, Duke University, Fuqua School of Business, October 2007.

12 Julian Birkinshaw, "Infosys: growing gains," *Labnotes*, May 2008, 8: 8–11. http://www.managementlab.org/publications/.

13 Quote taken from: J. Bonasia, "TopCoder finds tech top guns," *Investor's Business Daily*, October 26, 2007.

14 The Lincoln Electric story is taken from two Harvard Business School case studies: Norman A. Berg and Norman D. Fast, "Lincoln Electric Co.," 1975, ref. 376028; Jordan Siegel, "Lincoln Electric," 2006, ref. 707445.

15 Susan E. Jackson and Randall S. Schuler, *Managing Human Resources Through Strategic Partnerships*, 8th edition (Mason, OH: Southwestern, 2004), page 695.

16 Julian Birkinshaw and Stuart Crainer, "Game on: Theory Y meets Generation Y," *Business Strategy Review*, 2008, 19(4): 4–10.

17 http://www.seriousgames.org/index.html.

18 "Serious games," *The Economist*, October 23, 2001.

19 Historical examples include the 1714 Longitude Prize awarded to John Harrison for designing the marine chronometer, Napoleon's Food Preservation Prize of 1795, to help find a

way to better feed his army, and the Nobel Prizes for academic achievement.

20 The McKinsey & Company Report, "'And the winner is …' Capturing the promise of philanthropic prizes," released March 3, 2009. Downloadable from: www.mckinsey.com/ clientservice/../And_the_winner_is.pdf.

21 Oriflame material taken from the company's website, www. oriflame.com.

22 From the Oriflame India website, www.oriflame.co.in.

23 Taken from the Oriflame India website, op. cit.

24 Engagement data provided by Wendy Cartwright, Head of Human Resources for the ODA.

25 This example draws from two case studies on self-directed teams published by the CIPD in the UK. Self-directed teams at Rolls-Royce Gas Turbines and Learning through team reviews at Rolls-Royce, http://www.cipd.co.uk/ helpingpeoplelearn/_casestudies/.

26 "A shared learning programme for Rolls-Royce," http://www. cipd.co.uk/helpingpeoplelearn/_casestudies/_Arcrllsryc. htm.

27 "Self-directed teams at Rolls-Royce," http://www.cipd.co.uk/ helpingpeoplelearn/_rlsryc.htm.

28 Charles Handy, *The Elephant and Flea* (Boston, MA: Harvard Business School Press, 2002).

29 Katherine Blackford and Arthur Newcombe, *The Job, The Man, The Boss* (New York: Doubleday Page and Company, 1914).

30 Marcus Buckingham, *Now Discover Your Strengths* (New York: Simon & Schuster, 2001).

Chapter 7

1 A version of this matrix where the focus is on individual projects is presented in: Eddie Obeng and Christophe Gillet,

The Complete Leader: How to Lead to Results (London: London Business Press, 2008). The focus in this article is on the Management Model of the firm as a whole, rather than an individual project.

2 The surprisingly large number of companies in the Science quadrant is a reflection of the fact that the sample of companies included quite a few not-for-profit and public sector companies that scored themselves high on "intrinsic" motivation.

3 Bernard Girard, *The Google Way* (San Francisco, CA: No Starch Press, 2009), page 24.

4 Shona Brown and Kathleen M. Eisenhardt, *Competing on the Edge: Strategy As Structured Chaos* (Boston, MA: Harvard Business School Press, 1998).

5 Girard op. cit., pages 107–108.

6 Gary Hamel with Bill Breen, *The Future of Management* (Boston, MA: Harvard Business School Press, 2007), page 111.

7 Hamel, ibid., page 109.

8 Interview with Eric Schmidt at Future of Management Conference. Printed in full in: *Labnotes*, September 2008, 9: 6–9. See www.managementlab.org/publications.

9 The executive in question, Sheryl Sandberg, went on to become COO of Facebook. See: Adam Lashinsky, "Chaos by design," *Fortune*, October 2, 2006.

10 Girard, op. cit., page 115.

11 Hamel, op. cit., page 117.

12 http://www.google.com/corporate/tenthings.html.

13 Great Places to Work Institute, http://www.greatplacetowork. com/best/100best2007-google.php.

14 Eric Schmidt interview, op. cit.

15 Girard, op. cit., pages 66, 79.

16 Great Places to Work Institute, op. cit.

17 Jessica E. Vascellaro, "Google searches for ways to keep big ideas at home," *Wall Street Journal*, June 18, 2009.

18 Julian Birkinshaw and Stuart Crainer, "The danger of desks," *Labnotes*, August 2007, 5: 8–9.

19 John F. Love, *McDonald's: Behind the Arches* (New York: Bantam Books, 1986, 1995), page 150.

20 Eric Schlosser, *Fast Food Nation* (London: Penguin Books, 2002), page 230.

21 John F. Love, op. cit., page 140.

22 Paul Facella with Adina Genn, *Everything I Know About Business I Learned at McDonald's* (New York: McGraw Hill, 2009), pages 62–63.

23 Love, op. cit., page 263.

24 From a consumer poll by *Restaurants and Institutions* in 2000, cited by Eric Schlosser, op. cit., page 260.

25 "Skinner's winning McDonald's recipe," *BusinessWeek* online extra, February 5, 2007, http://www.businessweek.com/magazine/content/07_06/b4020007.htm.

26 Paul Facella, op. cit., page 178.

27 Jerry Newman, *My Secret Life on the McJob: Management Lessons from Behind the Counter* (New York: McGraw Hill, 2007).

28 Philip Augar, *The Greed Merchants* (London: Penguin Books), page 49.

29 Ref my article in S+B, explain there is also externalization of risk management.

30 Andrew Kuritzkes, "Risk governance: seeing the forest for the trees," MMC Knowledge Center, January 2009, http://www.mmc.com/knowledgecenter/viewpoint/Risk_Governance.php.

31 G. Tett, "Anthropology that explains varying banking behaviour," *Financial Times*, January 18, 20, 2008.

32 Russell Walker, "Managing in a downturn. Fortune favours the well prepared," *Financial Times*, January 30, 2009. Felix Salmon, "Market movers," September 3, 2008, http://www.portfolio.com/views/blogs/market-movers/2008/09/03/how-jamie-dimon-manages-risk?tid=true.

33 Rodney Chase speaking at LBS event, recorded on DVD, available from author.

34 Simon Caulkin, "The Idea Exchange at UBS," *Labnotes*, June 2009, 12: 1–4.

35 David Owen, "The anti-gravity men," *New Yorker*, June 25, 2007. Other useful sources for this discussion of Arup were: the website, www.arup.com; Evelyn Fenton and Andrew Pettigrew, "Integrating a global professional services organization: the case of Ove Arup Partnership," in A. Pettigrew and E. Fenton (eds), *The Innovating Organization* (Thousand Oaks, CA: Sage Publications, 2000), pages 47–60.

36 Cited in the *New Yorker* article, ibid., taken from *Ove Arup: Master Builder of the Twentieth Century*, 2006, Peter Jones.

37 Company website arup.com.

38 *New Yorker* article op. cit.

39 "Key Speech," Ove Arup, 1970, arup.com.

40 Arup Corporate Report 2008.

41 Quoted in the *New Yorker* article op. cit.

42 2007 Action Planning Session Summary Report for Arup Group, May 2007, prepared by HayGroup.

43 "Case study: Arup," by Colin Henson, Inside Knowledge, Vol. 10, Issue 7, posted April 12, 2007, http://www.ikmagazine.com/xq/asp/sid.0/articleid.3C219ACD-8D7E-462B-A136–98F17A73397C/eTitle.Case_study_Arup/qx/display.htm.

44 Key Speech, Ove Arup, op. cit.

45 Case study: Arup, op. cit.

46 arup.com.

47 Arup Five-Year Plan, available from the company website at arup.com.

48 arup.com.

49 arup.com.

50 HayGroup Summary Report op. cit.

Chapter 8

1 Robert S. Kaplan, David P. Norton, "Putting the Balanced Scorecard to Work," *Harvard Business Review*, September 1993: 2–16.

2 This case study of Art Schneiderman and the Balanced Scorecard is taken from: Michael J. Mol and Julian Birkinshaw, *Giant Steps in Management* (London: Financial Times/Prentice Hall, 2007); see also Schneiderman's own website, www.schneiderman.com.

3 Gary Hamel uses the term "Gray Haired Revolutionaries" for Change Agents in his book, *Leading the Revolution* (Boston: Harvard Business School Press, 2000, 2002). Other similar terms are Innovation Champions and Intrapreneurs.

4 This case study comes from Julian Birkinshaw and Stuart Crainer, "When Gen Y meets Theory Y," *Business Strategy Review*, 2008, 19(4): 4–10.

5 John F. Helliwell and Haifang Huang, "Well-Being and Trust in the Workplace," Working Paper 14589, (Cambridge, MA: National Bureau of Economic Research, December 2008).

6 Interest in the work of the team continues to spread across Microsoft and beyond, through a "Friends of 42Projects" email alias. Readers can join Friends@42projects.org by going to http://www.42projects.org/4.html.

7 "Trust, innovation and minimalist management: Ross Smith Redux", Charles Green, June 27, 2011, Trustedadvisor.com.

Chapter 9

1 For more details on the process of management innovation, see Julian Birkinshaw, Gary Hamel and Michael Mol, "Management innovation," *Academy of Management Review*, 2008.

2 This example is drawn from: Julian Birkinshaw, "Breaking away from budgeting", *Labnotes*, February 2007, 3: 2–5.

3 Julian Birkinshaw, "Mothership, Inc.," *Labnotes*, May 2008, 8: 12–13.

4 Note that this blocker was taken from Gary Hamel's "Moon shots for management," *Harvard Business Review*, 2009, 87, February: 108–109.

5 The results of this survey had not been published at the time this book went to press. Please refer to www.managementlab. org where the results will be posted. Parenthetically, this finding echoes one of the key points in W. Edwards Deming's "14 point plan" for Total Quality Management, namely to "Drive out fear."

6 Stuart Crainer and Julian Birkinshaw, "Covert operations," *Business Strategy Review*, 2009(3): 76–81.

7 Andrew Hargadon, *How Breakthroughs Happen* (Boston, MA: Harvard Business School Press, 2003), page 17.

8 Hargadon op. cit., page 35.

9 Job swapping may sound unusual but in fact it is a recognized practice for facilitating personal development and gaining new insights. For example, see: http://en.wordpress.com/tag/job-swapping/.

Index

Index compiled by Indexing Specialists (UK) Ltd